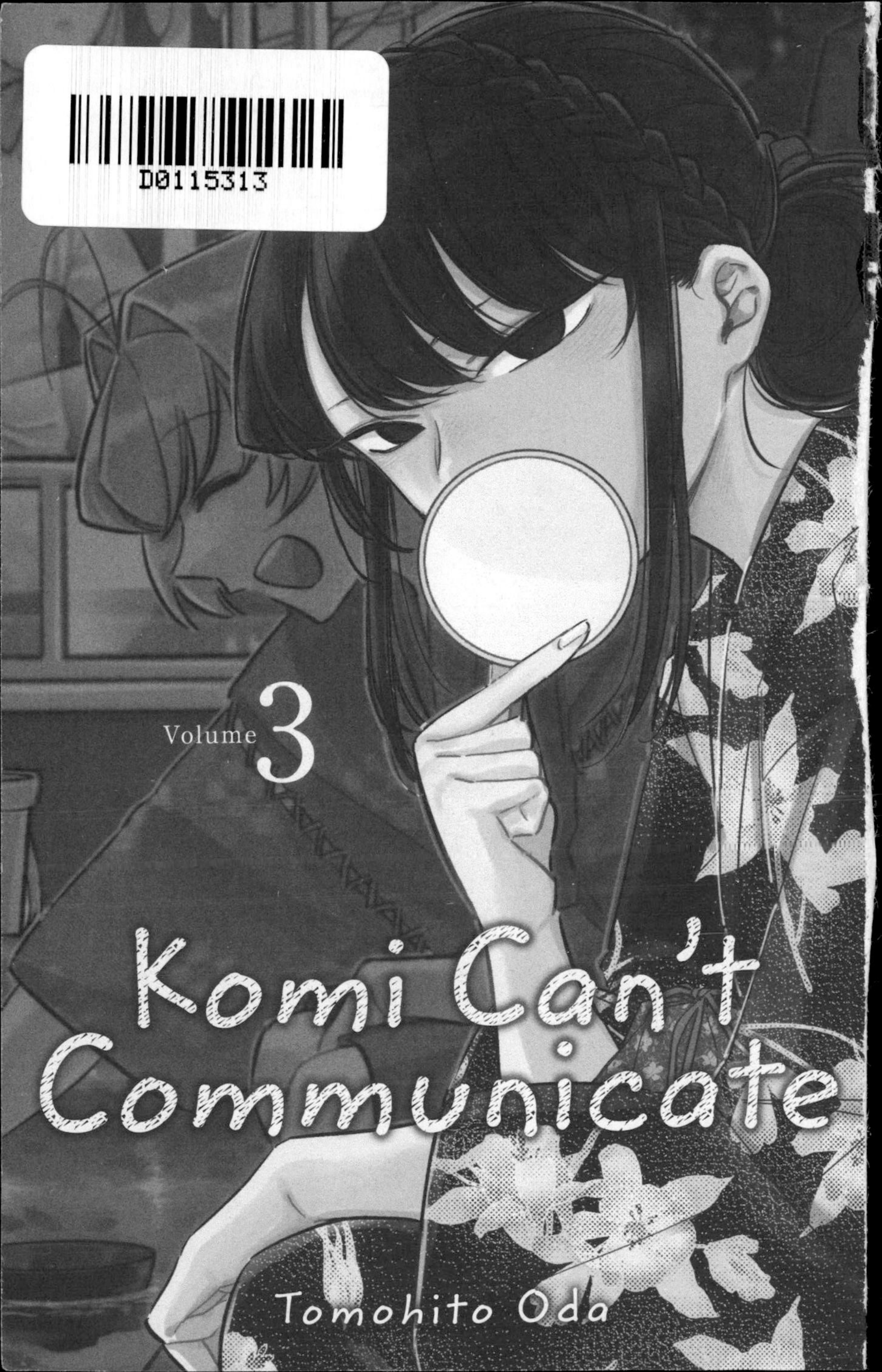

Volume 3

Komi Can't Communicate

Tomohito Oda

Contents

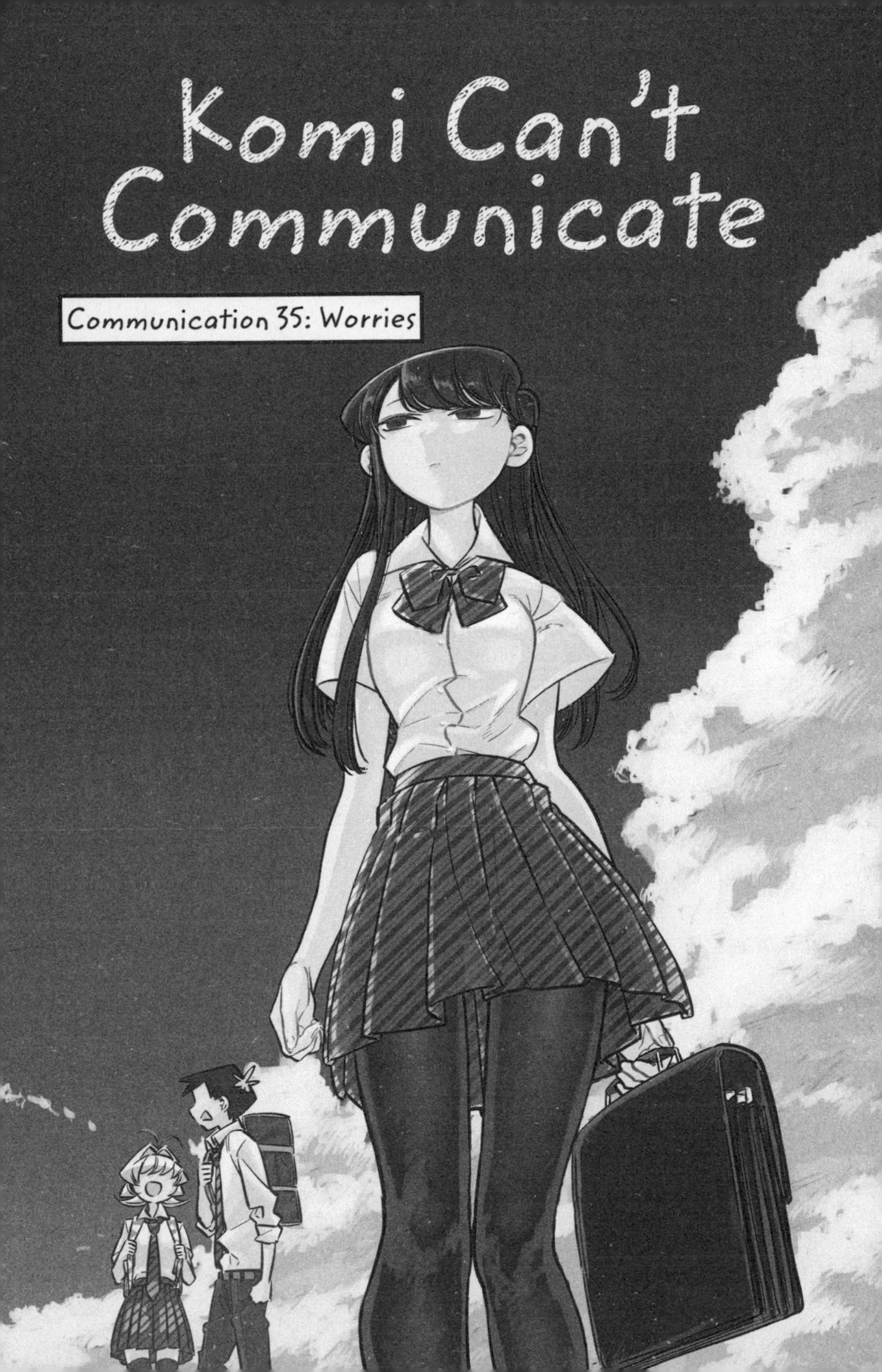
Komi Can't Communicate
Communication 35: Worries

SPARKLE SPARKLE

SPARKLE

Komi Can't Communicate

Komi Can't Communicate

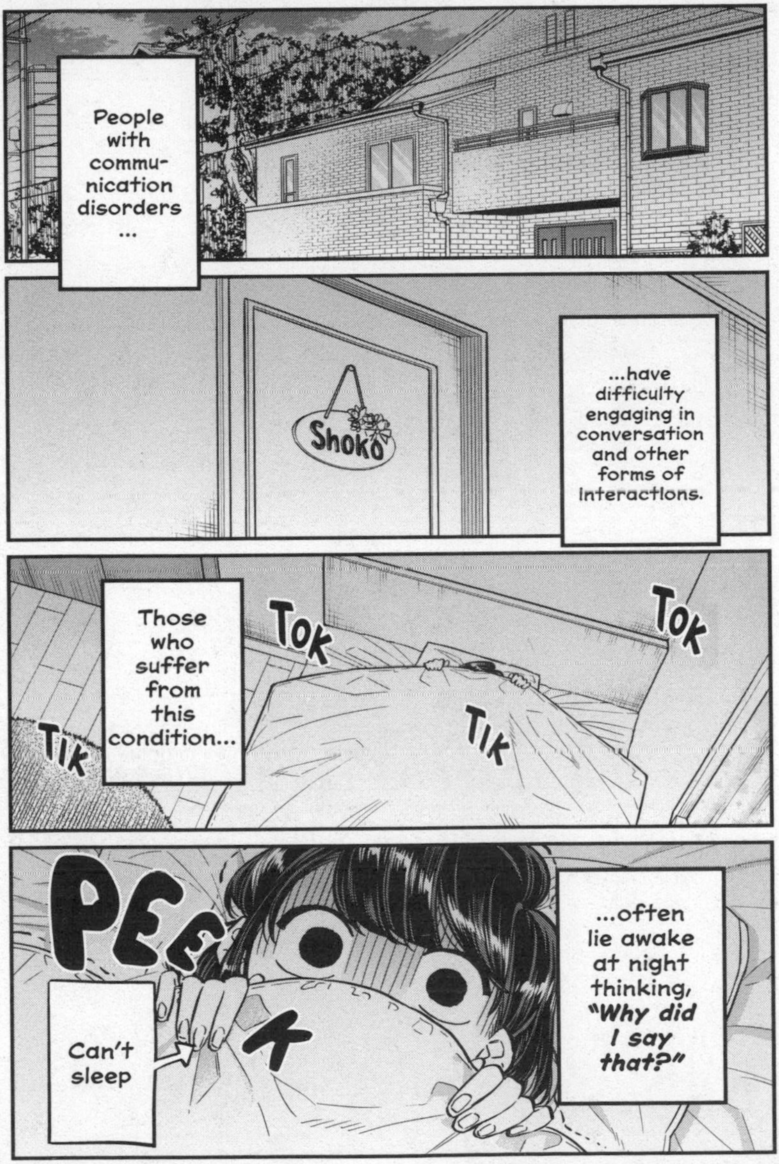
People with communication disorders...
...have difficulty engaging in conversation and other forms of interactions.
Shoko
TOK
TOK
Those who suffer from this condition...
TIK
TIK
...often lie awake at night thinking, "Why did I say that?"
PEEK
Can't sleep

Memory 1: Conversation with Yamai

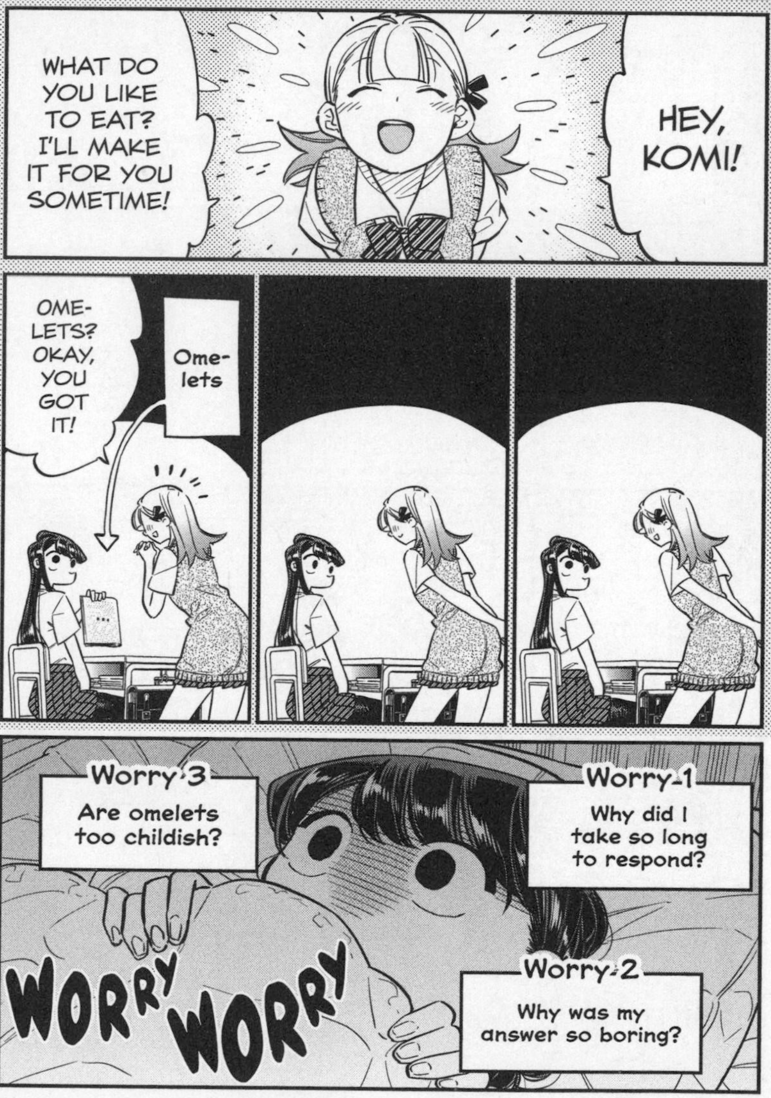
HEY, KOMI!
WHAT DO YOU LIKE TO EAT? I'LL MAKE IT FOR YOU SOMETIME!
Ome-lets
OME-LETS? OKAY, YOU GOT IT!
Worry 1
Why did I take so long to respond?
Worry 2
Why was my answer so boring?
Worry 3
Are omelets too childish?
WORRY WORRY

Memory 2: Conversation with Najimi

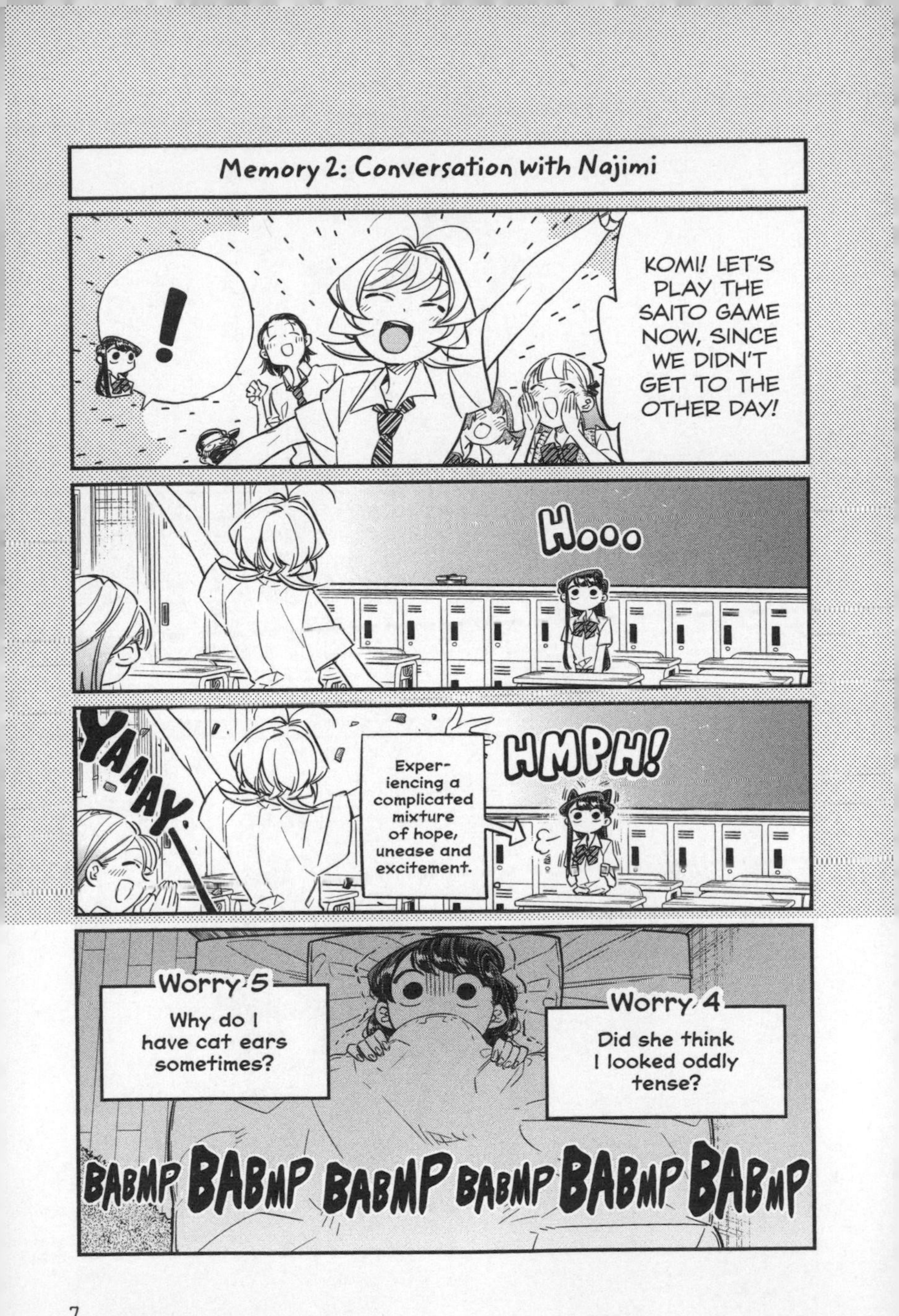
KOMI! LET'S PLAY THE SAITO GAME NOW, SINCE WE DIDN'T GET TO THE OTHER DAY!
!
Hooo
HMPH!
Experiencing a complicated mixture of hope, unease and excitement.
YAAAAY
Worry 4
Did she think I looked oddly tense?
Worry 5
Why do I have cat ears sometimes?
BABMP BABMP BABMP BABMP BABMP BABMP

Memory 3: Conversation with Agari

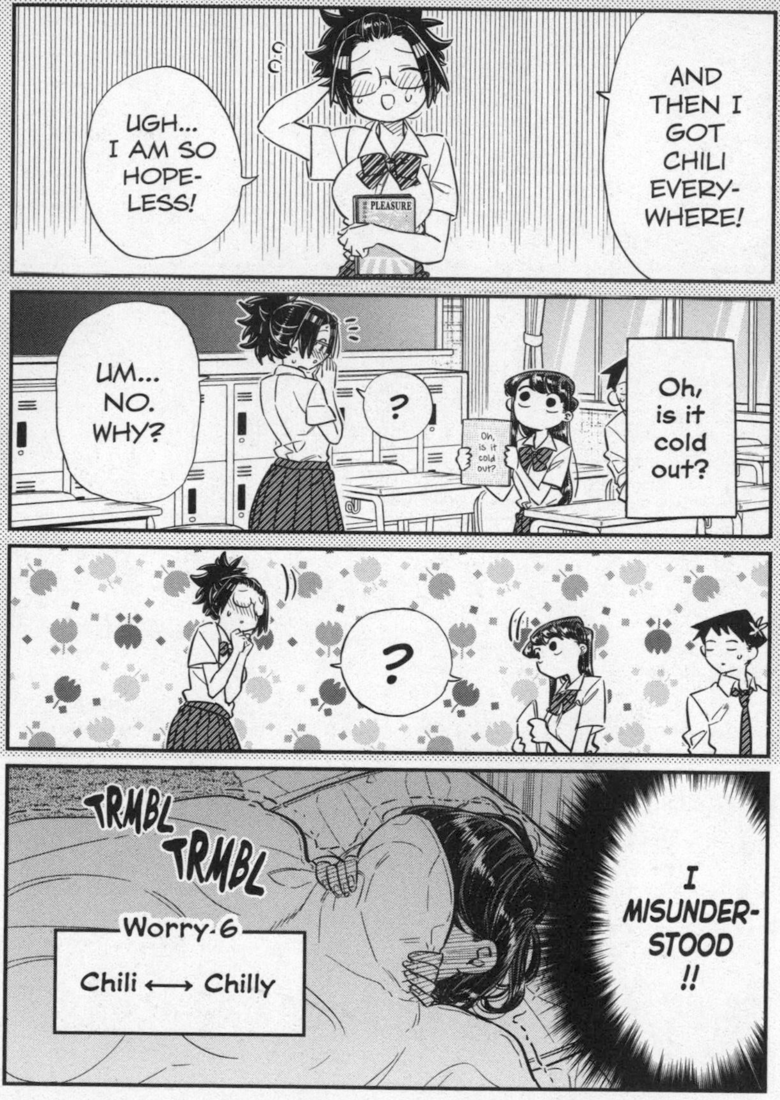
AND THEN I GOT CHILI EVERY-WHERE!
UGH... I AM SO HOPE-LESS!
PLEASURE
Oh, is it cold out?
Oh, is it cold out?
?
UM... NO. WHY?
?
I MISUNDER-STOOD !!
TRMBL TRMBL
Worry 6
Chili ⟷ Chilly

Memory 4: Conversation with Tadano

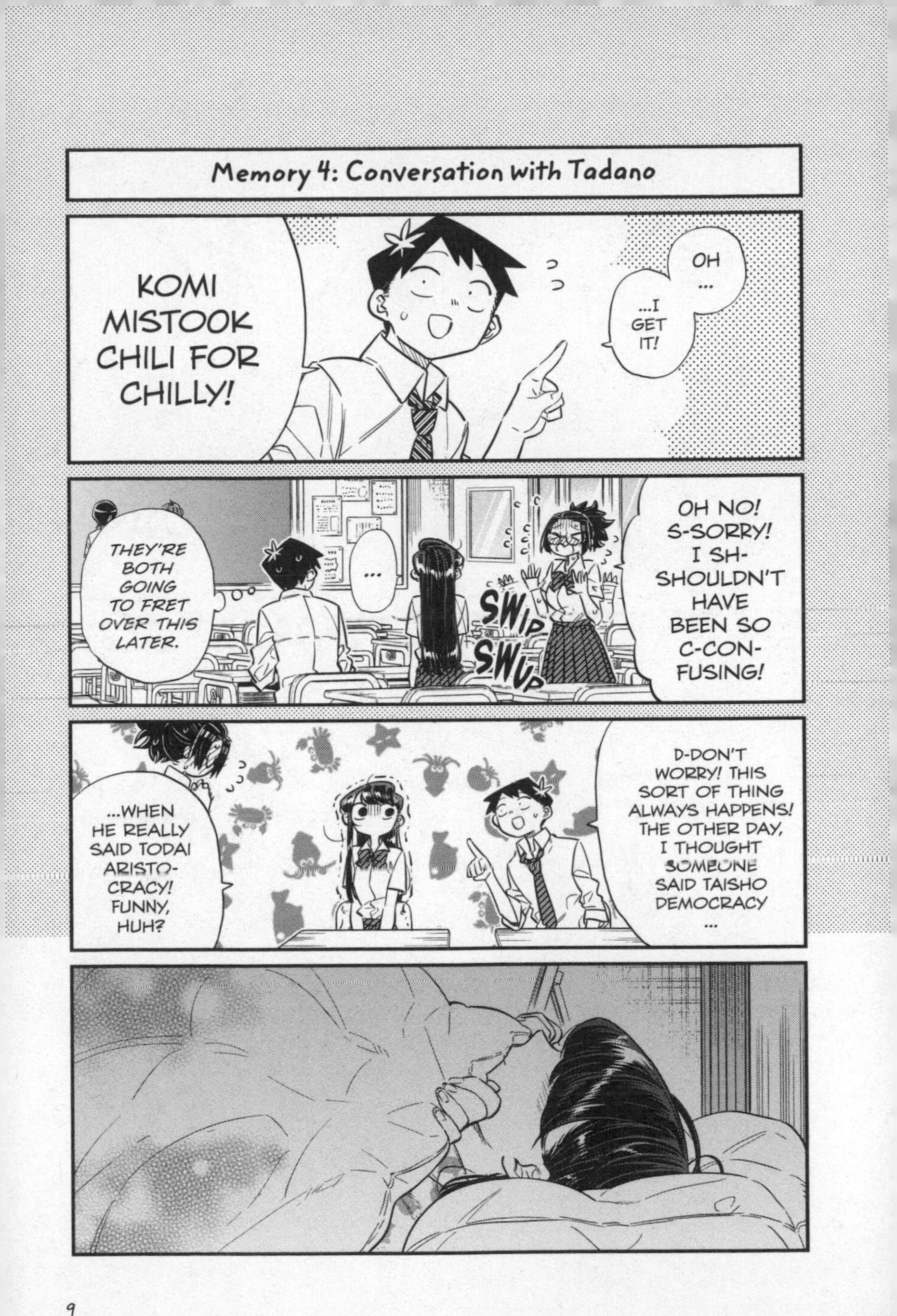
OH ...
...I GET IT!
KOMI MISTOOK CHILI FOR CHILLY!
OH NO! S-SORRY! I SH-SHOULDN'T HAVE BEEN SO C-CON-FUSING!
SWIP SWUP
...
THEY'RE BOTH GOING TO FRET OVER THIS LATER.
D-DON'T WORRY! THIS SORT OF THING ALWAYS HAPPENS! THE OTHER DAY, I THOUGHT SOMEONE SAID TAISHO DEMOCRACY ...
...WHEN HE REALLY SAID TODAI ARISTO-CRACY! FUNNY, HUH?

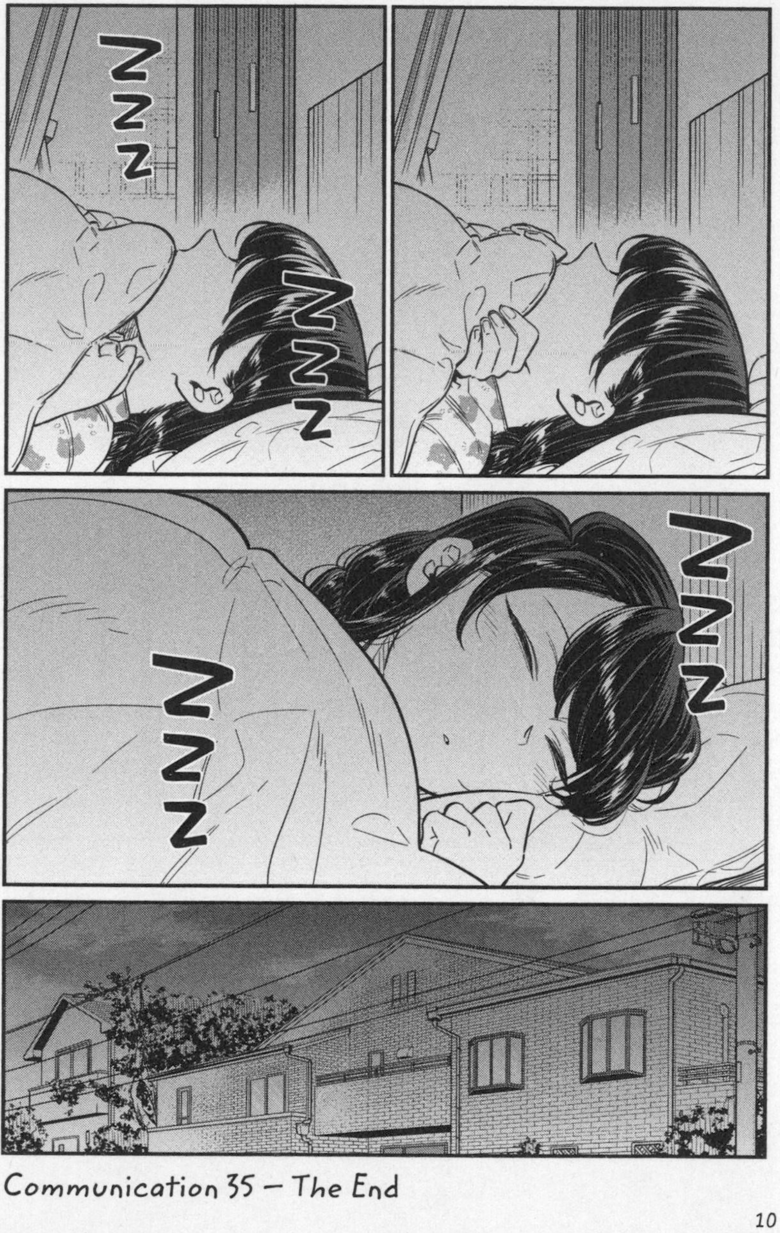
ZZZ
ZZZ
ZZZ
ZZZ

Communication 35 — The End

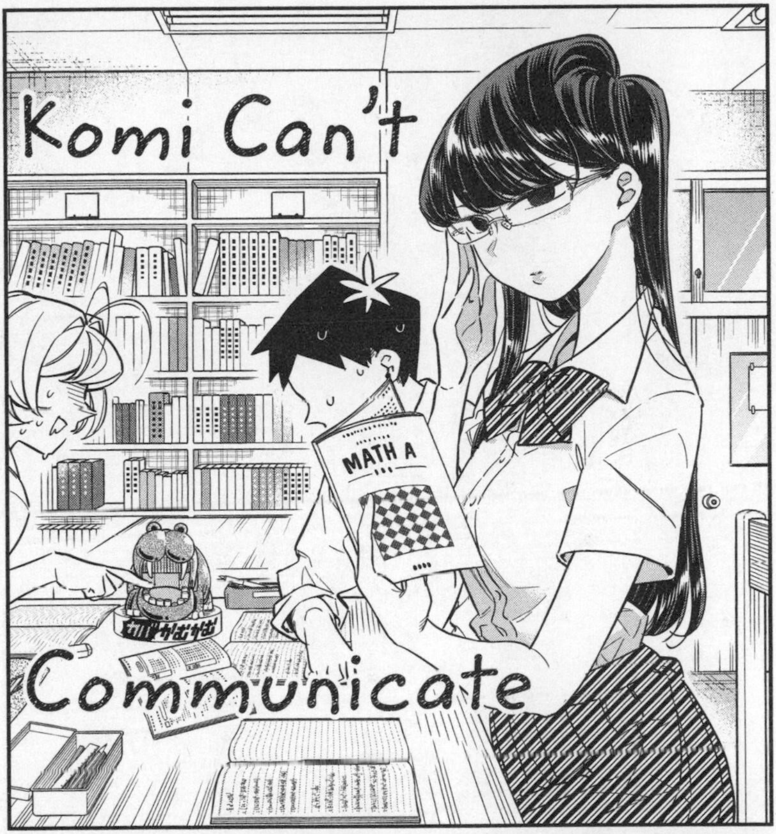
Komi Can't
MATH A
Communicate

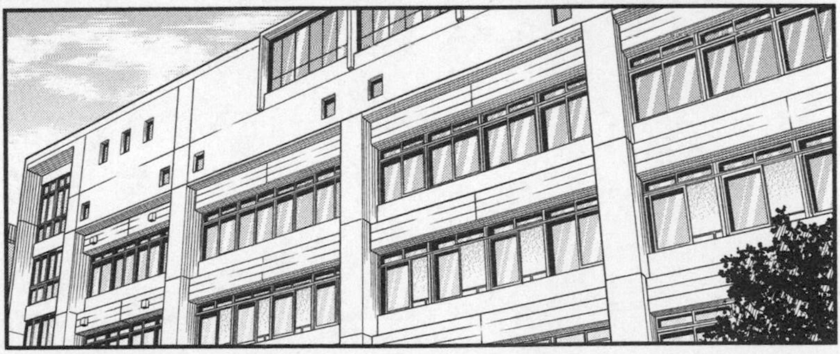

Communication 36: Studying for Tests

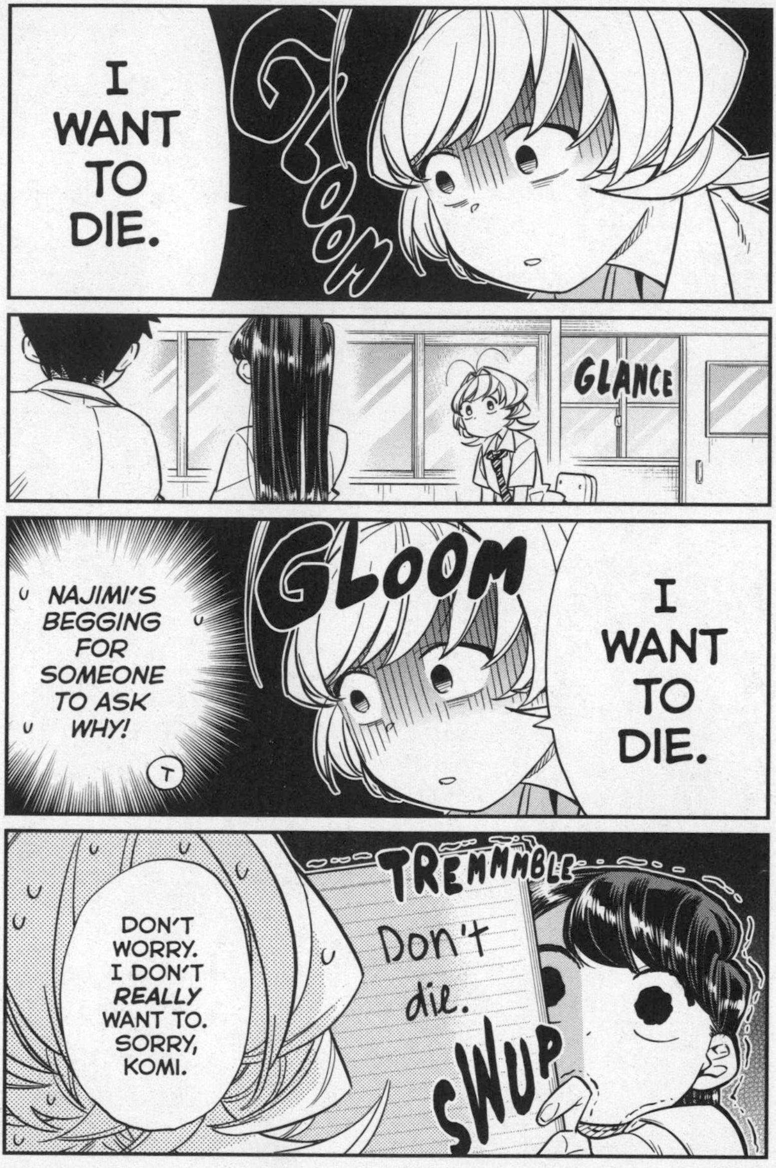
GLOOM
I WANT TO DIE.
GLANCE
I WANT TO DIE.
GLOOM
NAJIMI'S BEGGING FOR SOMEONE TO ASK WHY!
T
TREMMMBLE
Don't die.
SWUP
DON'T WORRY. I DON'T *REALLY* WANT TO. SORRY, KOMI.

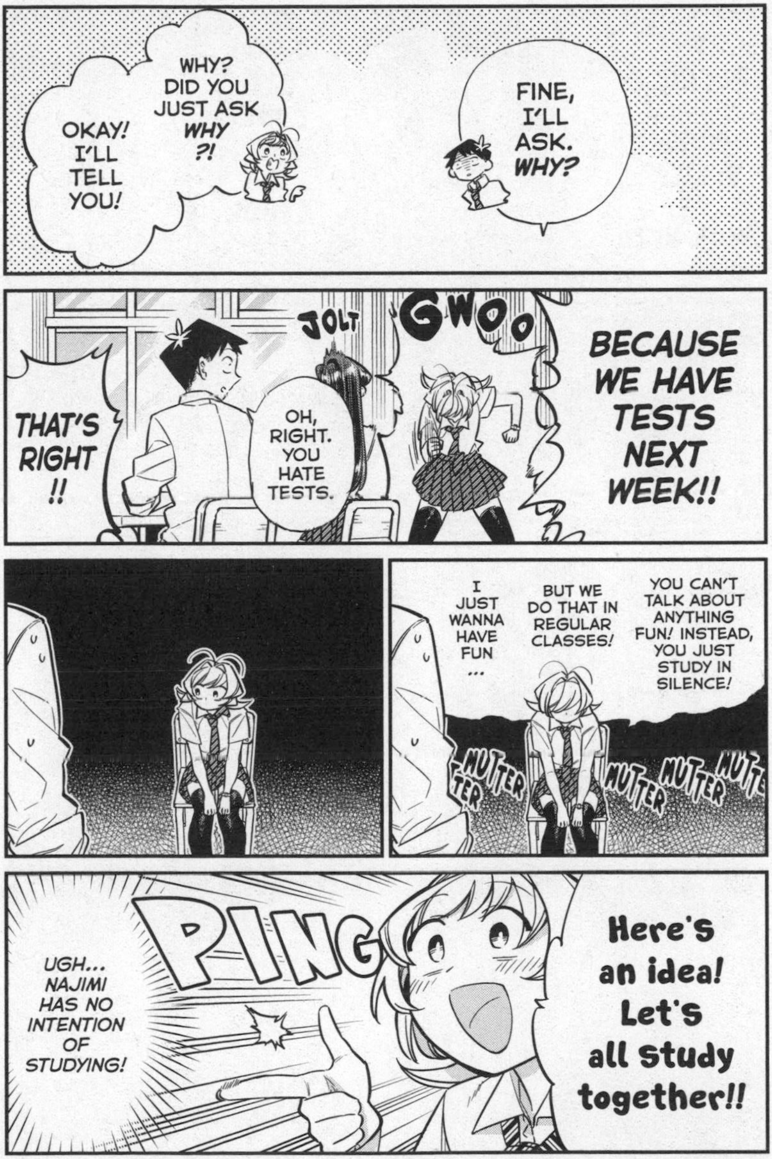
FINE, I'LL ASK. WHY?
WHY? DID YOU JUST ASK WHY?!
OKAY! I'LL TELL YOU!
BECAUSE WE HAVE TESTS NEXT WEEK!!
GWOO
JOLT
OH, RIGHT. YOU HATE TESTS.
THAT'S RIGHT!!
YOU CAN'T TALK ABOUT ANYTHING FUN! INSTEAD, YOU JUST STUDY IN SILENCE!
BUT WE DO THAT IN REGULAR CLASSES!
I JUST WANNA HAVE FUN...
MUTTER MUTTER MUTTER MUTTER
Here's an idea! Let's all study together!!
PING
UGH... NAJIMI HAS NO INTENTION OF STUDYING!

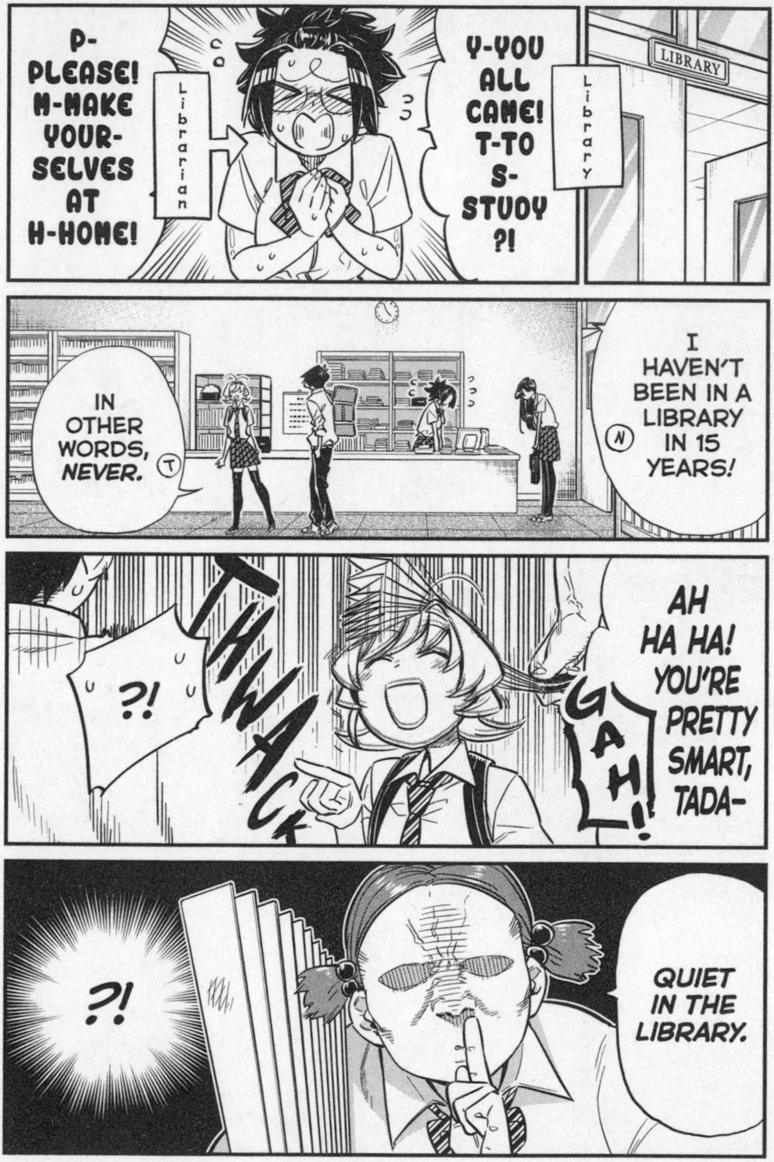
LIBRARY
Library
Y-YOU ALL CAME! T-TO S-STUDY?!
Librarian
P-PLEASE! M-MAKE YOURSELVES AT H-HOME!
I HAVEN'T BEEN IN A LIBRARY IN 15 YEARS!
N
IN OTHER WORDS, *NEVER.*
T
AH HA HA! YOU'RE PRETTY SMART, TADA-
GAH!
THWACK
?!
QUIET IN THE LIBRARY.
?!

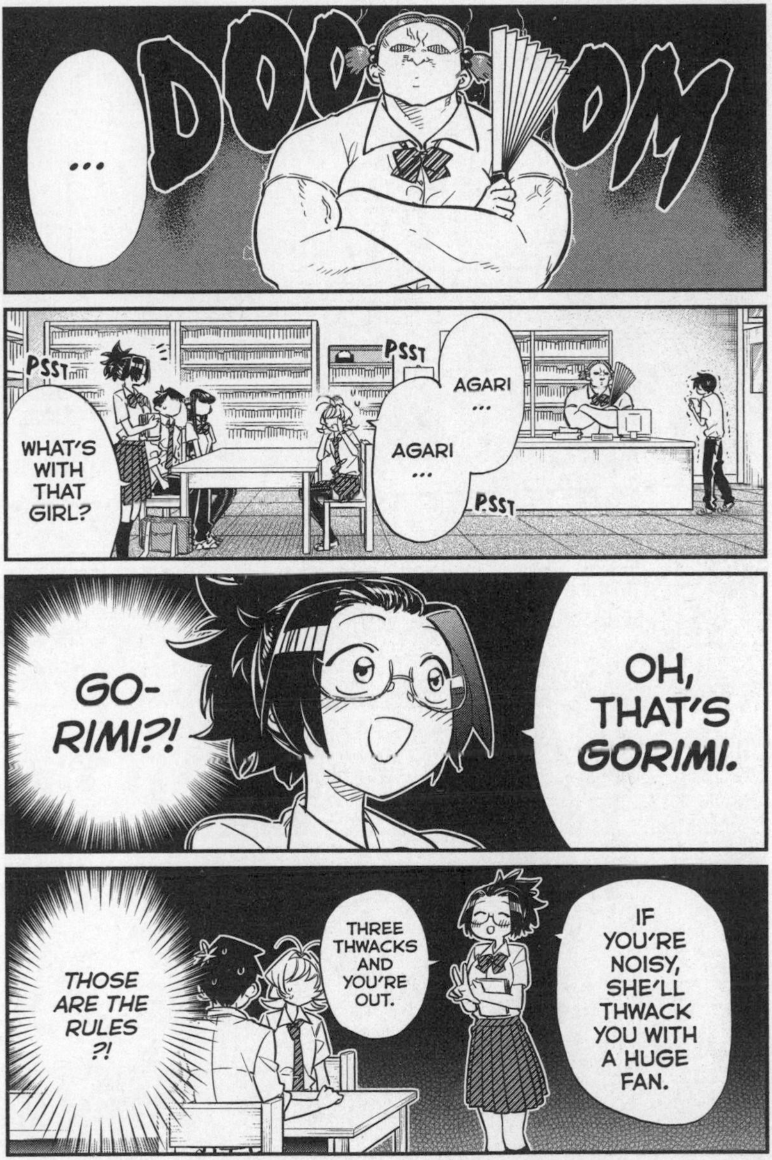
DOOOM
...
PSST
AGARI ...
AGARI ...
PSST
PSST
WHAT'S WITH THAT GIRL?
OH, THAT'S GORIMI.
GO-RIMI?!
IF YOU'RE NOISY, SHE'LL THWACK YOU WITH A HUGE FAN.
THREE THWACKS AND YOU'RE OUT.
THOSE ARE THE RULES ?!

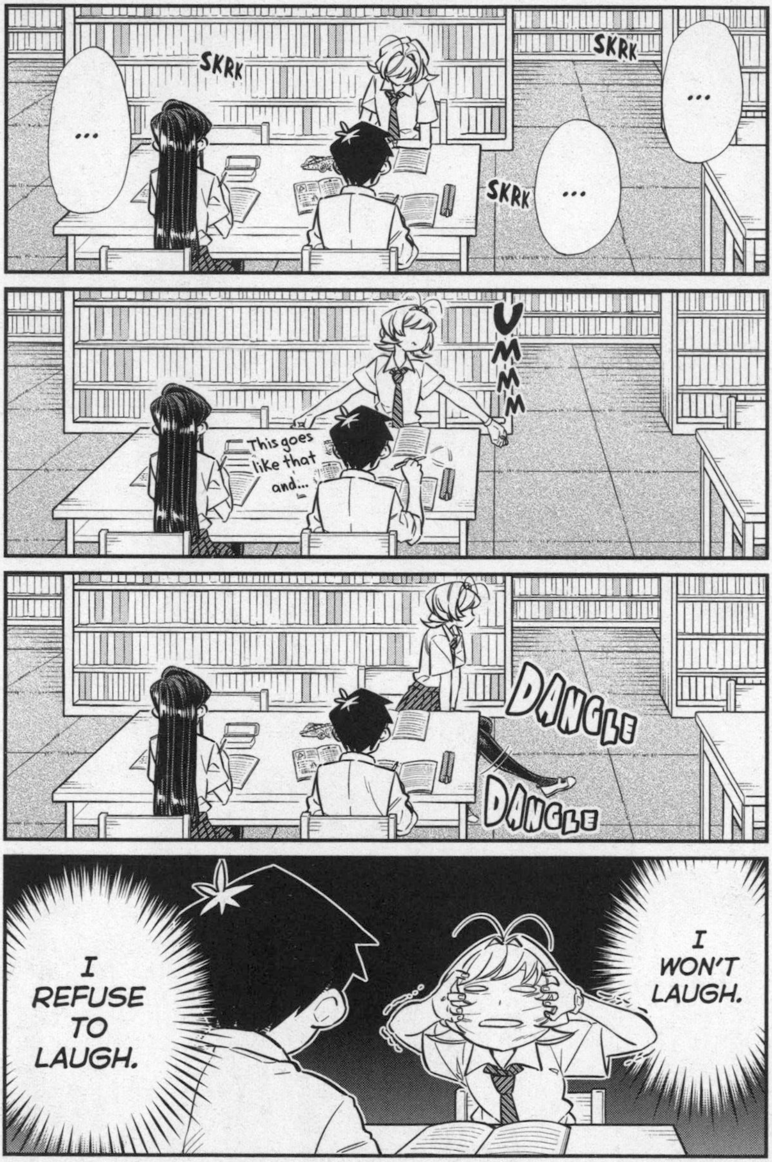
...
SKRK
...
SKRK
SKRK
...
UMMM
This goes like that and...
DANGLE
DANGLE
I WON'T LAUGH.
I REFUSE TO LAUGH.

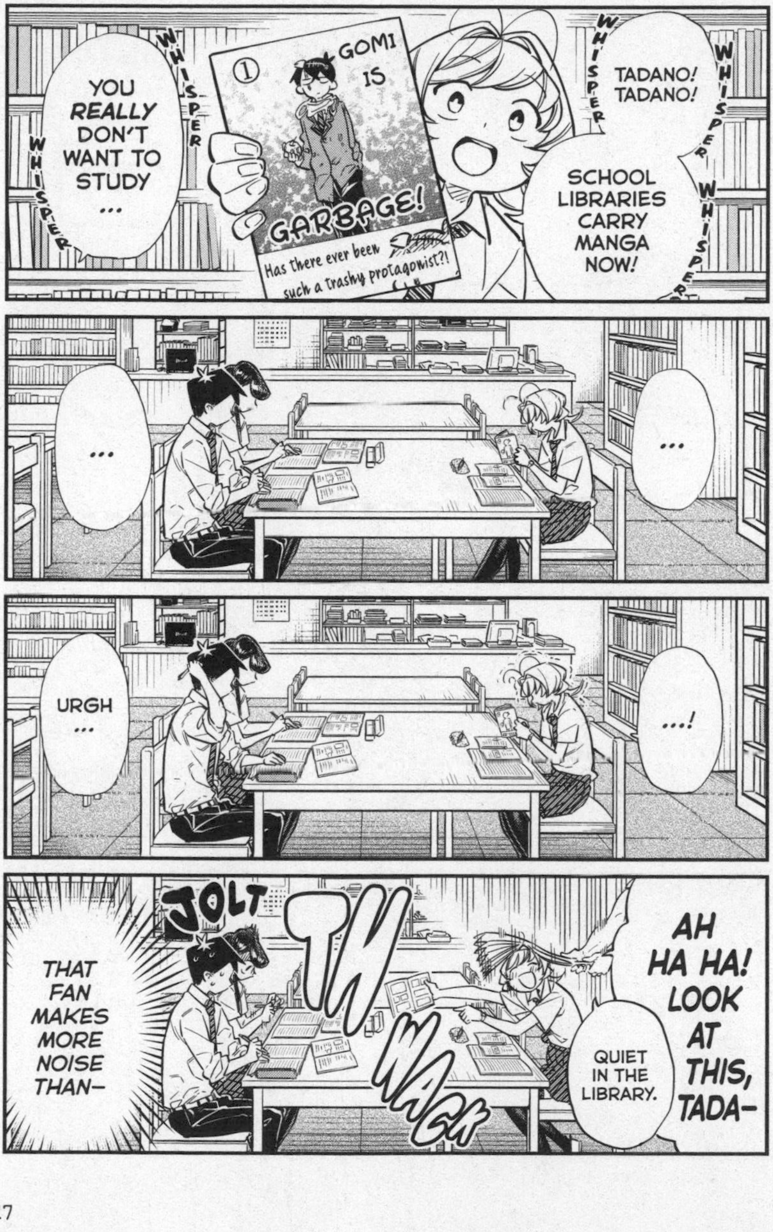
WHISPER
TADANO! TADANO!
WHISPER
SCHOOL LIBRARIES CARRY MANGA NOW!
WHISPER
① GOMI IS GARBAGE!
Has there ever been such a trashy protagonist?!
WHISPER
YOU REALLY DON'T WANT TO STUDY ...
WHISPER
...
...
...!
URGH ...
AH HA HA! LOOK AT THIS, TADA—
QUIET IN THE LIBRARY.
THWACK
JOLT
THAT FAN MAKES MORE NOISE THAN—

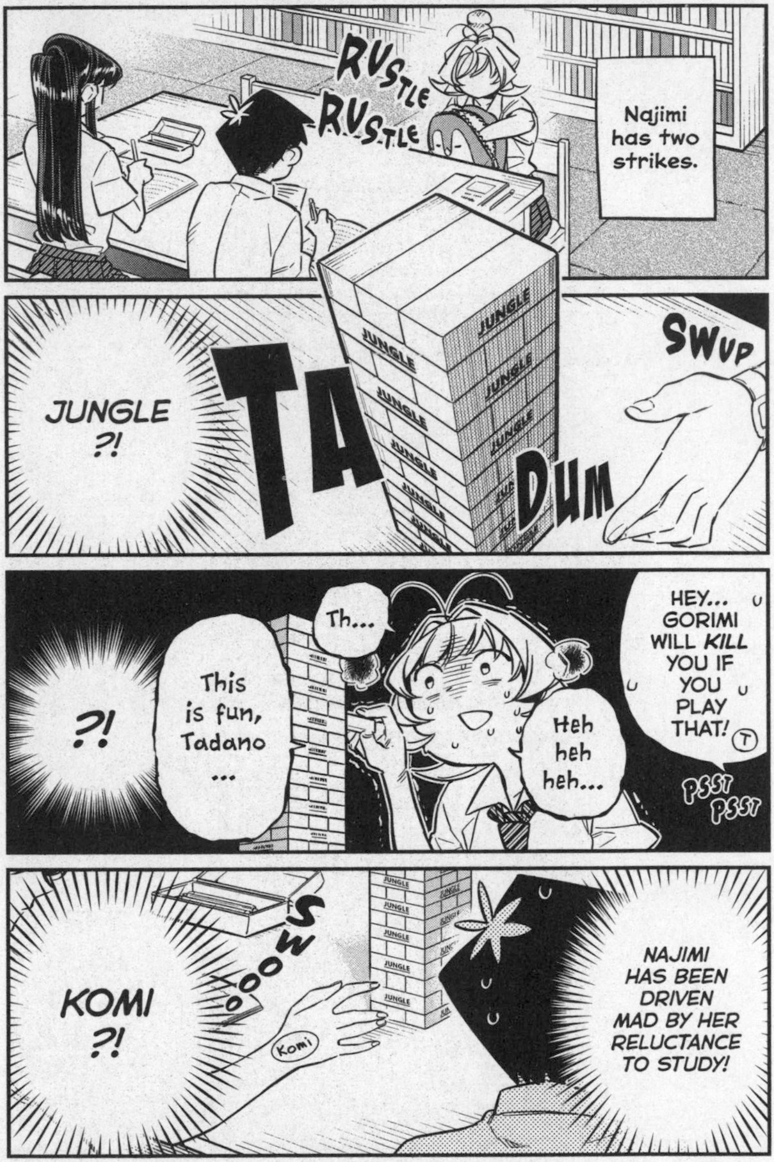
Najimi has two strikes.
RUSTLE RUSTLE
SWUP
TA DUM
JUNGLE ?!
HEY... GORIMI WILL KILL YOU IF YOU PLAY THAT!
PSST PSST
Heh heh heh...
Th...
This is fun, Tadano ...
?!
NAJIMI HAS BEEN DRIVEN MAD BY HER RELUCTANCE TO STUDY!
SWOOOO
Komi
KOMI ?!

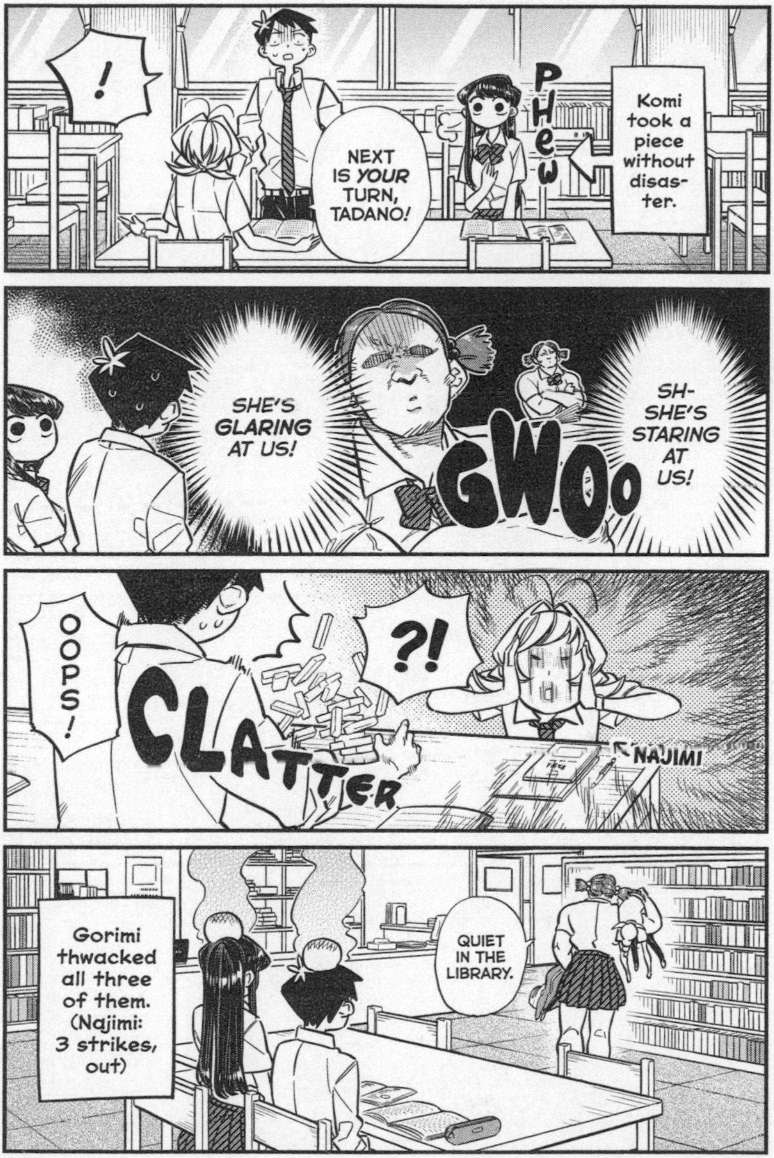
Komi took a piece without disaster.
PHEW
NEXT IS YOUR TURN, TADANO!
!
SH- SHE'S STARING AT US!
GWOO
SHE'S GLARING AT US!
NAJIMI
?!
CLATTER
OOPS!
QUIET IN THE LIBRARY.
Gorimi thwacked all three of them. (Najimi: 3 strikes, out)

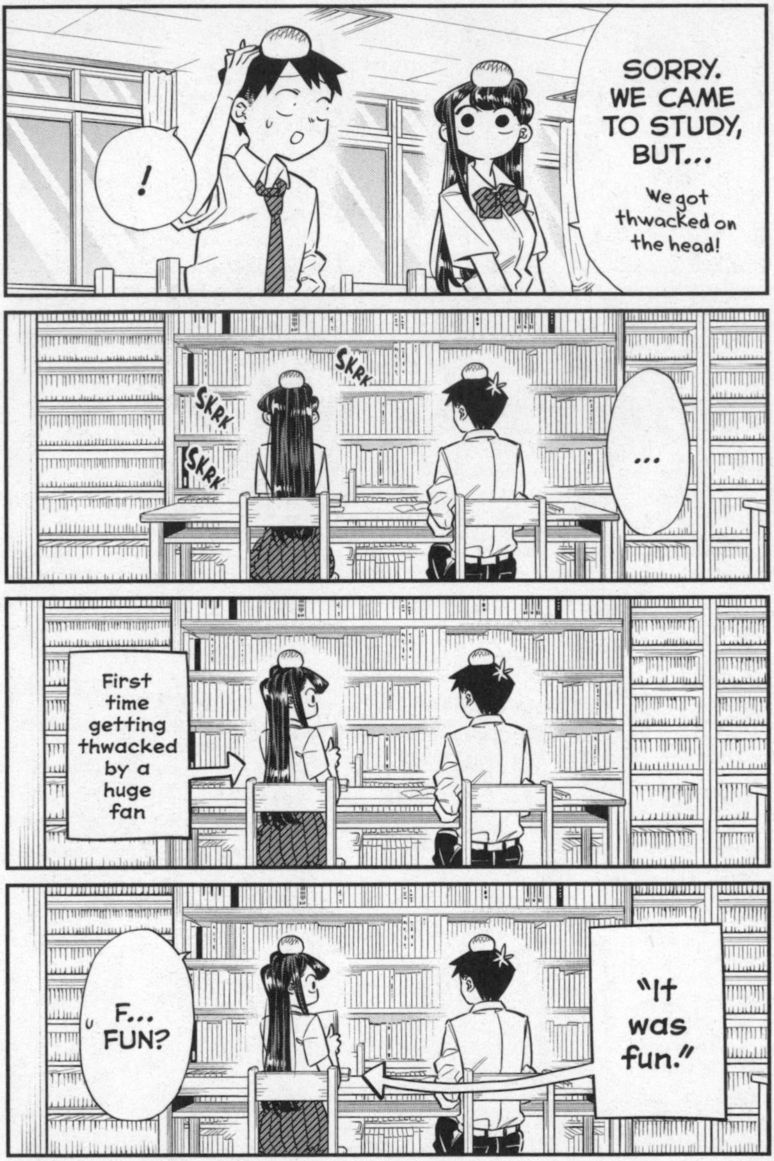
SORRY. WE CAME TO STUDY, BUT...
We got thwacked on the head!
!
SKRK
SKRK
SKRK
...
First time getting thwacked by a huge fan
"It was fun."
F... FUN?

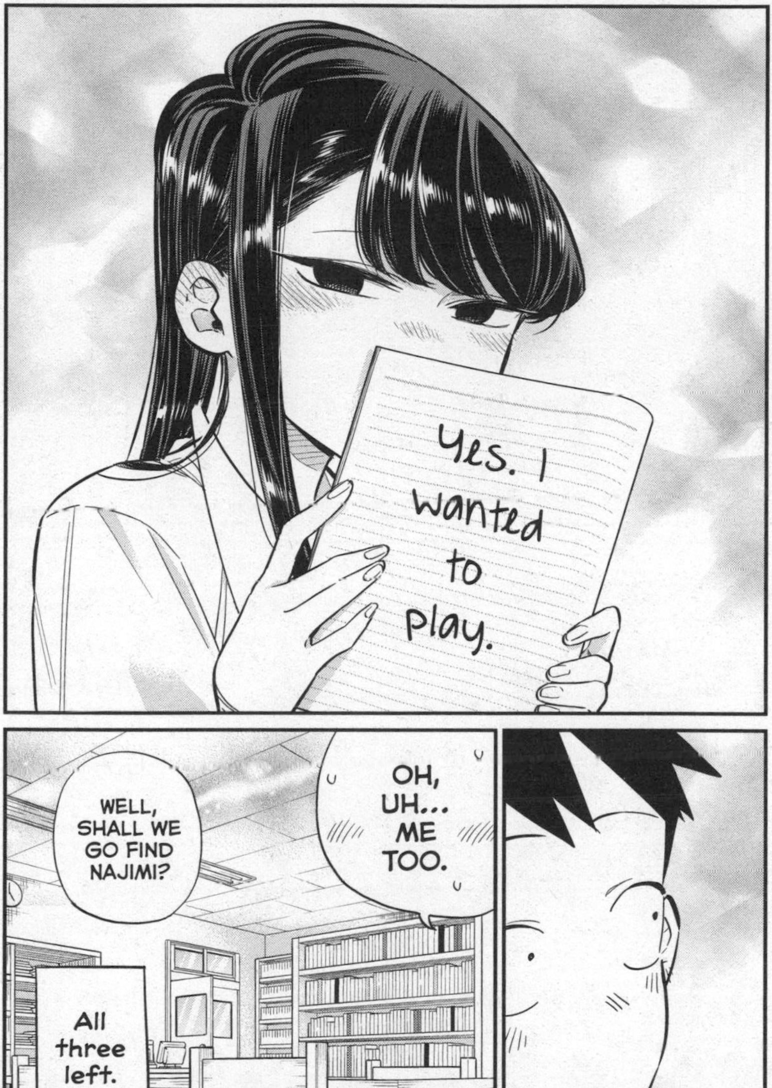
Yes. I wanted to play.
OH, UH... ME TOO.
WELL, SHALL WE GO FIND NAJIMI?
All three left.

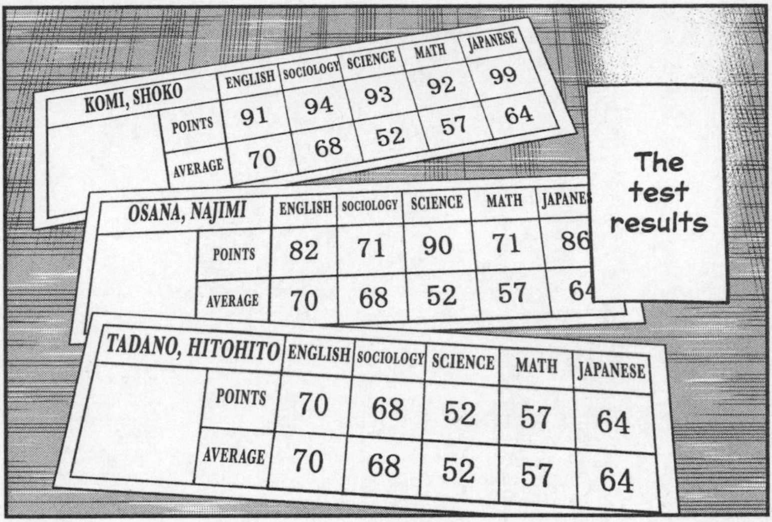
The test results
KOMI, SHOKO | ENGLISH | SOCIOLOGY | SCIENCE | MATH | JAPANESE
POINTS | 91 | 94 | 93 | 92 | 99
AVERAGE | 70 | 68 | 52 | 57 | 64
OSANA, NAJIMI | ENGLISH | SOCIOLOGY | SCIENCE | MATH | JAPANES
POINTS | 82 | 71 | 90 | 71 | 86
AVERAGE | 70 | 68 | 52 | 57 | 64
TADANO, HITOHITO | ENGLISH | SOCIOLOGY | SCIENCE | MATH | JAPANESE
POINTS | 70 | 68 | 52 | 57 | 64
AVERAGE | 70 | 68 | 52 | 57 | 64

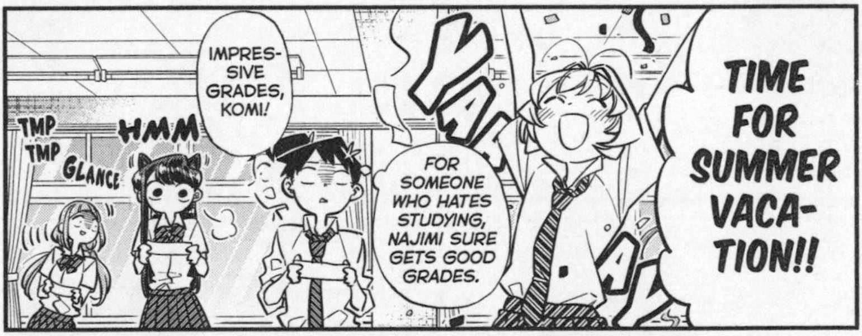
TIME FOR SUMMER VACA-TION!!
FOR SOMEONE WHO HATES STUDYING, NAJIMI SURE GETS GOOD GRADES.
IMPRES-SIVE GRADES, KOMI!
HMM
TMP TMP
GLANCE

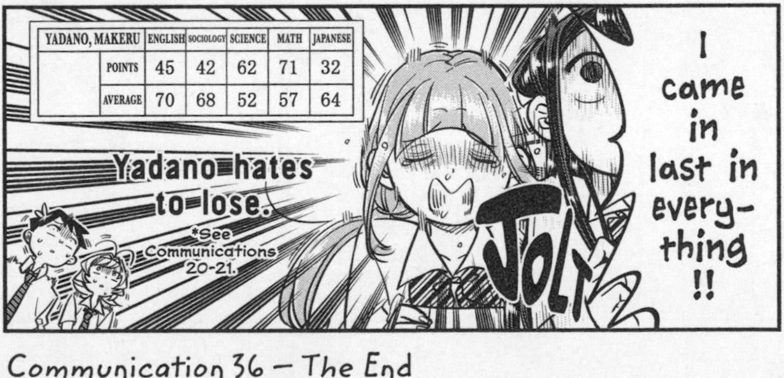
I came in last in every-thing!!
JOLT
YADANO, MAKERU | ENGLISH | SOCIOLOGY | SCIENCE | MATH | JAPANESE
POINTS | 45 | 42 | 62 | 71 | 32
AVERAGE | 70 | 68 | 52 | 57 | 64
Yadano hates to lose.
*See Communications 20-21.

Communication 36 – The End

Komi Can't Communicate

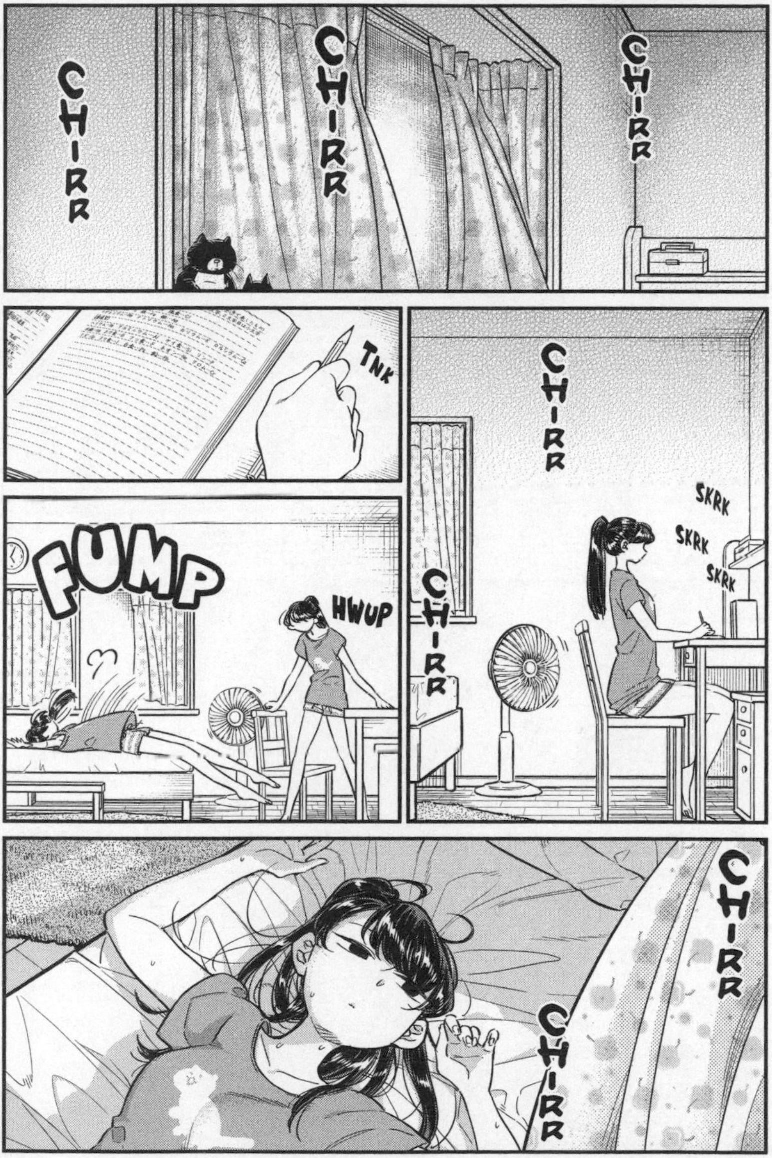
CHIRR
CHIRR
CHIRR
CHIRR
SKRK
SKRK
SKRK
CHIRR
TNK
HWUP
FUMP
CHIRR
CHIRR

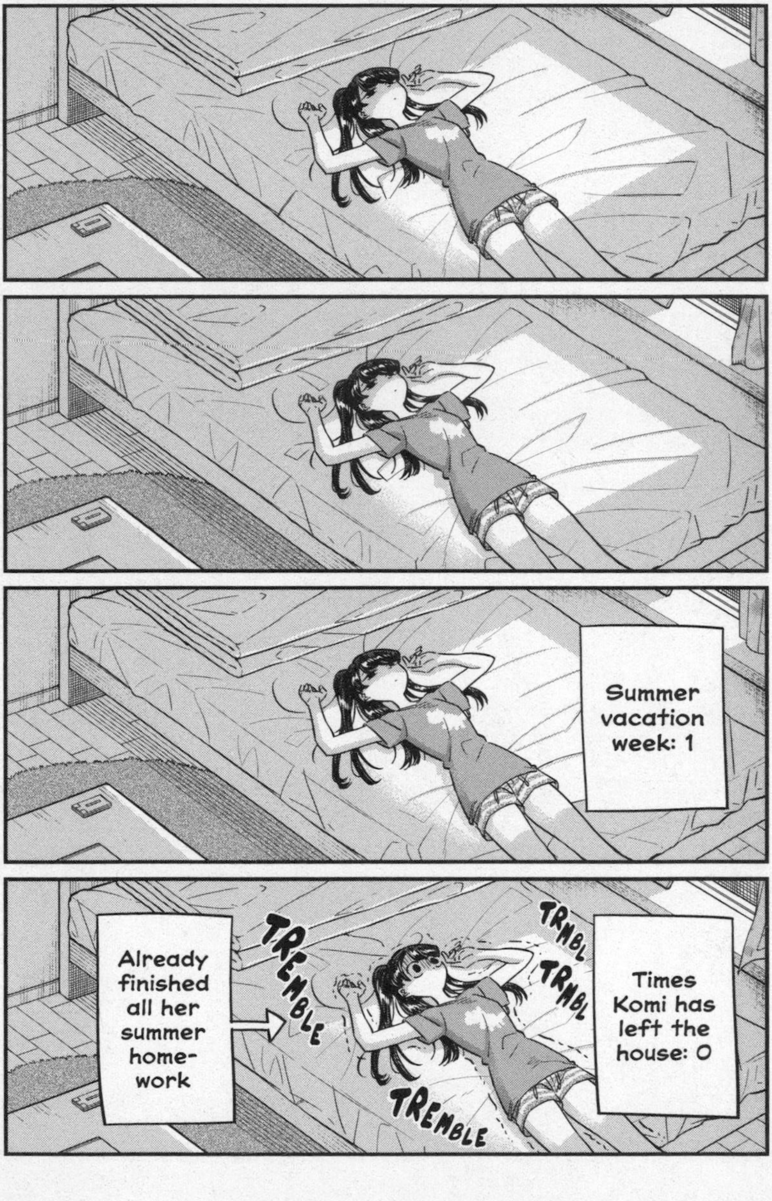
Summer vacation week: 1
TRMBL
Times Komi has left the house: 0
TRMBL
TREMBLE
Already finished all her summer home-work
TREMBLE

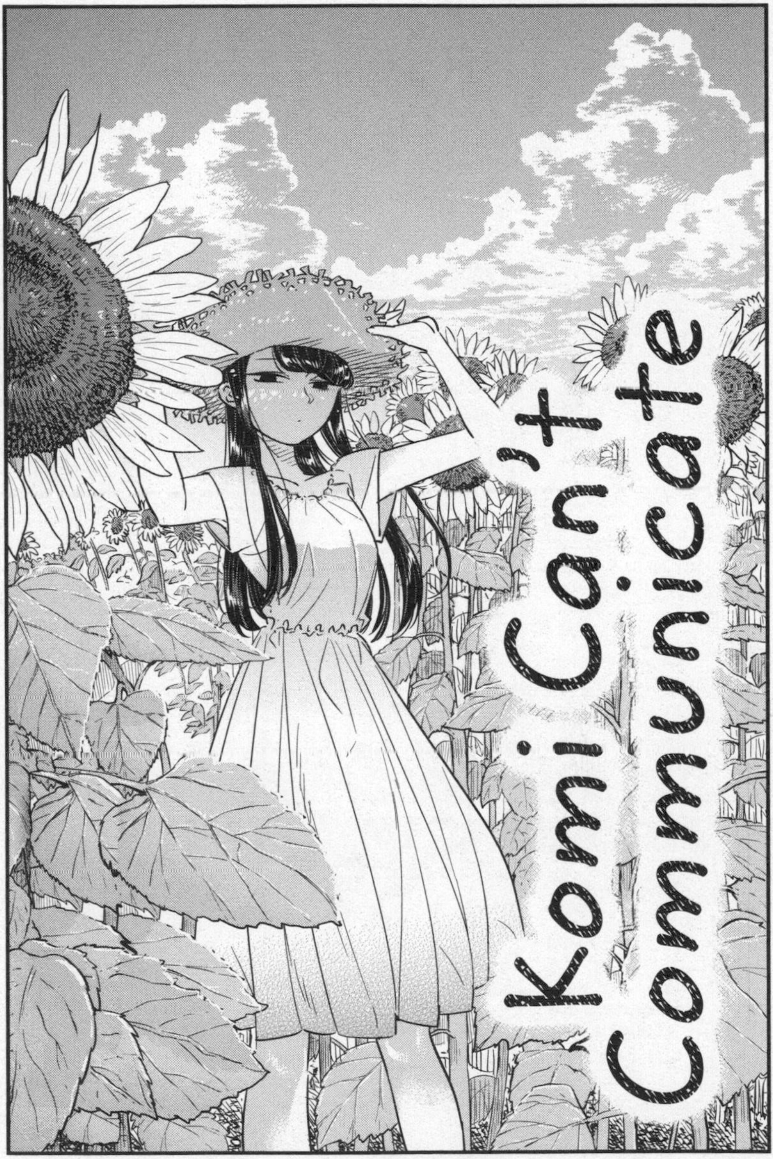
Komi Can't Communicate

Communication 37: Summer Vacation

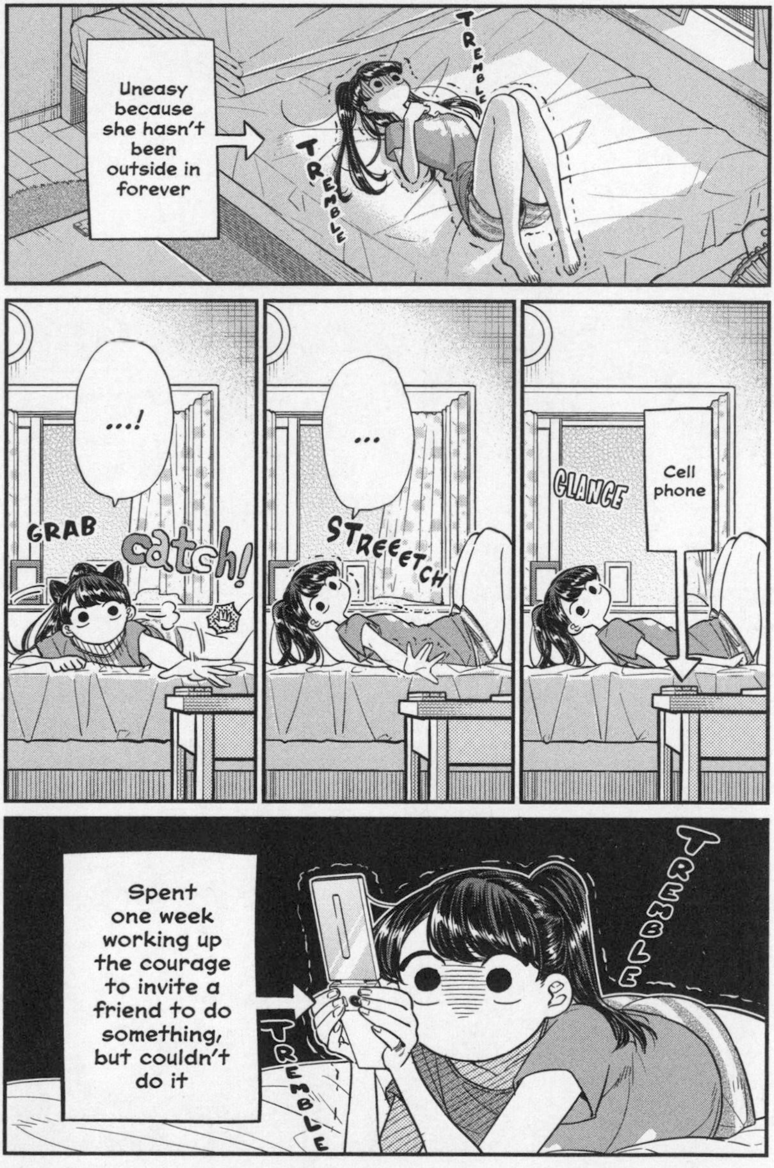
TREMBLE
Uneasy because she hasn't been outside in forever
TREMBLE
GLANCE
Cell phone
...
STREEETCH
...!
GRAB
catch!
TREMBLE
Spent one week working up the courage to invite a friend to do something, but couldn't do it
TREMBLE

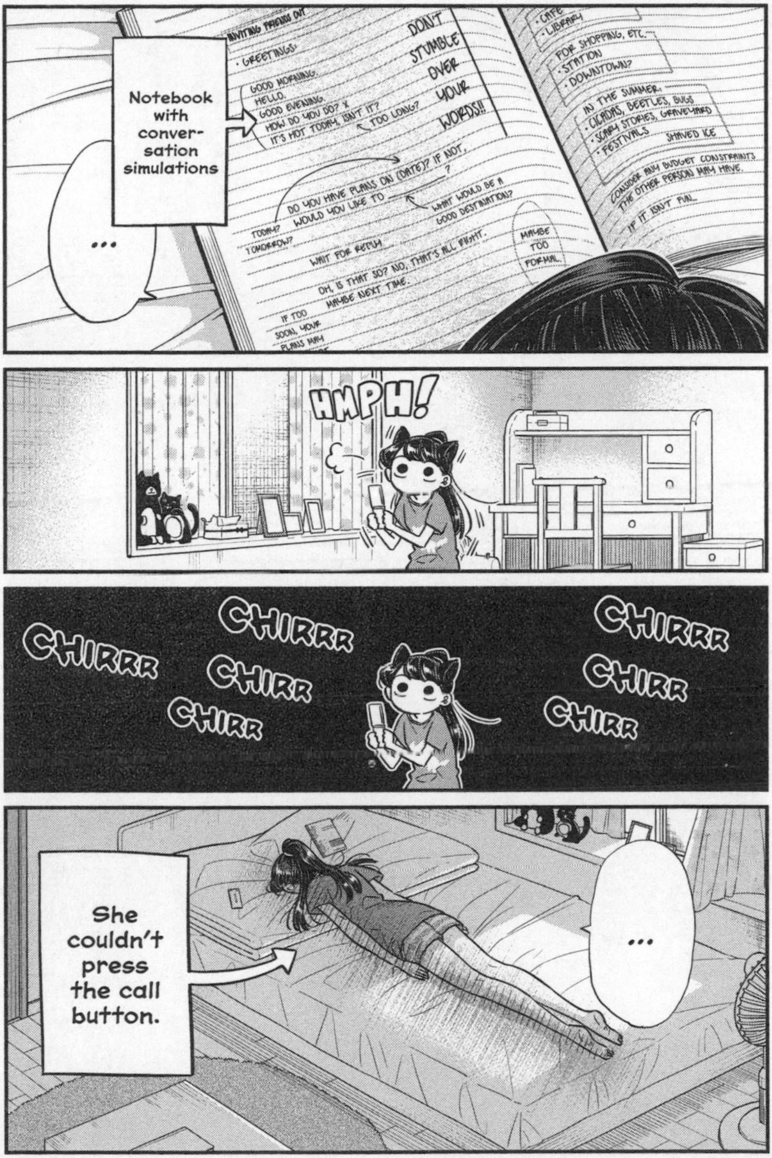

Notebook with conver-sation simulations
INVITING FRIENDS OUT
• GREETINGS:
GOOD MORNING.
HELLO.
GOOD EVENING.
HOW DO YOU DO? X
IT'S HOT TODAY, ISN'T IT?
TOO LONG?
DON'T STUMBLE OVER YOUR WORDS!!
DO YOU HAVE PLANS ON (DATE)? IF NOT, WOULD YOU LIKE TO ___?
TODAY? TOMORROW?
WHAT WOULD BE A GOOD DESTINATION?
WAIT FOR REPLY
OH, IS THAT SO? NO, THAT'S ALL RIGHT. MAYBE NEXT TIME.
MAYBE TOO FORMAL
IF TOO SOON, YOUR PLANS MAY
• CAFE
• LIBRARY
FOR SHOPPING, ETC.
• STATION
• DOWNTOWN?
IN THE SUMMER:
• CICADAS, BEETLES, BUGS
• SCARY STORIES, GRAVEYARD
• FESTIVALS
SHAVED ICE
CONSIDER ANY BUDGET CONSTRAINTS THE OTHER PERSON MAY HAVE.
IF IT ISN'T FUN
...
HMPH!
CHIRRR
CHIRR
CHIRR
CHIRRR
CHIRR
CHIRRR
CHIRR
...
She couldn't press the call button.

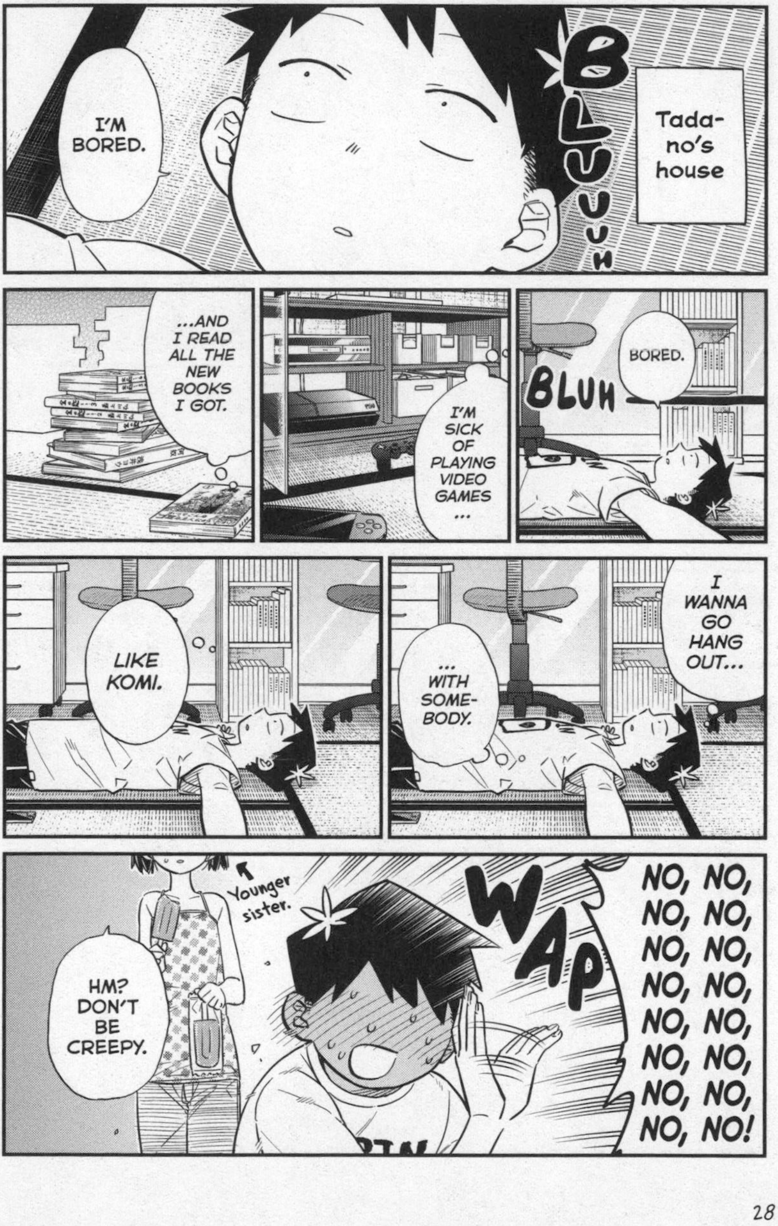

Tada-no's house
BLUUUUH
I'M BORED.
BORED.
BLUH
I'M SICK OF PLAYING VIDEO GAMES...
...AND I READ ALL THE NEW BOOKS I GOT.
I WANNA GO HANG OUT...
... WITH SOMEBODY.
LIKE KOMI.
NO, NO, NO, NO, NO, NO, NO, NO, NO, NO, NO, NO, NO, NO, NO, NO!
WAP
Younger sister.
HM? DON'T BE CREEPY.

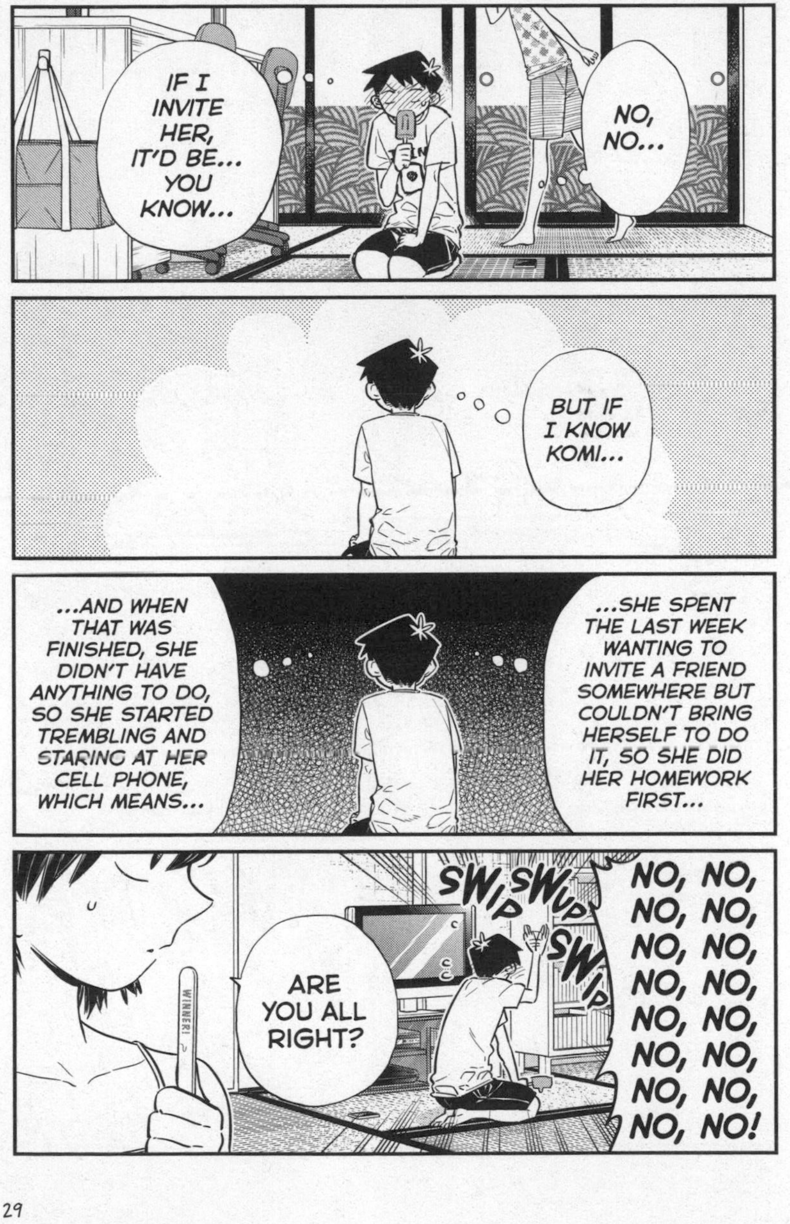
NO, NO...
IF I INVITE HER, IT'D BE... YOU KNOW...
BUT IF I KNOW KOMI...
...SHE SPENT THE LAST WEEK WANTING TO INVITE A FRIEND SOMEWHERE BUT COULDN'T BRING HERSELF TO DO IT, SO SHE DID HER HOMEWORK FIRST...
...AND WHEN THAT WAS FINISHED, SHE DIDN'T HAVE ANYTHING TO DO, SO SHE STARTED TREMBLING AND STARING AT HER CELL PHONE, WHICH MEANS...
NO, NO, NO, NO, NO, NO, NO, NO, NO, NO, NO, NO, NO, NO, NO, NO!
SWIP SWUP SWIP
ARE YOU ALL RIGHT?

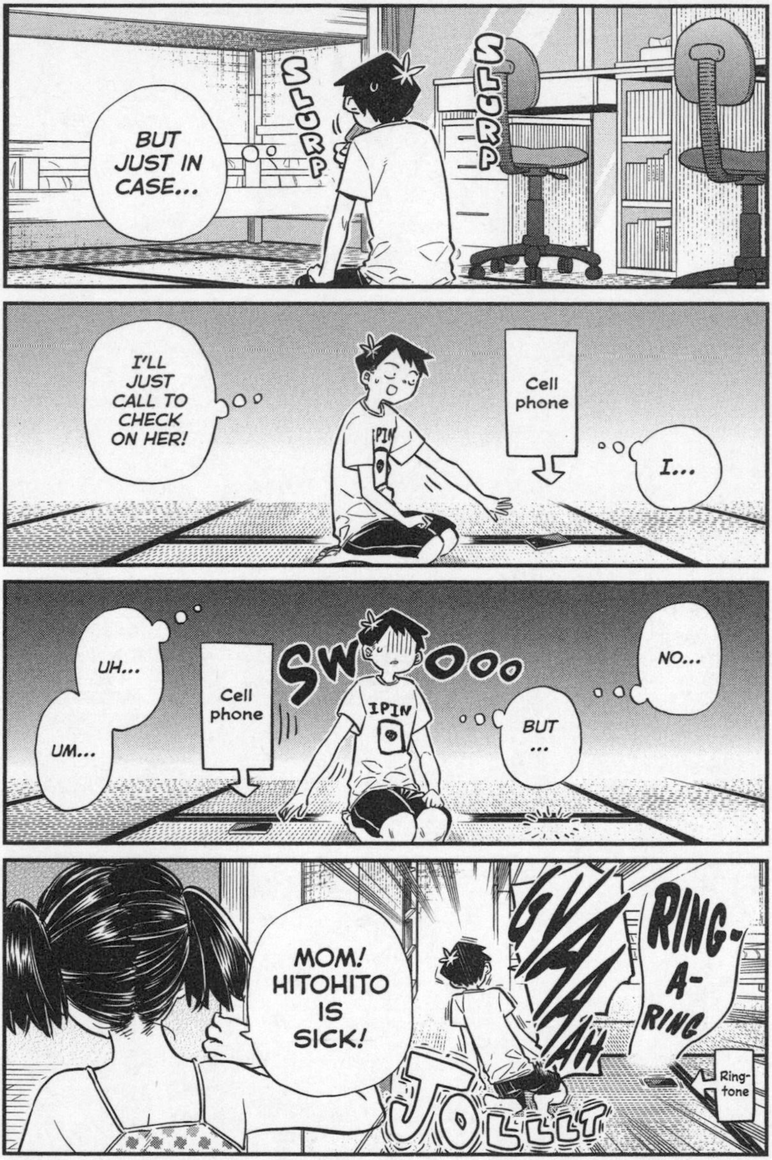
SLURP
SLURP
BUT JUST IN CASE...
I...
Cell phone
I'LL JUST CALL TO CHECK ON HER!
NO...
BUT ...
SWOOO
Cell phone
UH...
UM...
Ring-tone
RING-A-RING
GYAAAAH
JOLLLT
MOM! HITOHITO IS SICK!

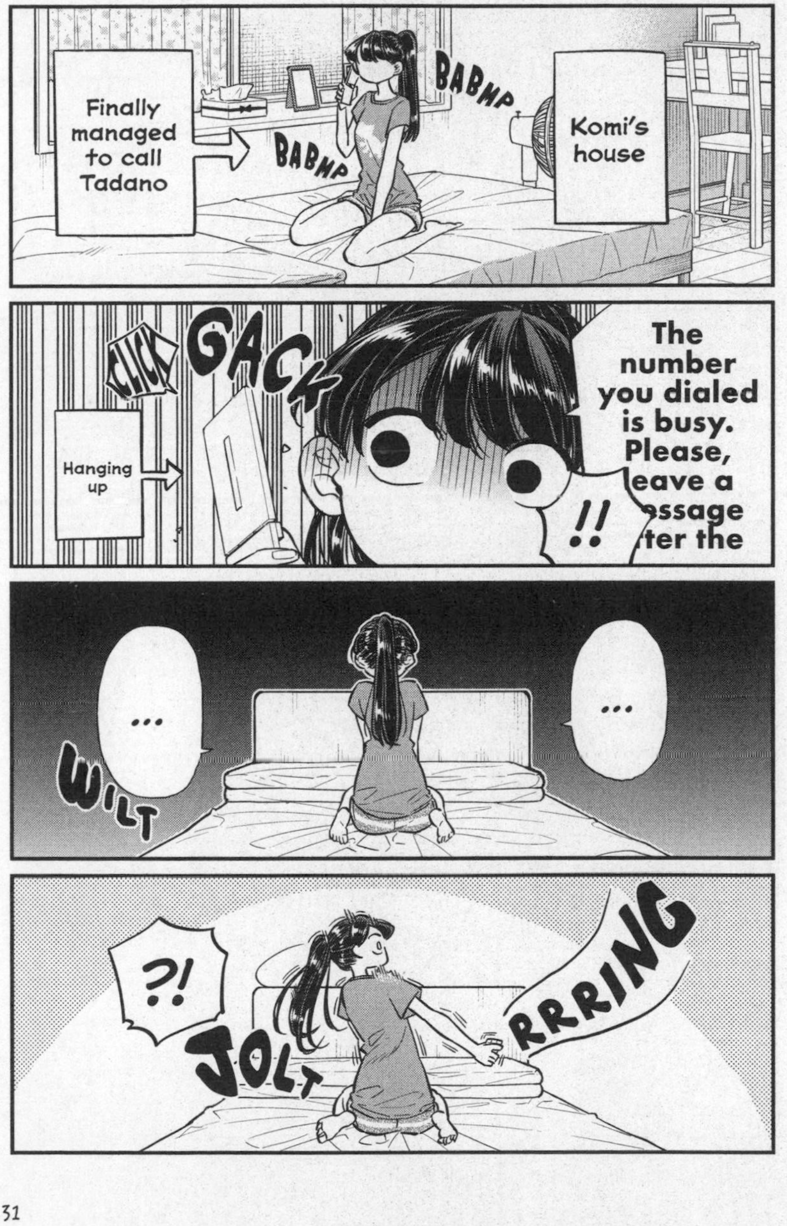
Komi's house
BABMP
BABMP
Finally managed to call Tadano
The number you dialed is busy. Please, leave a essage ter the
!!
GACK
CLICK
Hanging up
...
...
WILT
RRRING
?!
JOLT

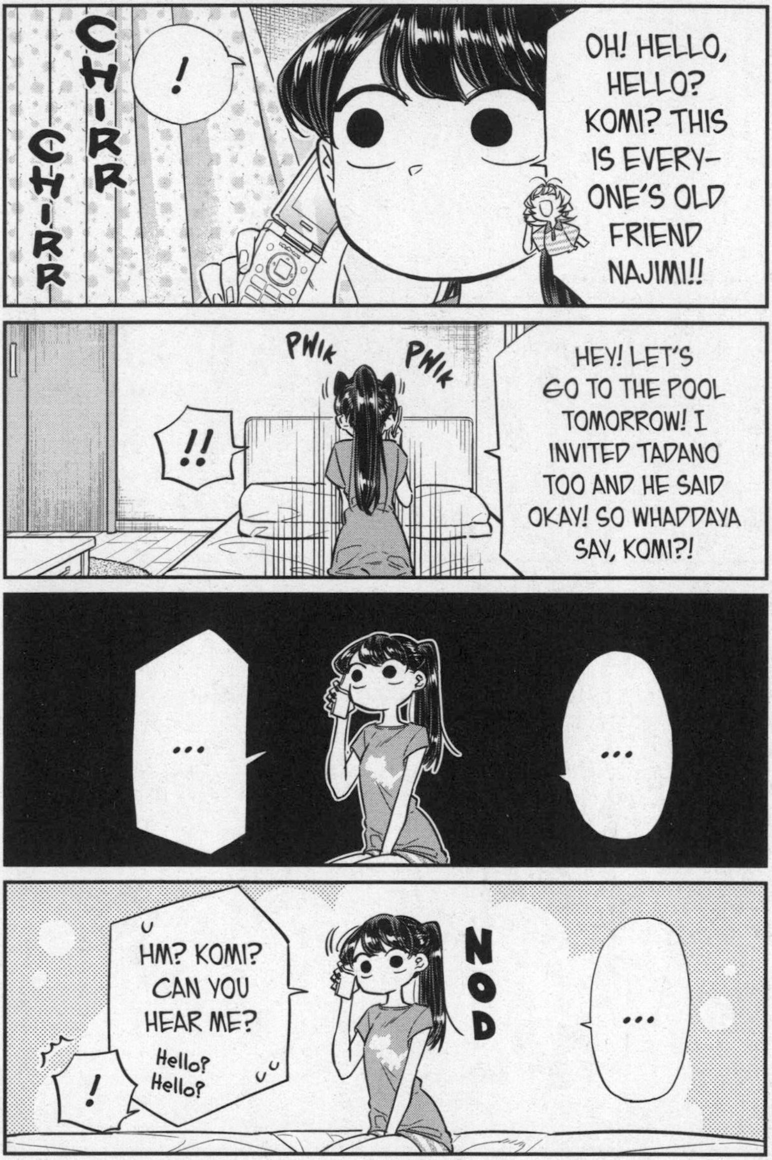
OH! HELLO, HELLO? KOMI? THIS IS EVERY-ONE'S OLD FRIEND NAJIMI!!
!
CHIRR
CHIRR
HEY! LET'S GO TO THE POOL TOMORROW! I INVITED TADANO TOO AND HE SAID OKAY! SO WHADDAYA SAY, KOMI?!
PWIK
PWIK
!!
...
...
...
NOD
HM? KOMI? CAN YOU HEAR ME?
Hello? Hello?
!

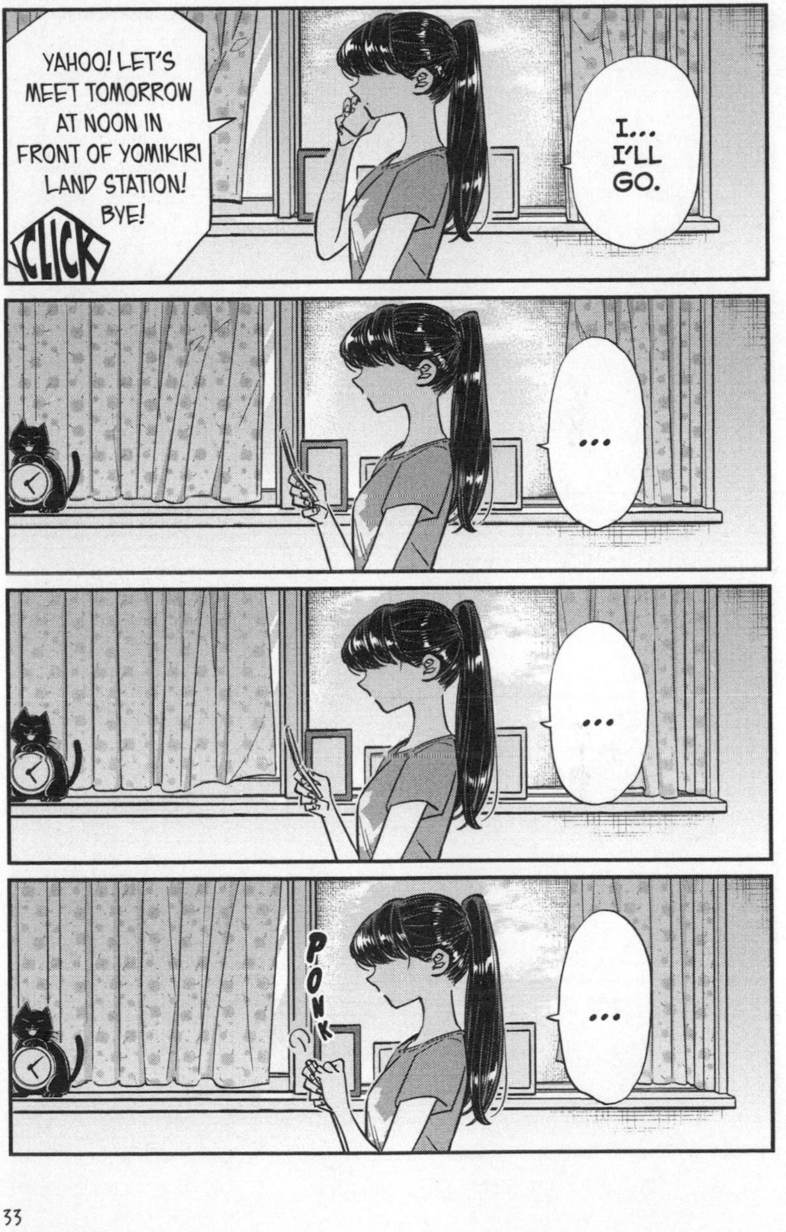
I... I'LL GO.
YAHOO! LET'S MEET TOMORROW AT NOON IN FRONT OF YOMIKIRI LAND STATION! BYE!
CLICK
...
...
...
POWK

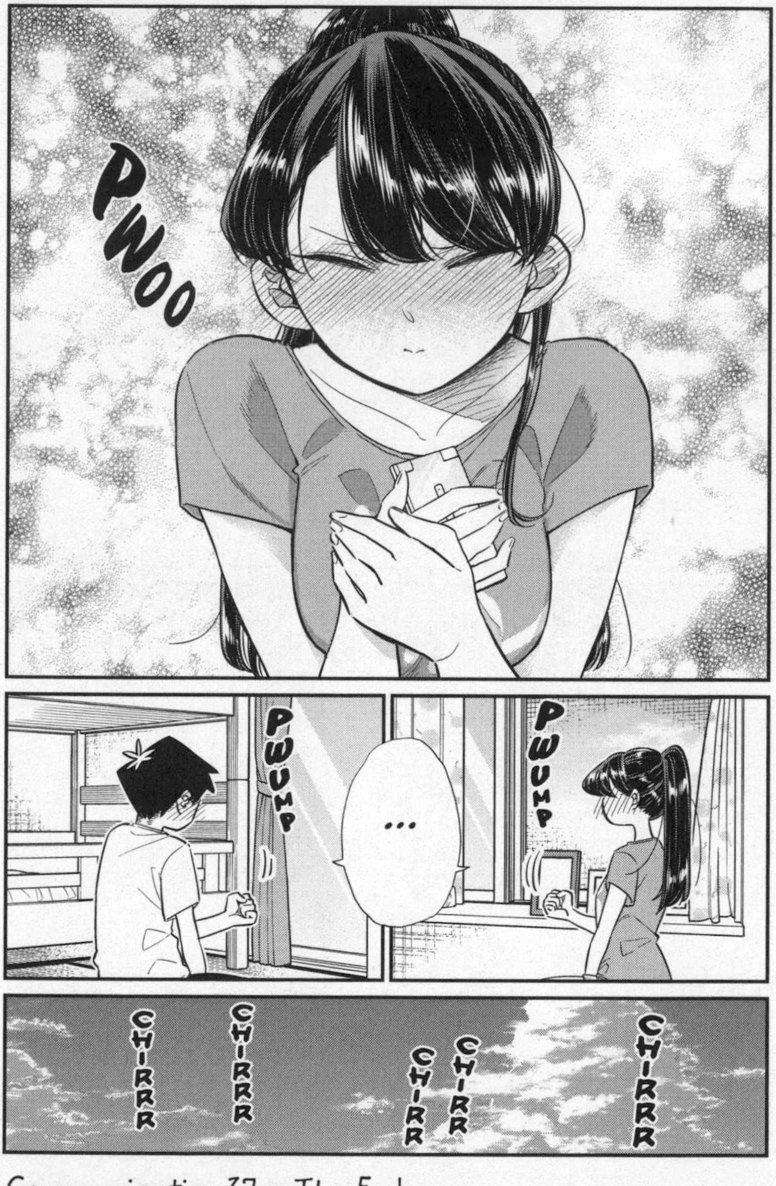
PWOO
PWUMP
...
PWUMP
CHIRRR
CHIRR
CHIRR
CHIRRR
CHIRRR

Communication 37 — The End

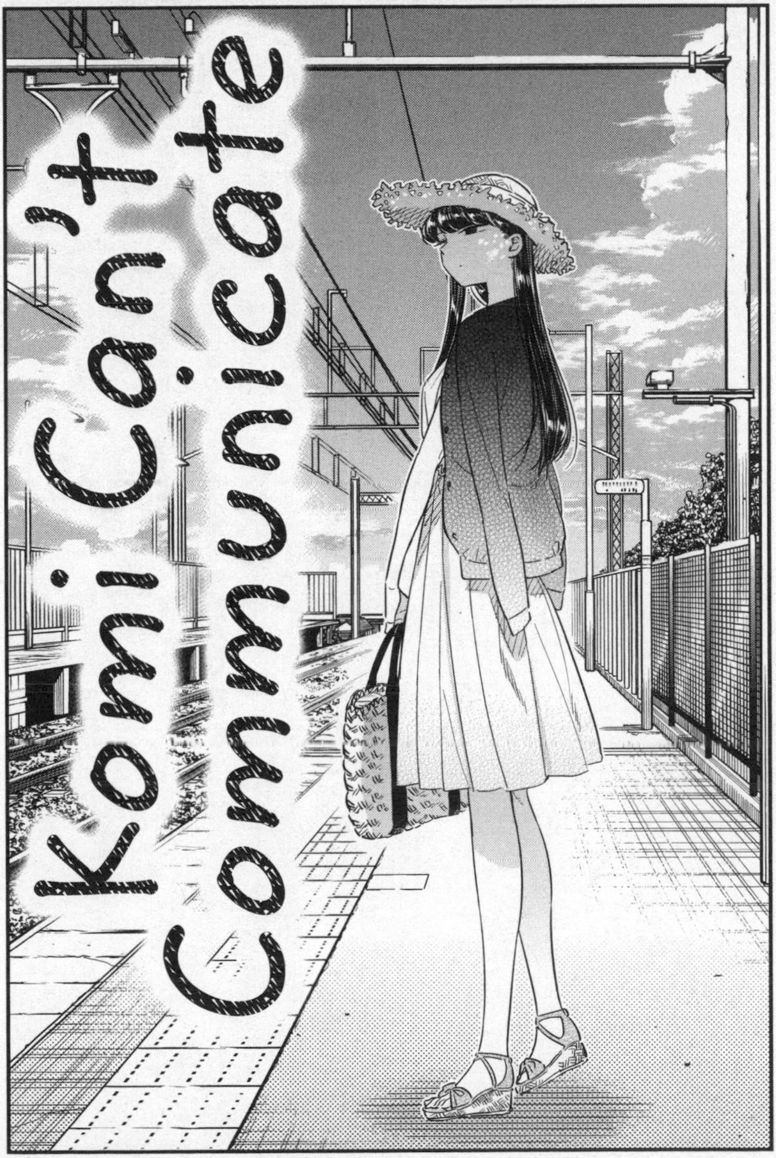
Komi Can't
Communicate
Communication 38: Meeting Up

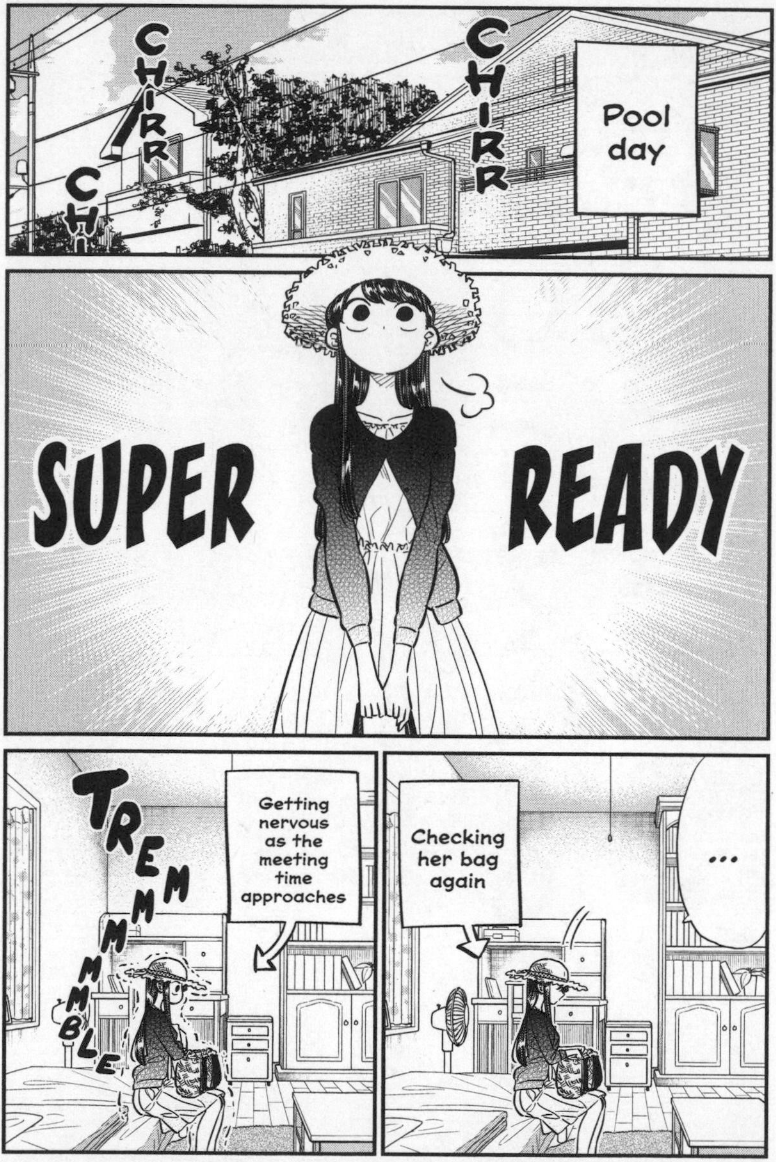
Pool day
CHIRR
CHIRR
CH
SUPER READY
...
Checking her bag again
Getting nervous as the meeting time approaches
TREMMMMMBLE

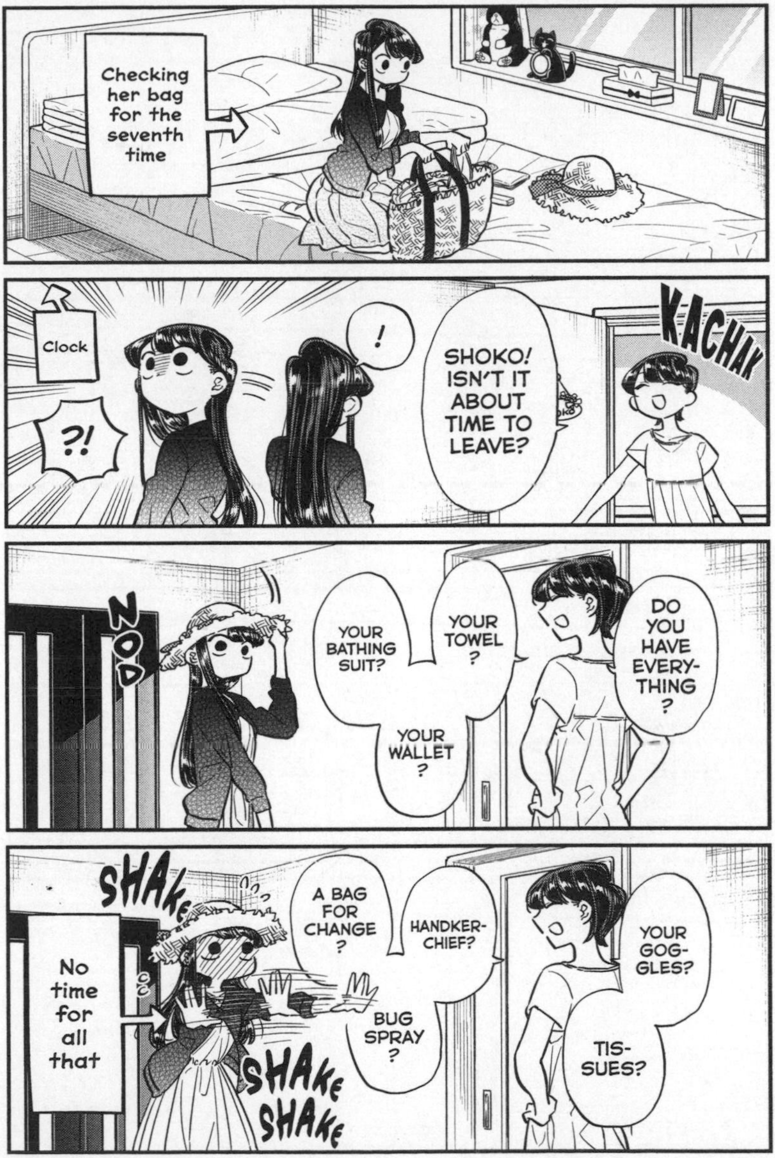

Checking her bag for the seventh time
KACHAK
SHOKO! ISN'T IT ABOUT TIME TO LEAVE?
!
Clock
?!
DO YOU HAVE EVERYTHING?
YOUR TOWEL?
YOUR BATHING SUIT?
YOUR WALLET?
NOD
YOUR GOGGLES?
TISSUES?
HANDKERCHIEF?
A BAG FOR CHANGE?
BUG SPRAY?
SHAKE
SHAKE SHAKE
No time for all that

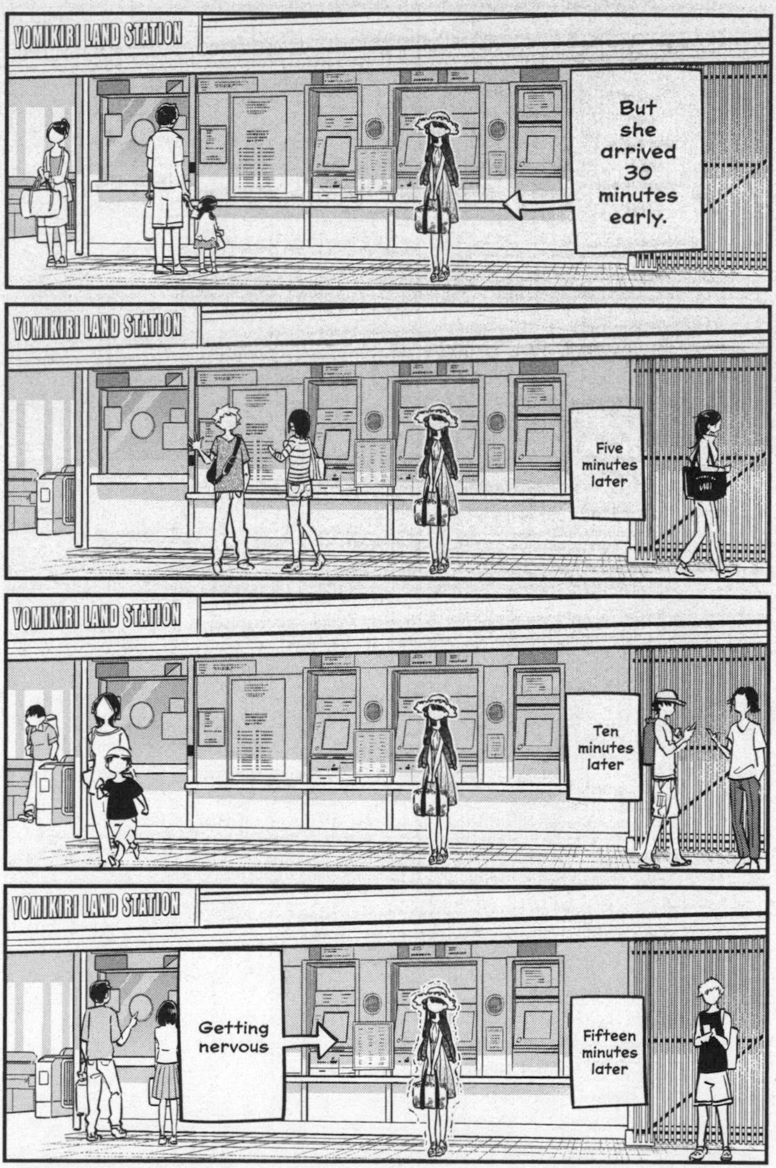
YOMIKIRI LAND STATION
But she arrived 30 minutes early.
YOMIKIRI LAND STATION
Five minutes later
YOMIKIRI LAND STATION
Ten minutes later
YOMIKIRI LAND STATION
Fifteen minutes later
Getting nervous

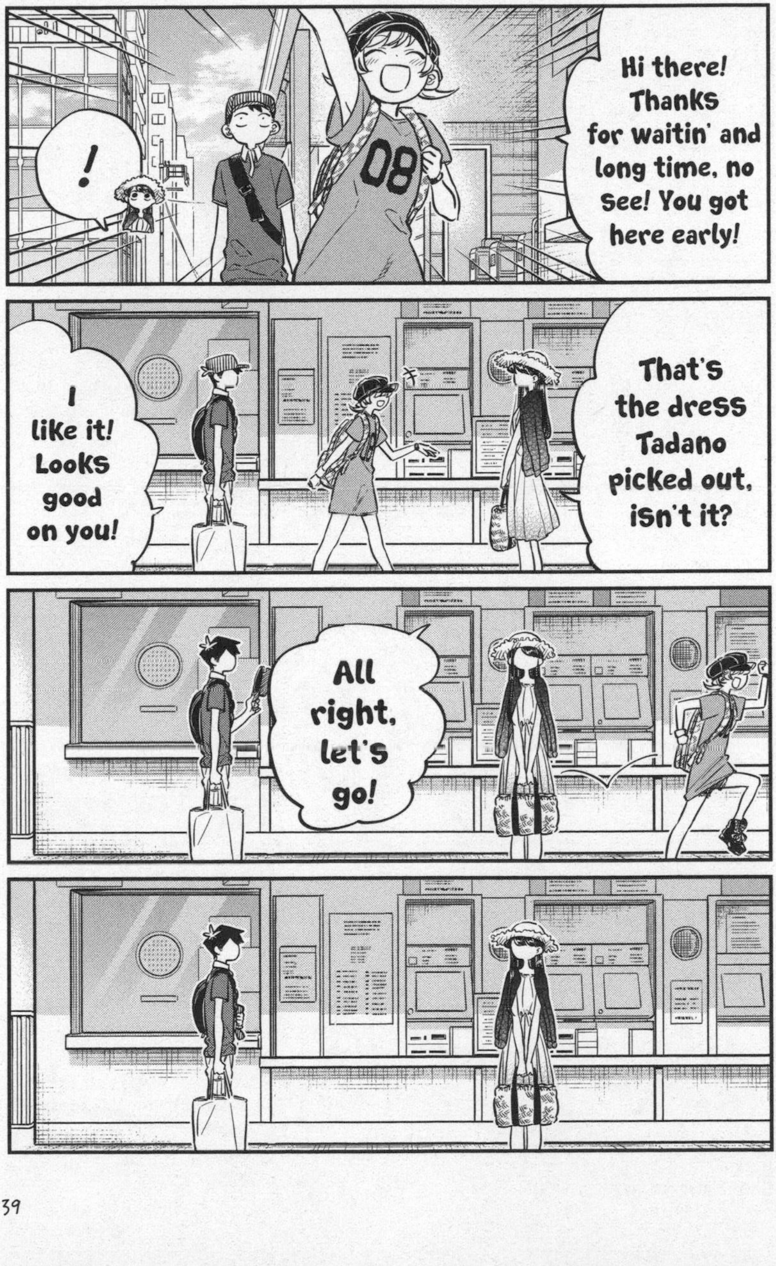
Hi there! Thanks for waitin' and long time, no see! You got here early!
!
That's the dress Tadano picked out, isn't it?
I like it! Looks good on you!
All right, let's go!

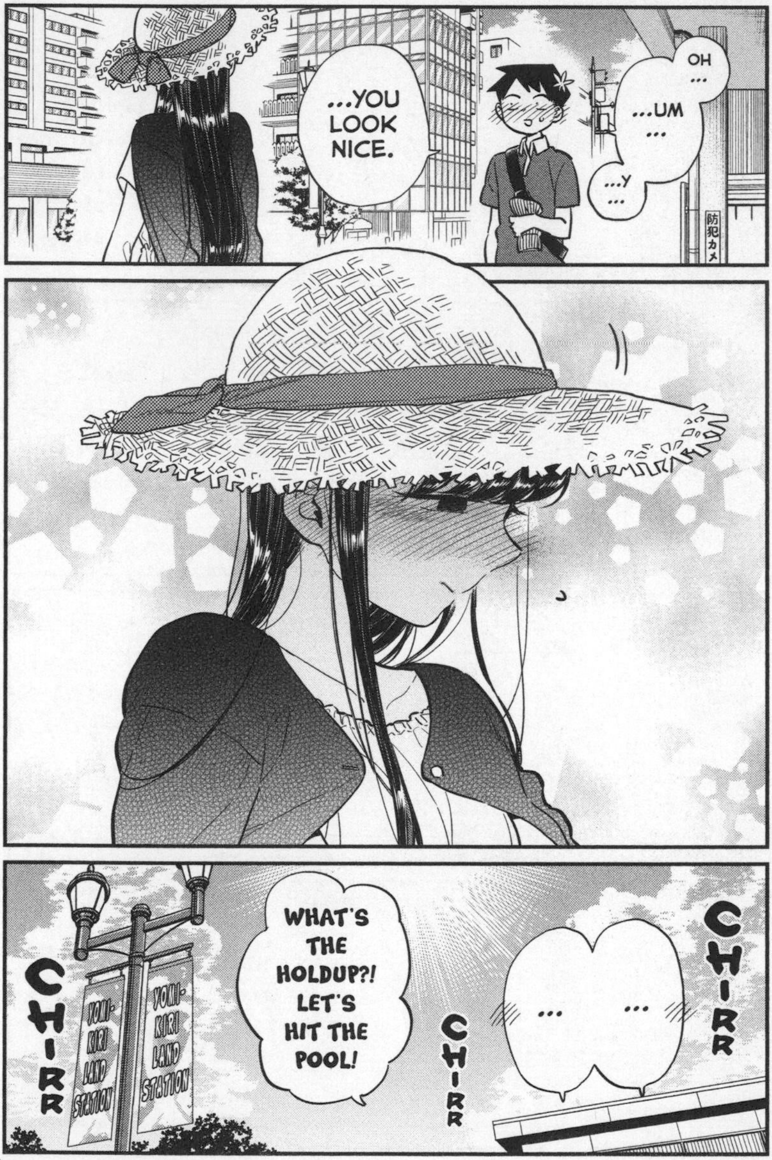
OH ... ...UM ... ...Y ...
防犯カメ
...YOU LOOK NICE.
CHIRR
... ...
CHIRR
WHAT'S THE HOLDUP?! LET'S HIT THE POOL!
YOMI-KIRI LAND STATION
YOMI-KIRI LAND STATION
CHIRR

Communication 38 — The End

Komi Can't Communicate

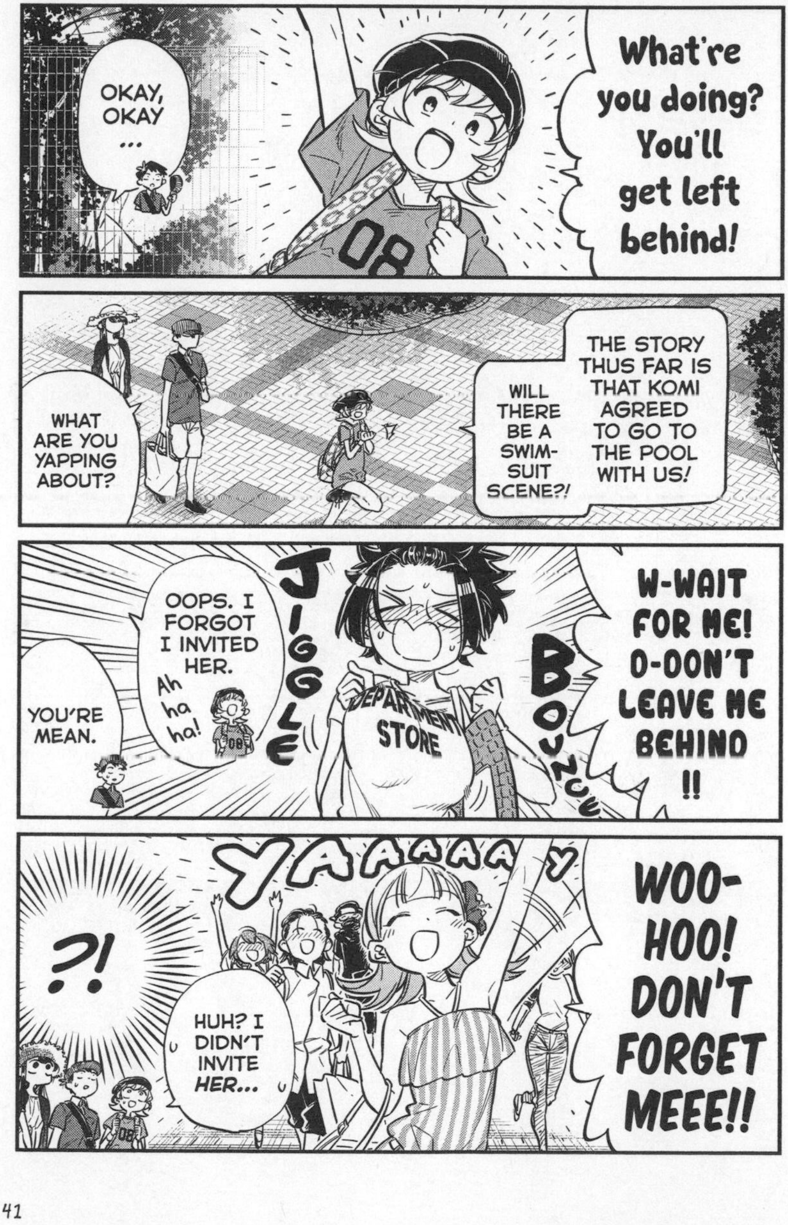
What're you doing? You'll get left behind!
OKAY, OKAY ...
THE STORY THUS FAR IS THAT KOMI AGREED TO GO TO THE POOL WITH US!
WILL THERE BE A SWIM-SUIT SCENE?!
WHAT ARE YOU YAPPING ABOUT?
W-WAIT FOR ME! D-DON'T LEAVE ME BEHIND !!
BOUNCE
DEPARTMENT STORE
JIGGLE
OOPS. I FORGOT I INVITED HER.
Ah ha ha!
YOU'RE MEAN.
WOO-HOO! DON'T FORGET MEEE!!
YAAAAAY
HUH? I DIDN'T INVITE HER...
?!

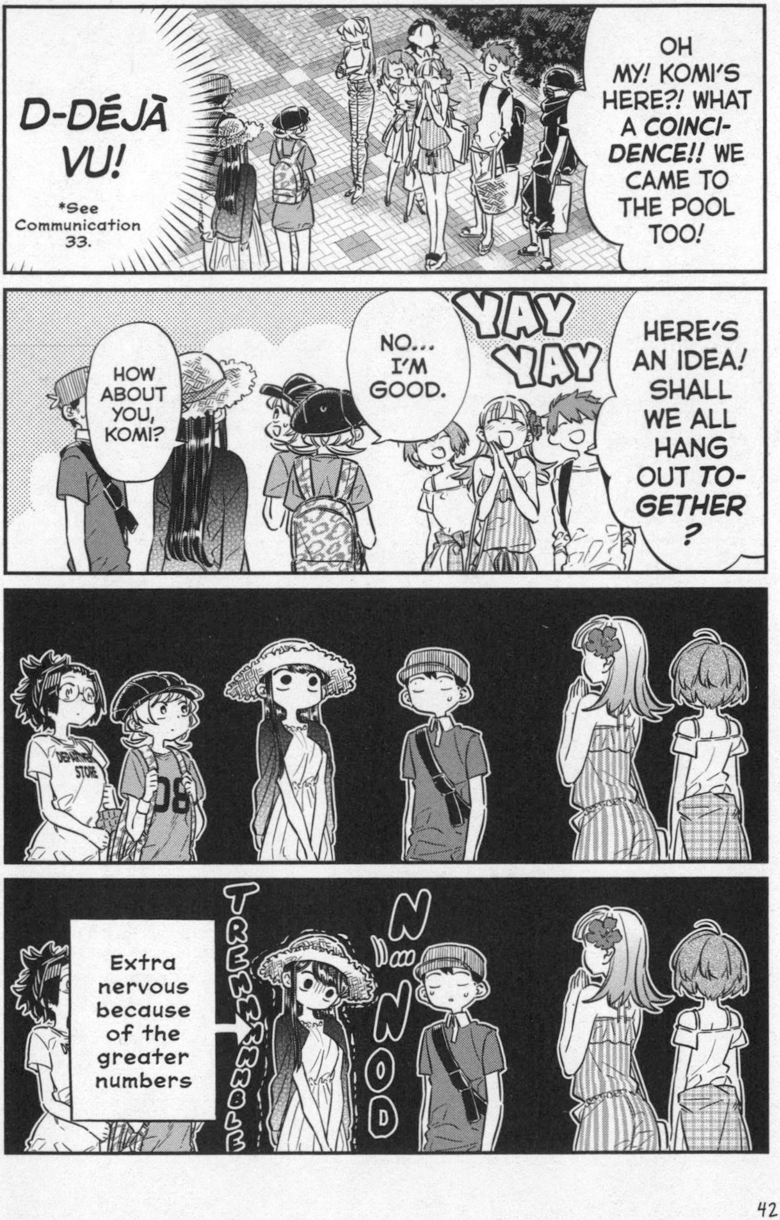
OH MY! KOMI'S HERE?! WHAT A COINCIDENCE!! WE CAME TO THE POOL TOO!
D-DÉJÀ VU!
*See Communication 33.
HERE'S AN IDEA! SHALL WE ALL HANG OUT TOGETHER?
YAY YAY
NO... I'M GOOD.
HOW ABOUT YOU, KOMI?
NOD NOD
TREMMMMBLE
Extra nervous because of the greater numbers

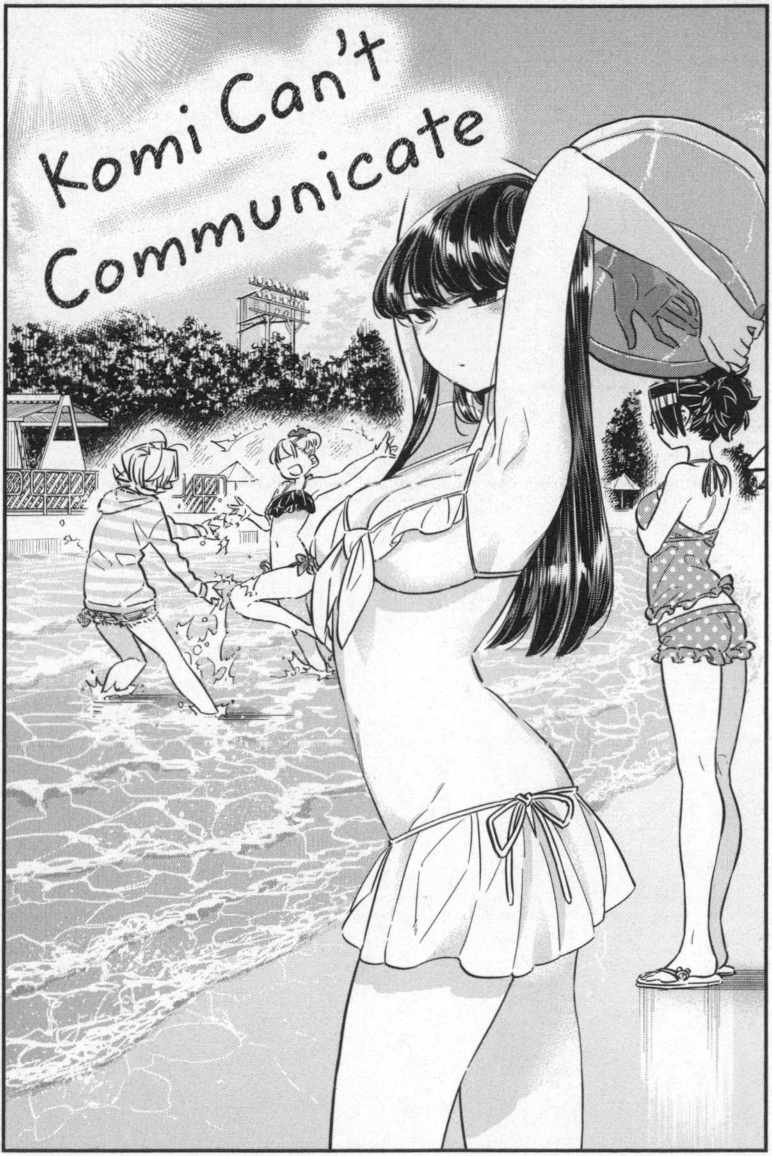
Komi Can't
Communicate

Communication 39: The Pool

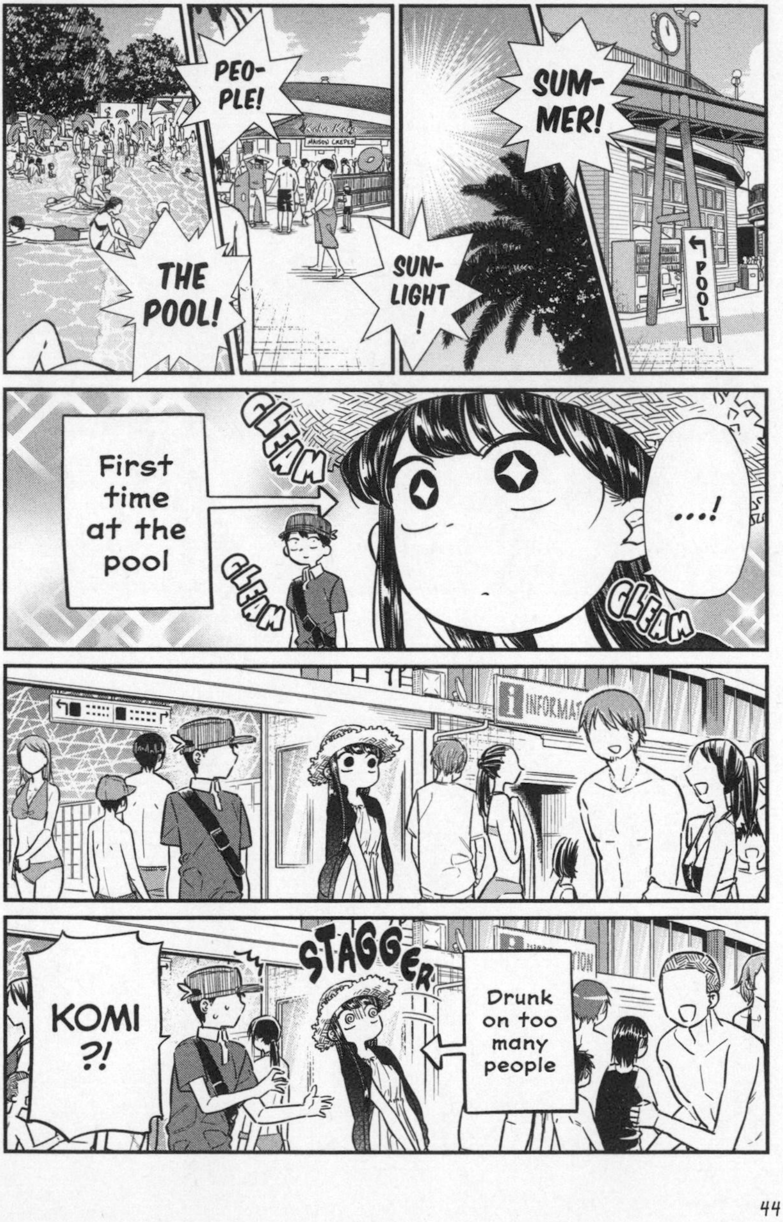
SUM-
MER!
POOL
SUN-
LIGHT
!
PEO-
PLE!
MAISON CREPES
THE
POOL!
...!
GLEAM
GLEAM
First time at the pool
GLEAM
INFORMAT
STAGGER
Drunk on too many people
KOMI
?!

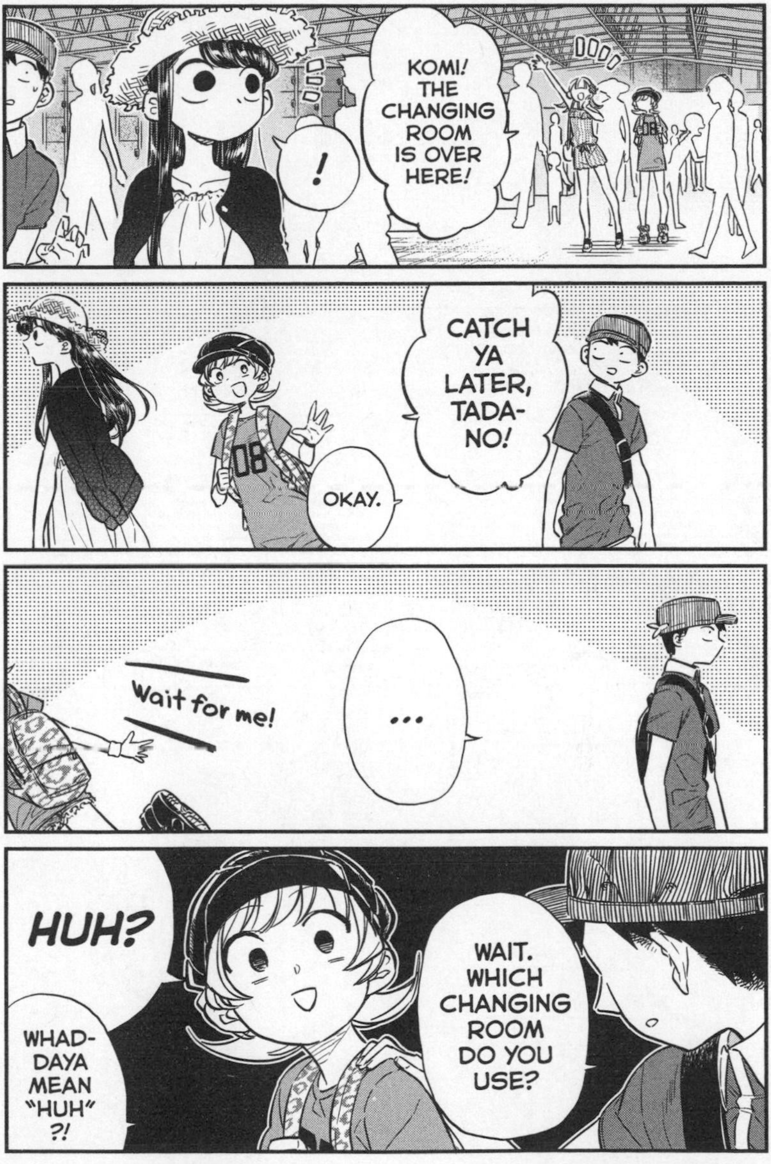
KOMI! THE CHANGING ROOM IS OVER HERE!
!
CATCH YA LATER, TADANO!
OKAY.
...
Wait for me!
WAIT. WHICH CHANGING ROOM DO YOU USE?
HUH?
WHADDAYA MEAN "HUH"?!

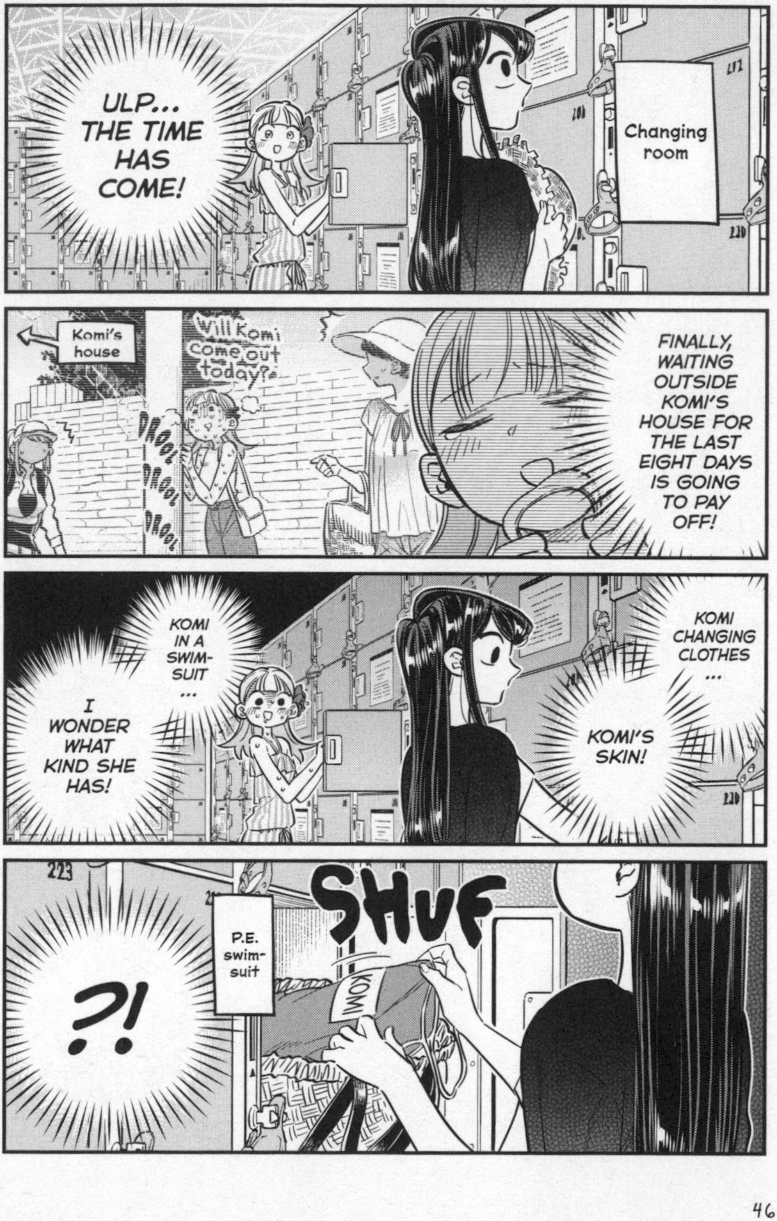
Changing room
ULP... THE TIME HAS COME!
FINALLY, WAITING OUTSIDE KOMI'S HOUSE FOR THE LAST EIGHT DAYS IS GOING TO PAY OFF!
Will Komi come out today?
DROOL DROOL DROOL DROOL
Komi's house
KOMI CHANGING CLOTHES ...
KOMI'S SKIN!
KOMI IN A SWIM-SUIT ...
I WONDER WHAT KIND SHE HAS!
SHUF
KOMI
P.E. swim-suit
?!

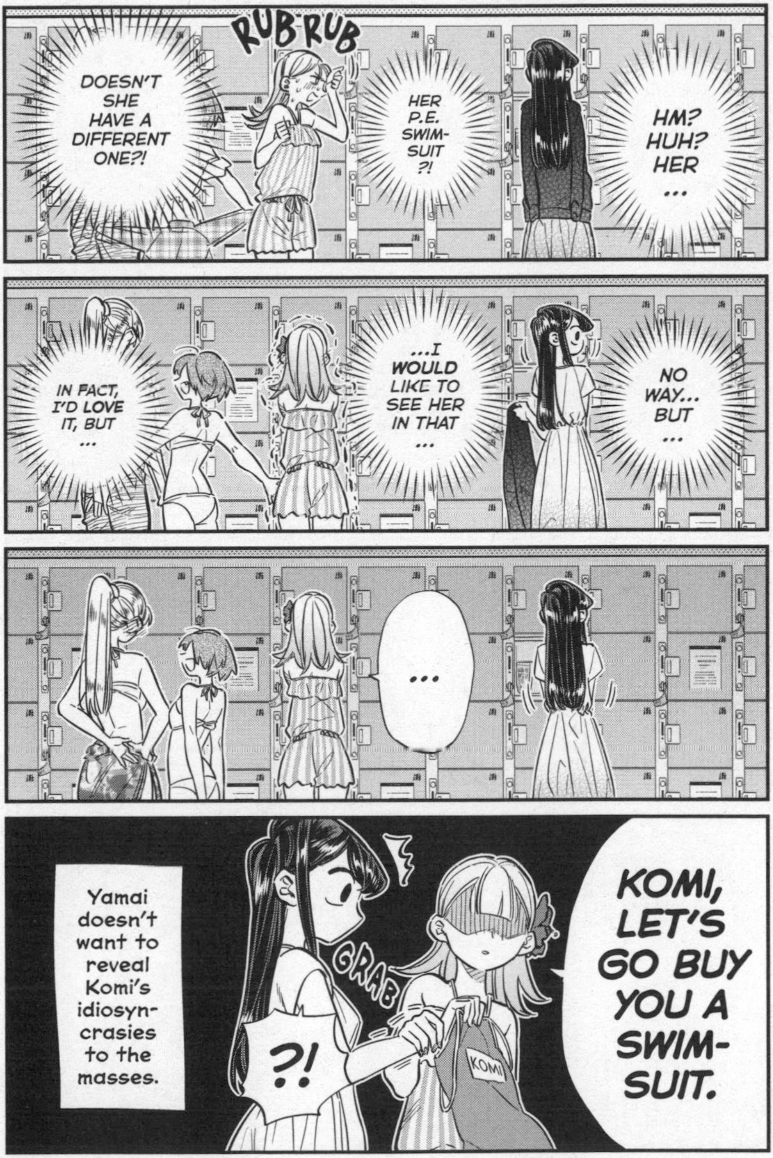
HM? HUH? HER ...
HER P.E. SWIM-SUIT ?!
RUB RUB
DOESN'T SHE HAVE A DIFFERENT ONE?!
NO WAY... BUT ...
...I WOULD LIKE TO SEE HER IN THAT ...
IN FACT, I'D LOVE IT, BUT ...
...
KOMI, LET'S GO BUY YOU A SWIM-SUIT.
GRAB
KOMI
?!
Yamai doesn't want to reveal Komi's idiosyn-crasies to the masses.

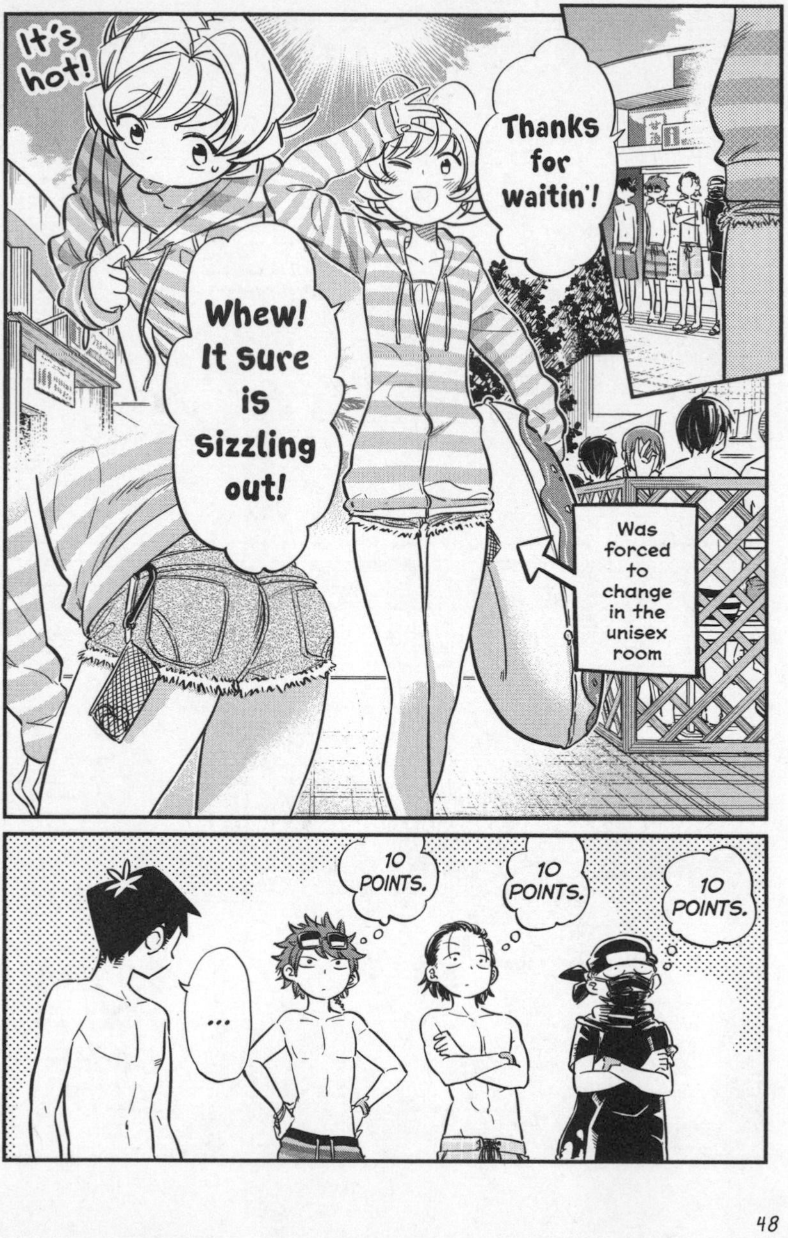

Thanks for waitin'!
Whew! It sure is sizzling out!
It's hot!
Was forced to change in the unisex room
10 POINTS.
10 POINTS.
10 POINTS.
...

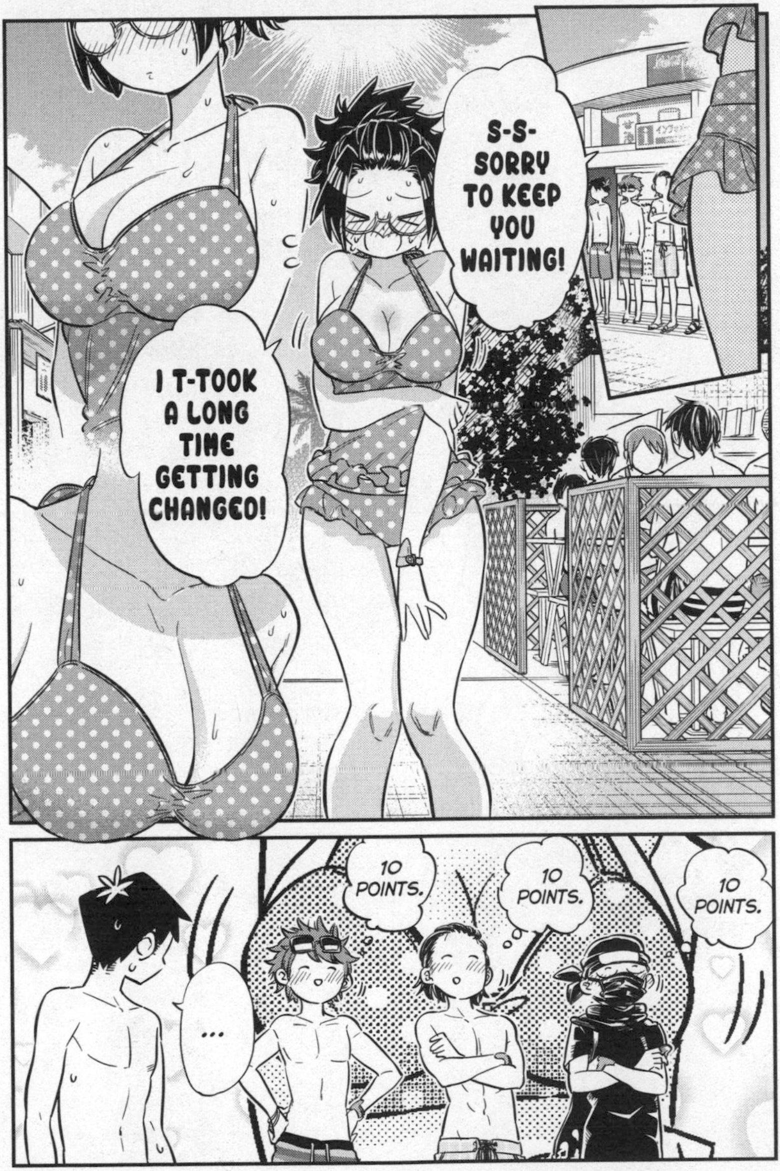
S-S-SORRY TO KEEP YOU WAITING!
I T-TOOK A LONG TIME GETTING CHANGED!
10 POINTS.
10 POINTS.
10 POINTS.
...

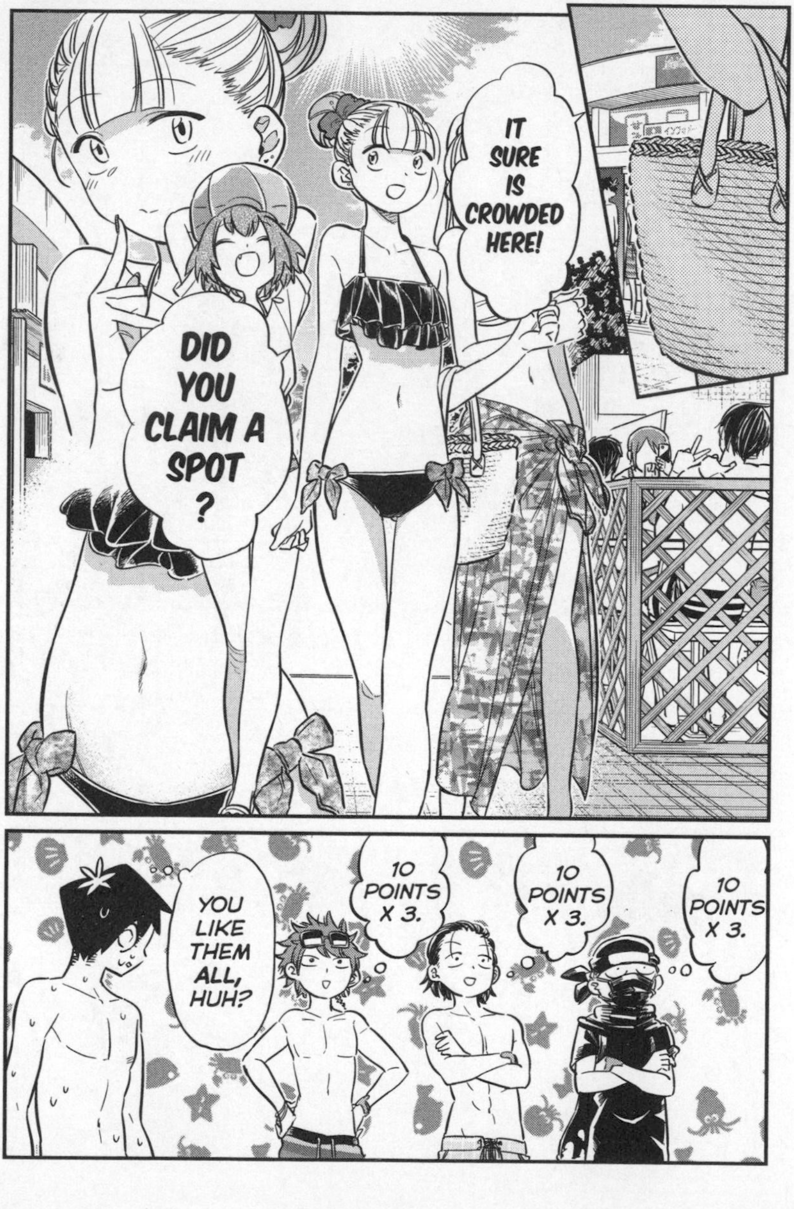
IT SURE IS CROWDED HERE!
DID YOU CLAIM A SPOT ?
10 POINTS X 3.
10 POINTS X 3.
10 POINTS X 3.
YOU LIKE THEM ALL, HUH?

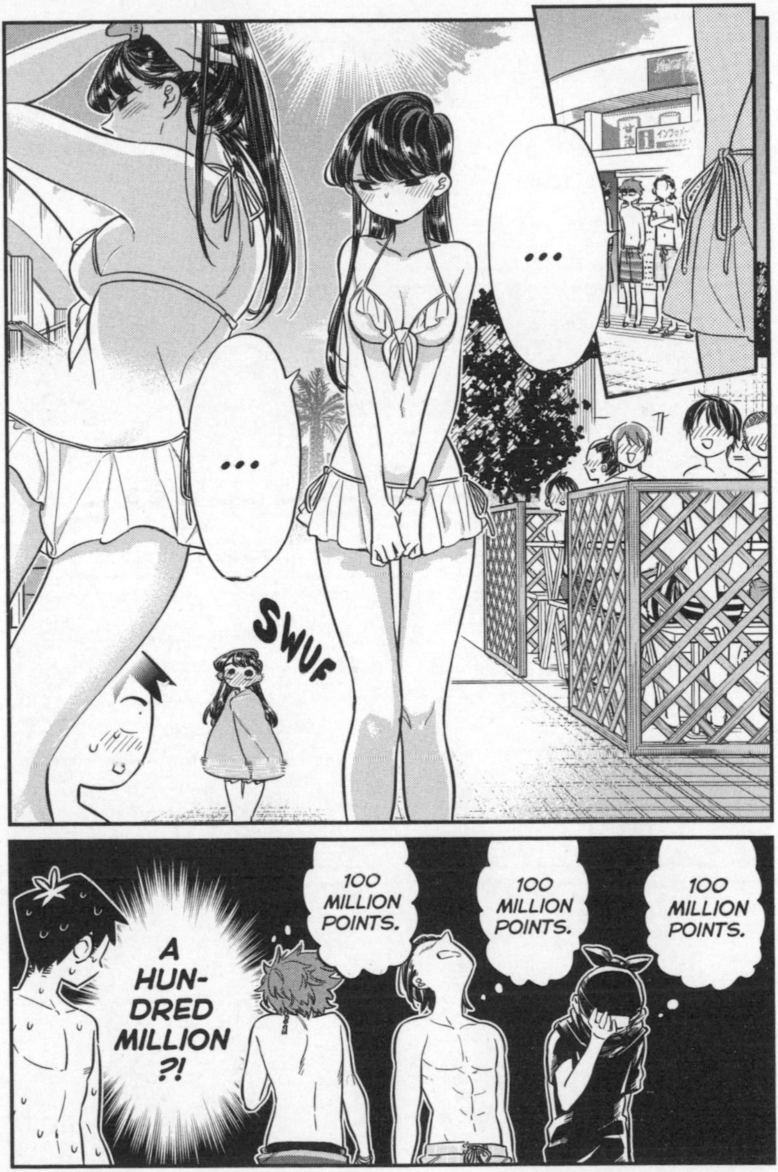
...
...
SWUF
100 MILLION POINTS.
100 MILLION POINTS.
100 MILLION POINTS.
A HUN-DRED MILLION ?!

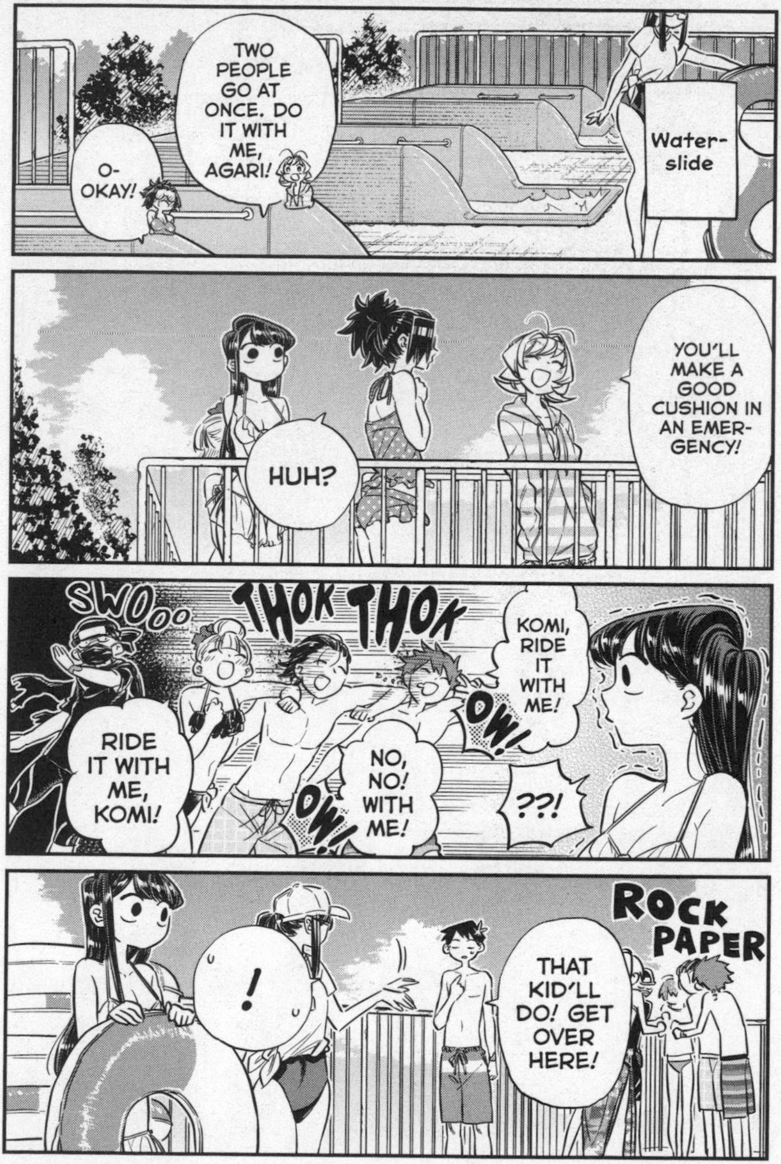
Water-slide
TWO PEOPLE GO AT ONCE. DO IT WITH ME, AGARI!
O-OKAY!
YOU'LL MAKE A GOOD CUSHION IN AN EMERGENCY!
HUH?
KOMI, RIDE IT WITH ME!
THOK THOK
SWOooo
OW!
??!
NO, NO! WITH ME!
OW!
RIDE IT WITH ME, KOMI!
ROCK PAPER
THAT KID'LL DO! GET OVER HERE!
!

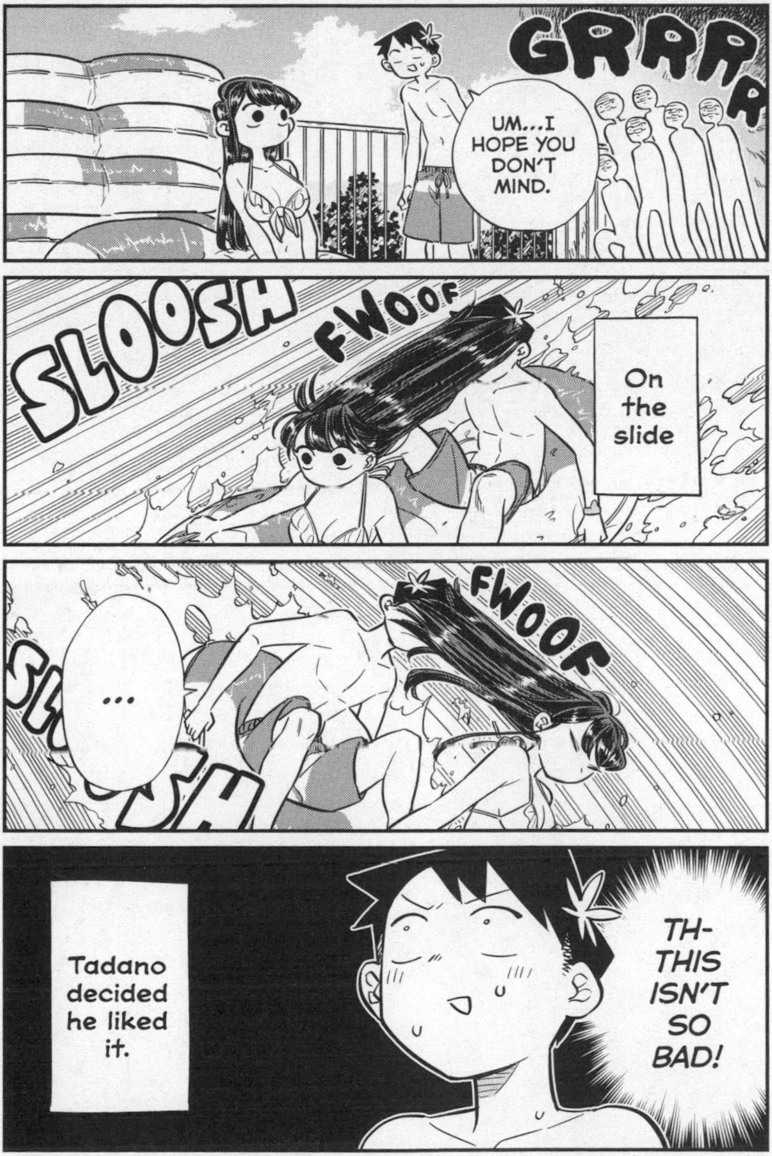
GRRRR
UM...I HOPE YOU DON'T MIND.
On the slide
FWOOF
SLOOSH
FWOOF
...
TH- THIS ISN'T SO BAD!
Tadano decided he liked it.

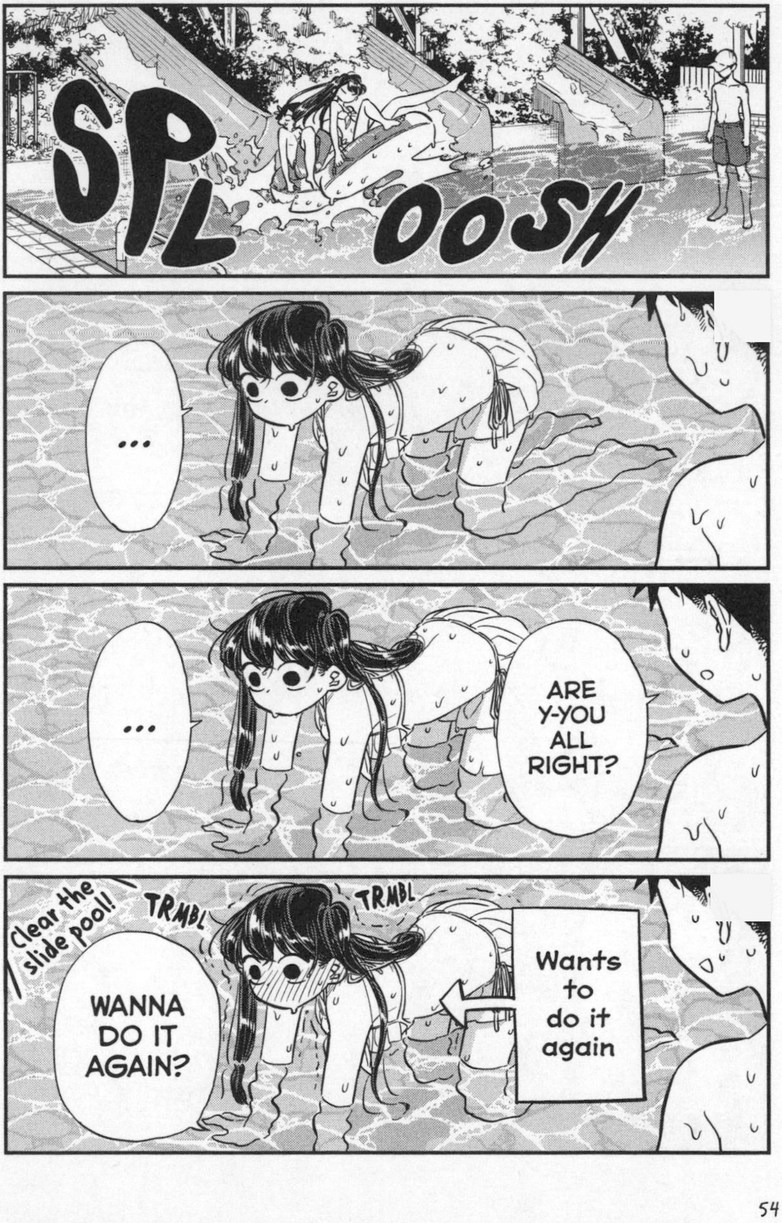
SPLOOSH
...
ARE Y-YOU ALL RIGHT?
...
TRMBL
Wants to do it again
TRMBL
WANNA DO IT AGAIN?
Clear the slide pool!

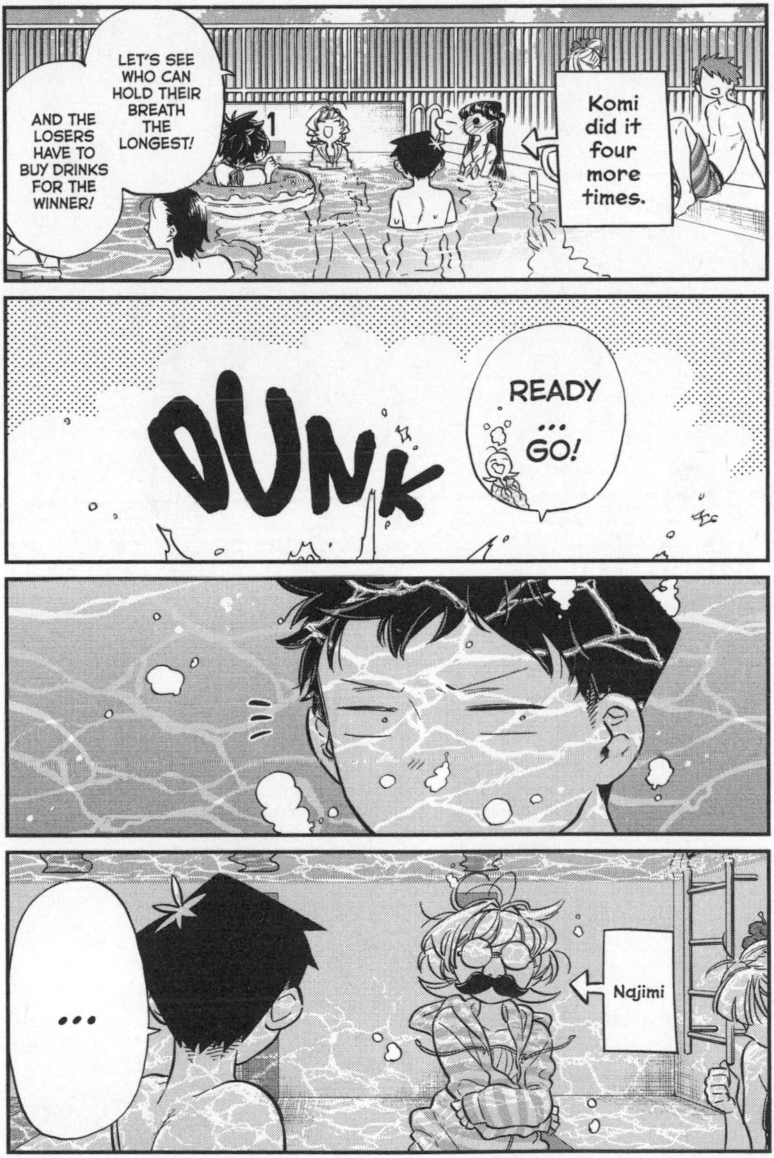
Komi did it four more times.
LET'S SEE WHO CAN HOLD THEIR BREATH THE LONGEST!
AND THE LOSERS HAVE TO BUY DRINKS FOR THE WINNER!
READY ... GO!
DUNK
Najimi
...

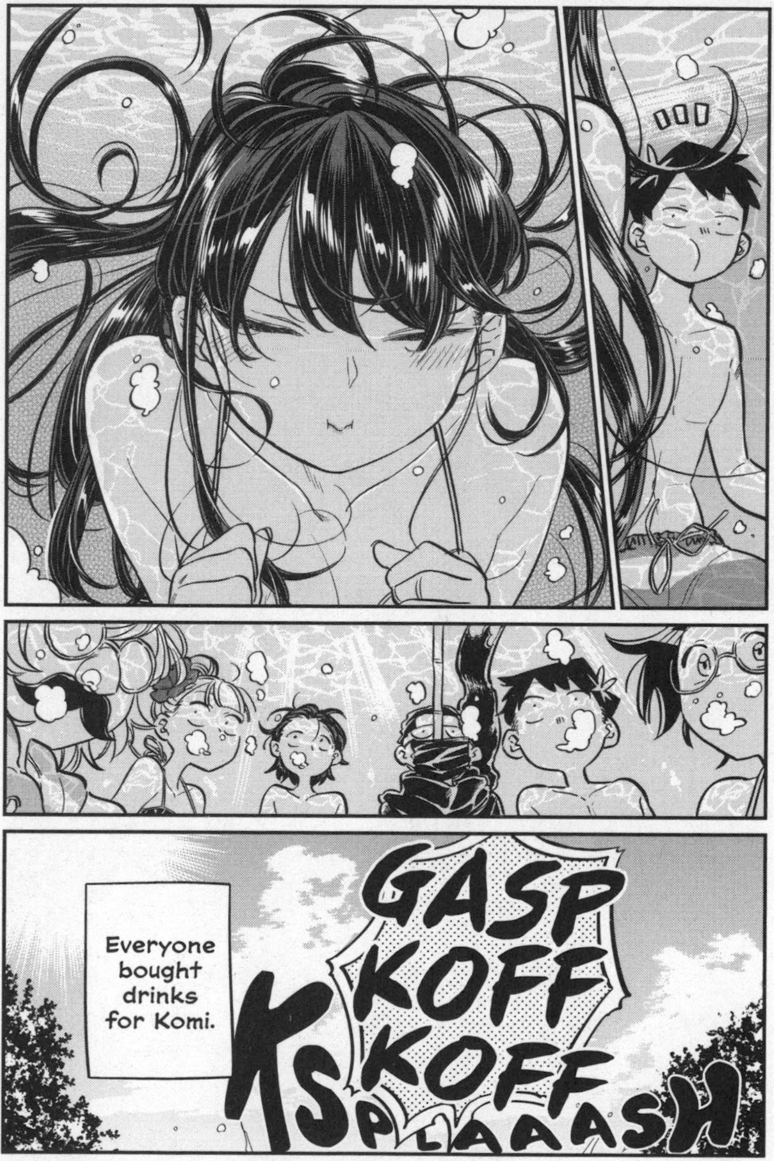
GASP
KOFF
KOFF
SPLAAASH
Everyone bought drinks for Komi.

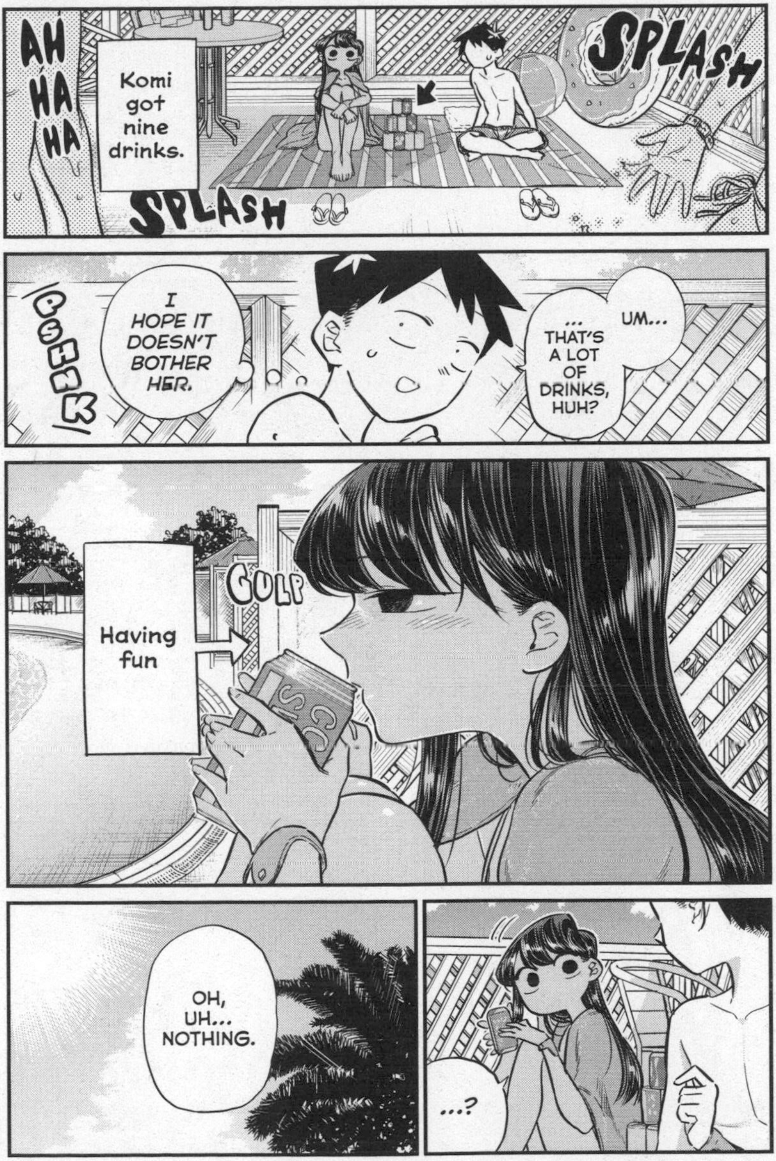
SPLASH
Komi got nine drinks.
AH HA HA
SPLASH
UM...
... THAT'S A LOT OF DRINKS, HUH?
I HOPE IT DOESN'T BOTHER HER.
PSHNK
GULP
Having fun
...?
OH, UH... NOTHING.

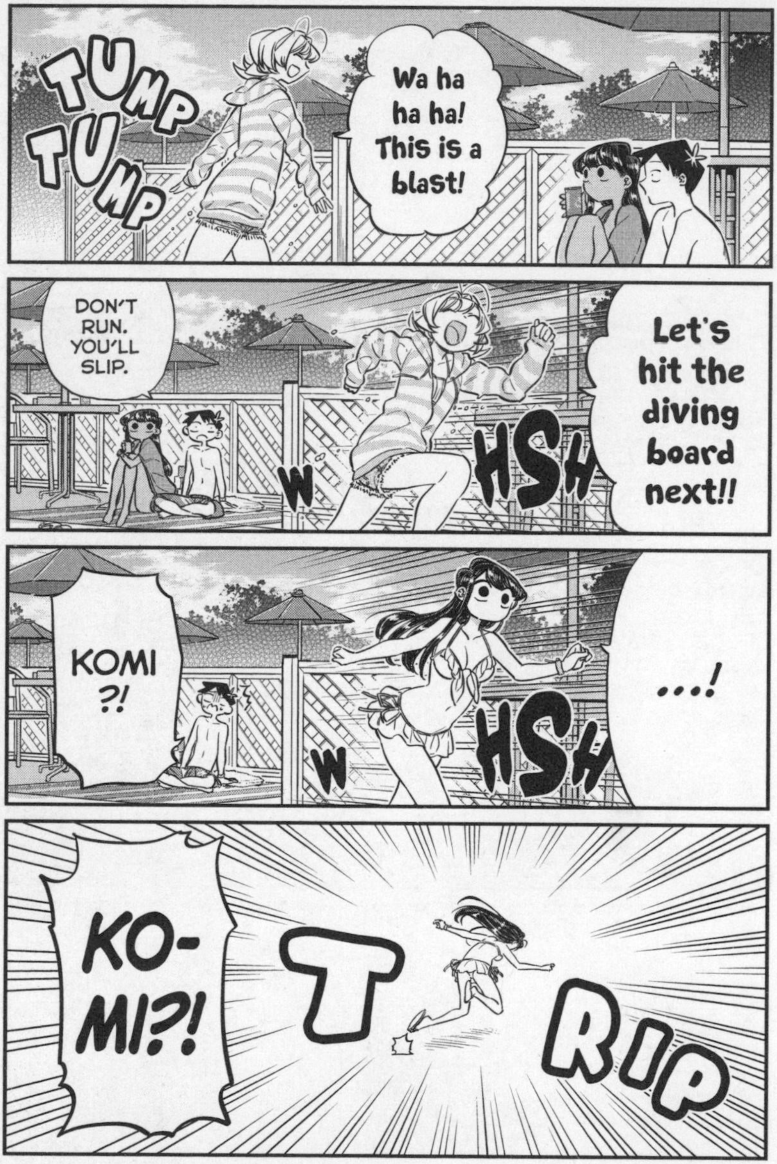
Wa ha ha ha! This is a blast!
TUMP TUMP
Let's hit the diving board next!!
WHSH
DON'T RUN. YOU'LL SLIP.
...!
WHSH
KOMI ?!
TRIP
KO-MI?!

Communication 39 – The End

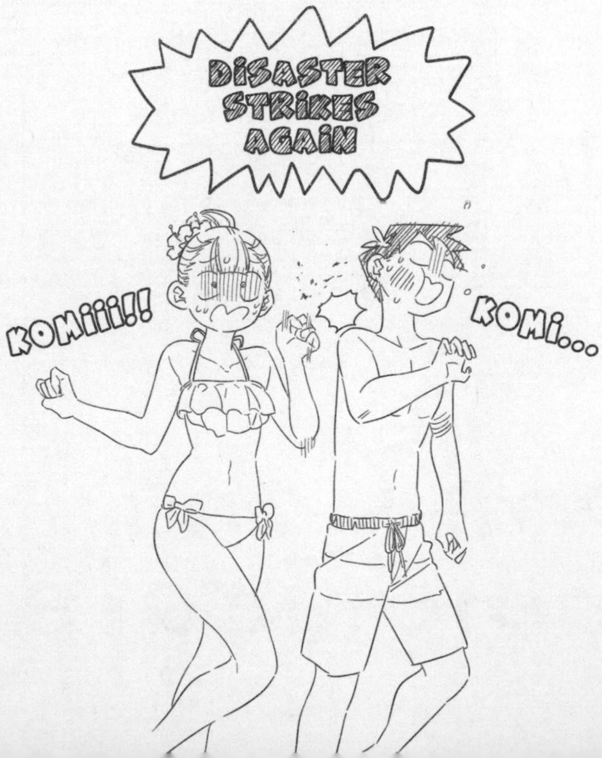
DiSASTER STRiKES AGAiN
KOMiii!!
KOMi...

Komi Can't
Communicate

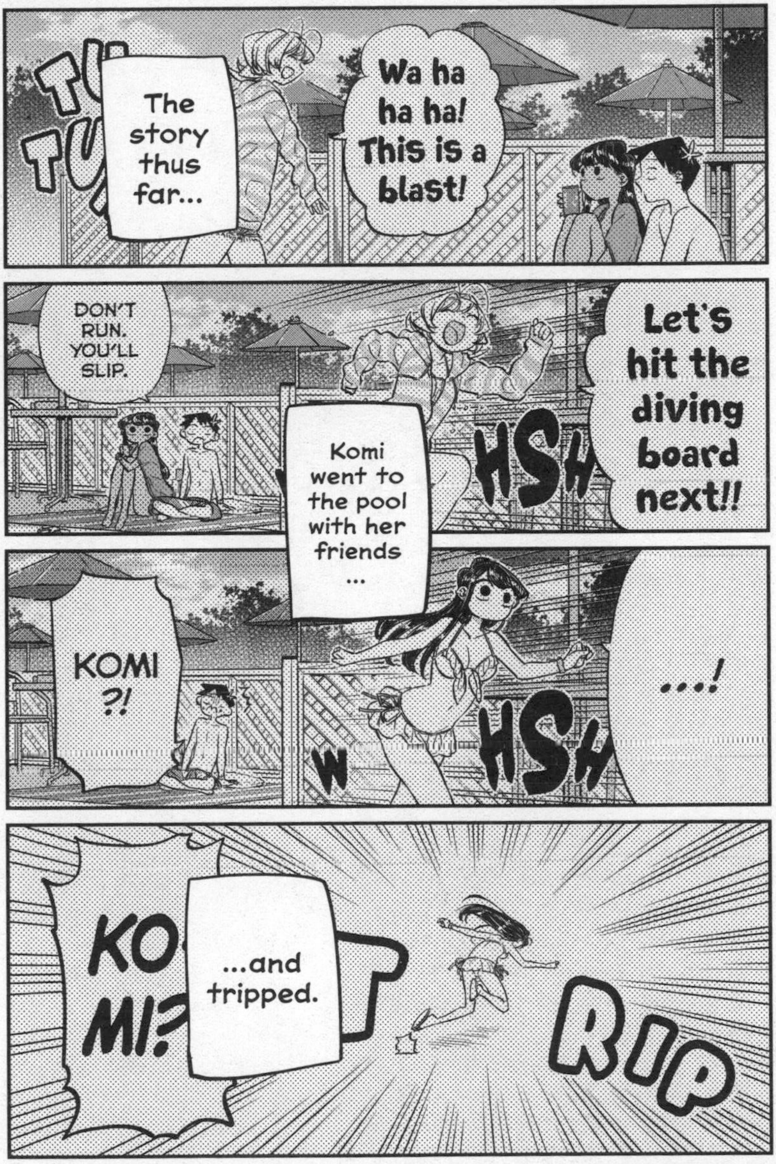

Wa ha ha ha! This is a blast!
The story thus far...
Let's hit the diving board next!!
DON'T RUN. YOU'LL SLIP.
Komi went to the pool with her friends ...
...!
WHSH
KOMI ?!
RIP
...and tripped.
KOMI!?

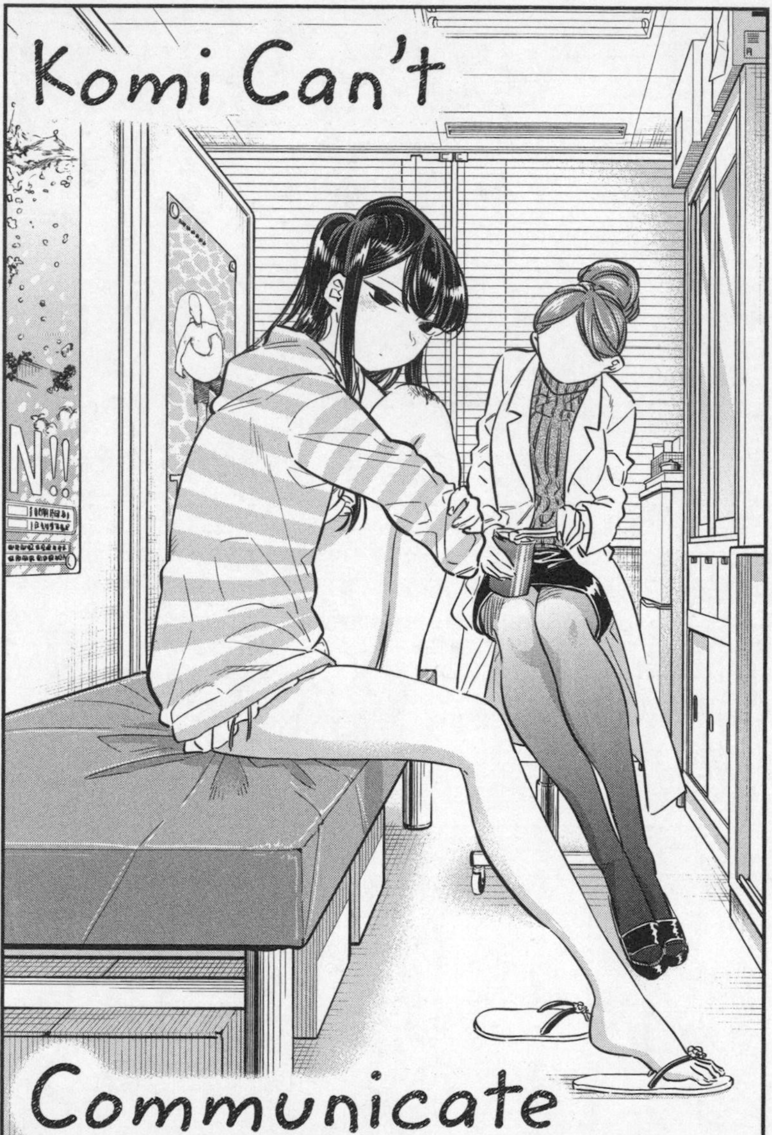
Komi Can't
Communicate

Communication 40: Just a Scrape

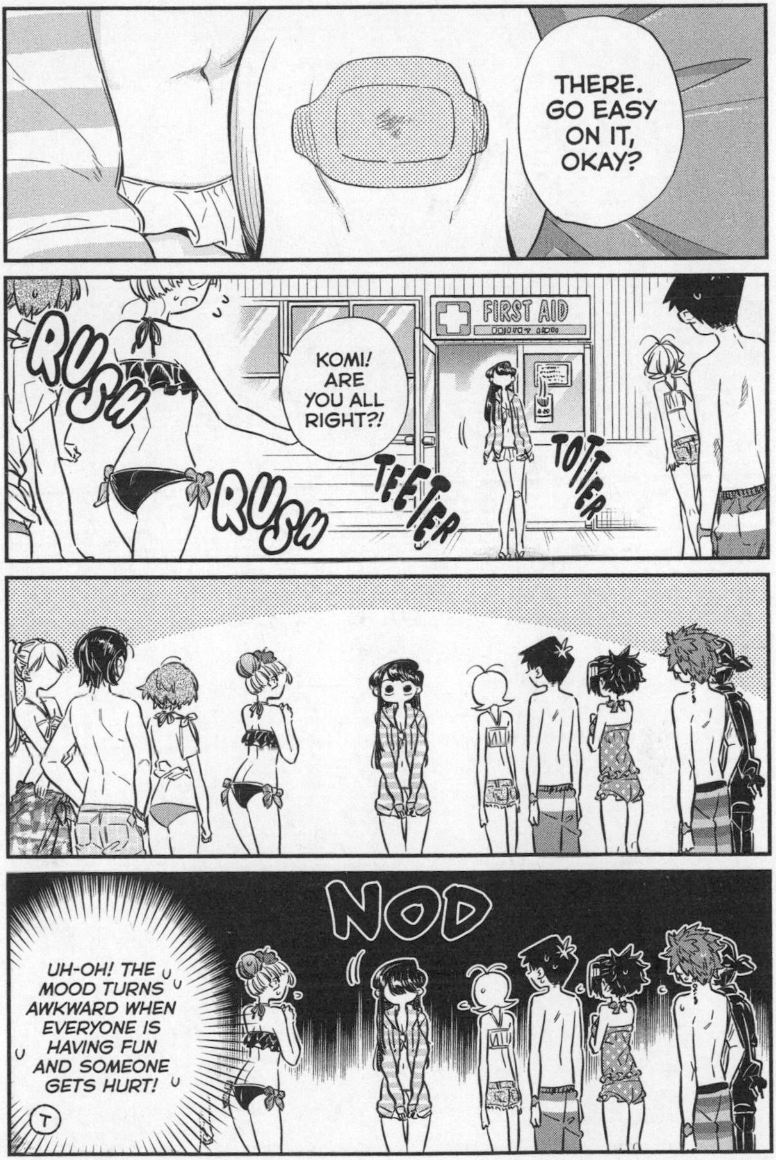
THERE. GO EASY ON IT, OKAY?
FIRST AID
TOTTER
TEETER
KOMI! ARE YOU ALL RIGHT?!
RUSH
RUSH
NOD
UH-OH! THE MOOD TURNS AWKWARD WHEN EVERYONE IS HAVING FUN AND SOMEONE GETS HURT!

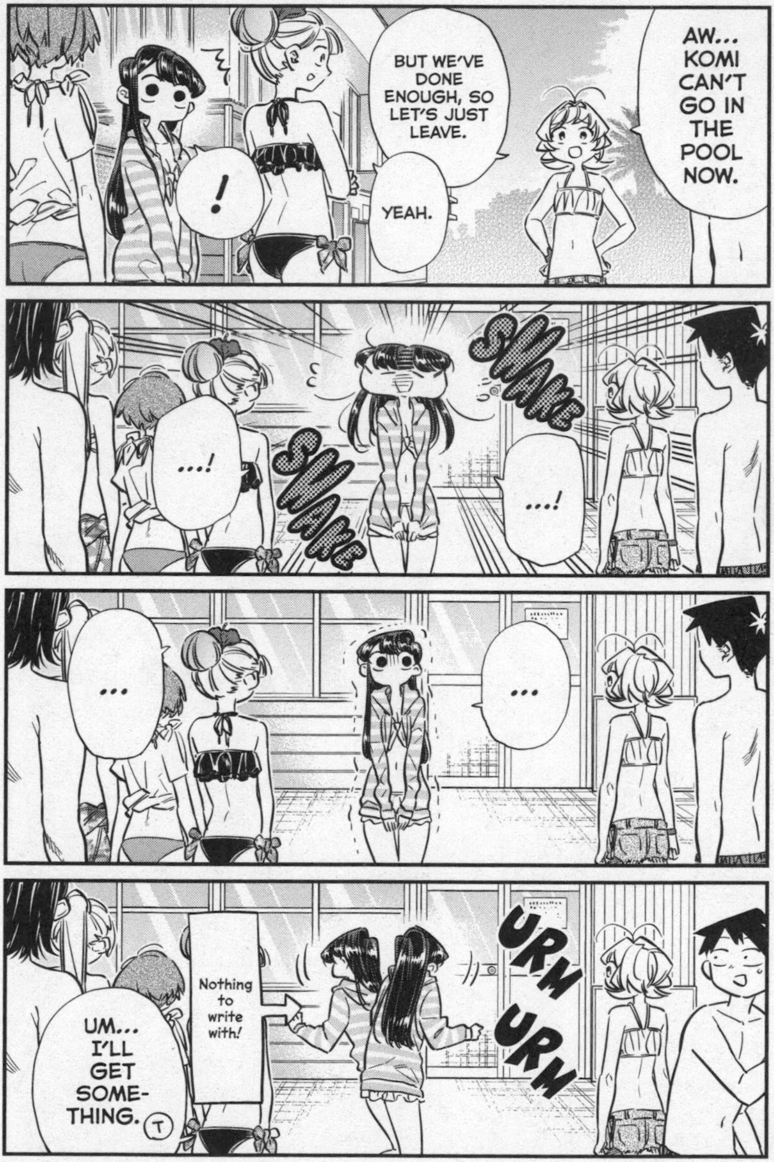
AW... KOMI CAN'T GO IN THE POOL NOW.
BUT WE'VE DONE ENOUGH, SO LET'S JUST LEAVE.
YEAH.
!
SWAKE
...!
SWAKE
...!
...
...
URM URM
Nothing to write with!
UM... I'LL GET SOME-THING.

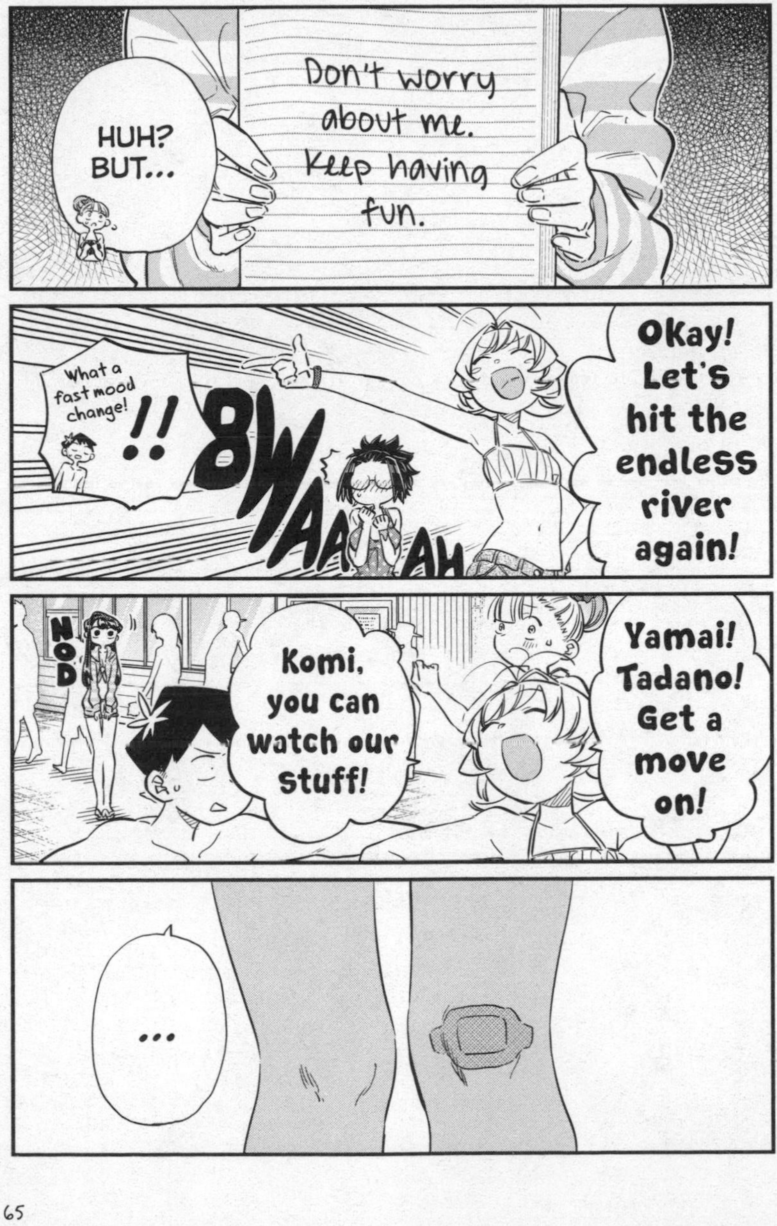
Don't worry about me. Keep having fun.
HUH? BUT...
Okay! Let's hit the endless river again!
BWAAAAH
!!
What a fast mood change!
Yamai! Tadano! Get a move on!
Komi, you can watch our stuff!
NOD
...

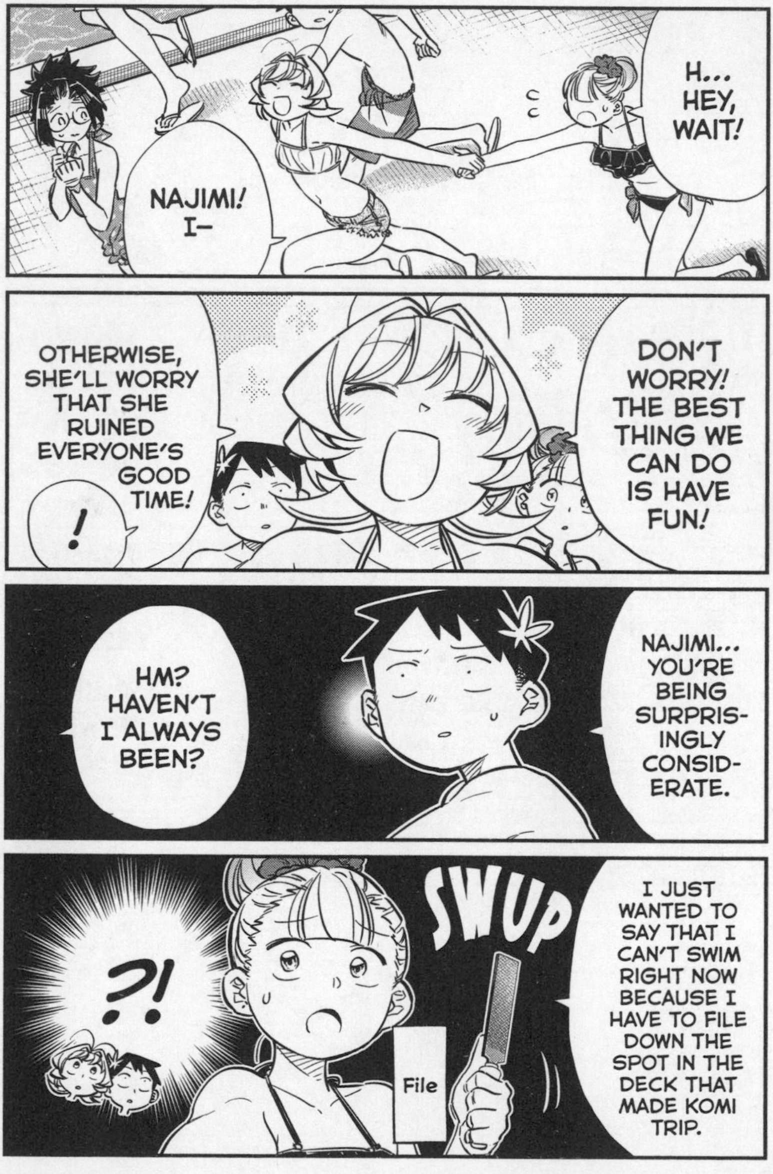
H... HEY, WAIT!
NAJIMI! I–
DON'T WORRY! THE BEST THING WE CAN DO IS HAVE FUN!
OTHERWISE, SHE'LL WORRY THAT SHE RUINED EVERYONE'S GOOD TIME!
!
NAJIMI... YOU'RE BEING SURPRISINGLY CONSIDERATE.
HM? HAVEN'T I ALWAYS BEEN?
I JUST WANTED TO SAY THAT I CAN'T SWIM RIGHT NOW BECAUSE I HAVE TO FILE DOWN THE SPOT IN THE DECK THAT MADE KOMI TRIP.
SWUP
File
?!

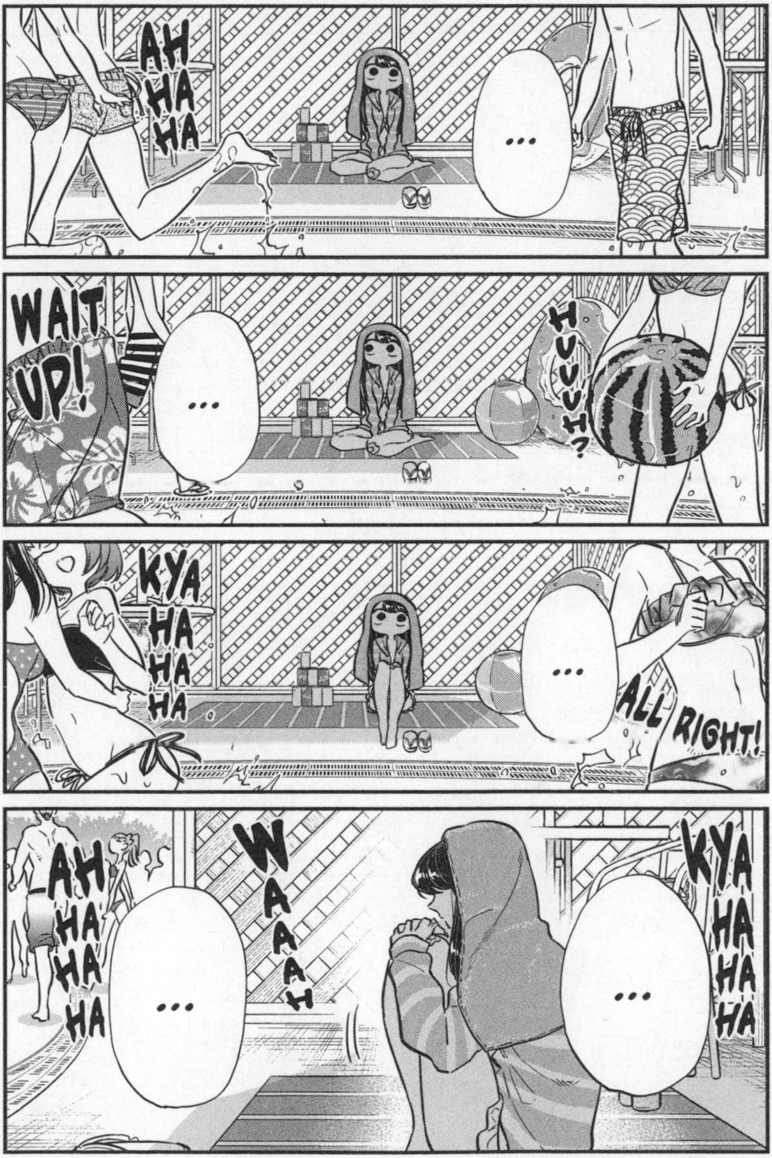
...
AH HA HA HA
HUUUH?
...
WAIT UP!
ALL RIGHT!
...
KYA HA HA HA
KYA HA HA HA HA
...
WAAAAH
...
AH HA HA HA HA

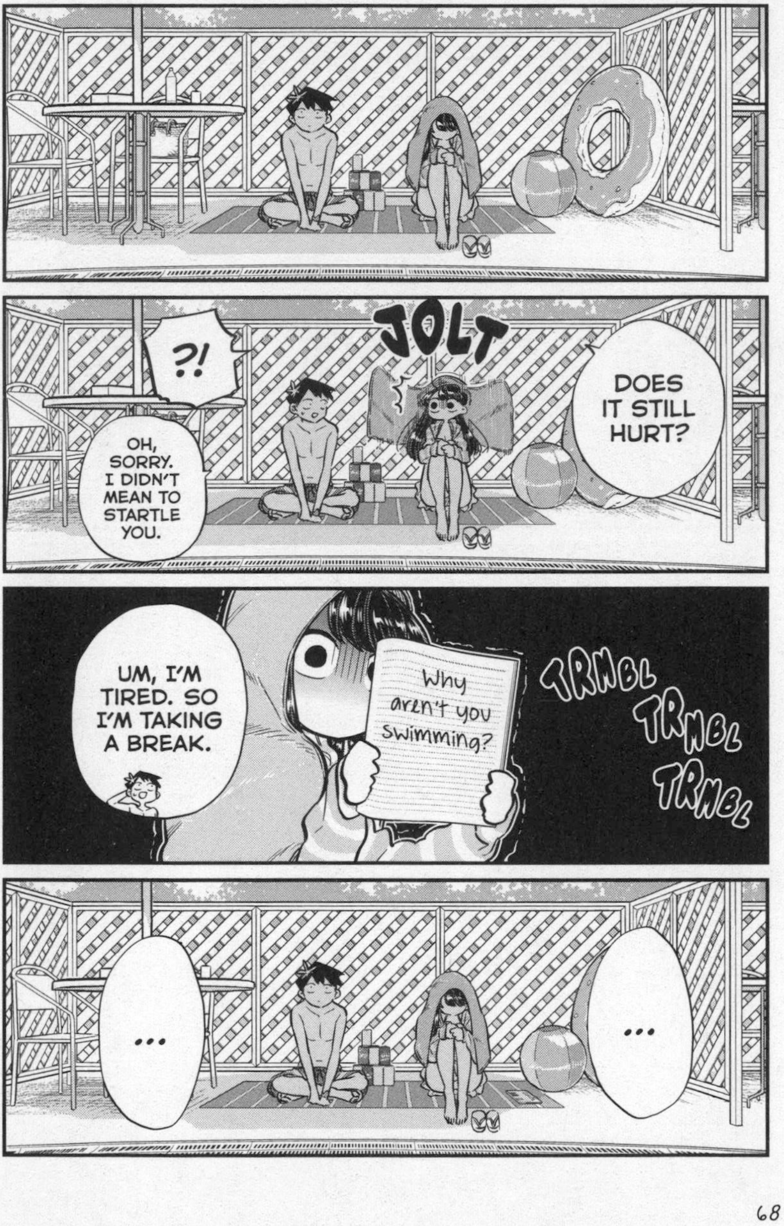
DOES IT STILL HURT?
JOLT
?!
OH, SORRY. I DIDN'T MEAN TO STARTLE YOU.
TRMBL TRMBL TRMBL
Why aren't you swimming?
UM, I'M TIRED. SO I'M TAKING A BREAK.
...
...

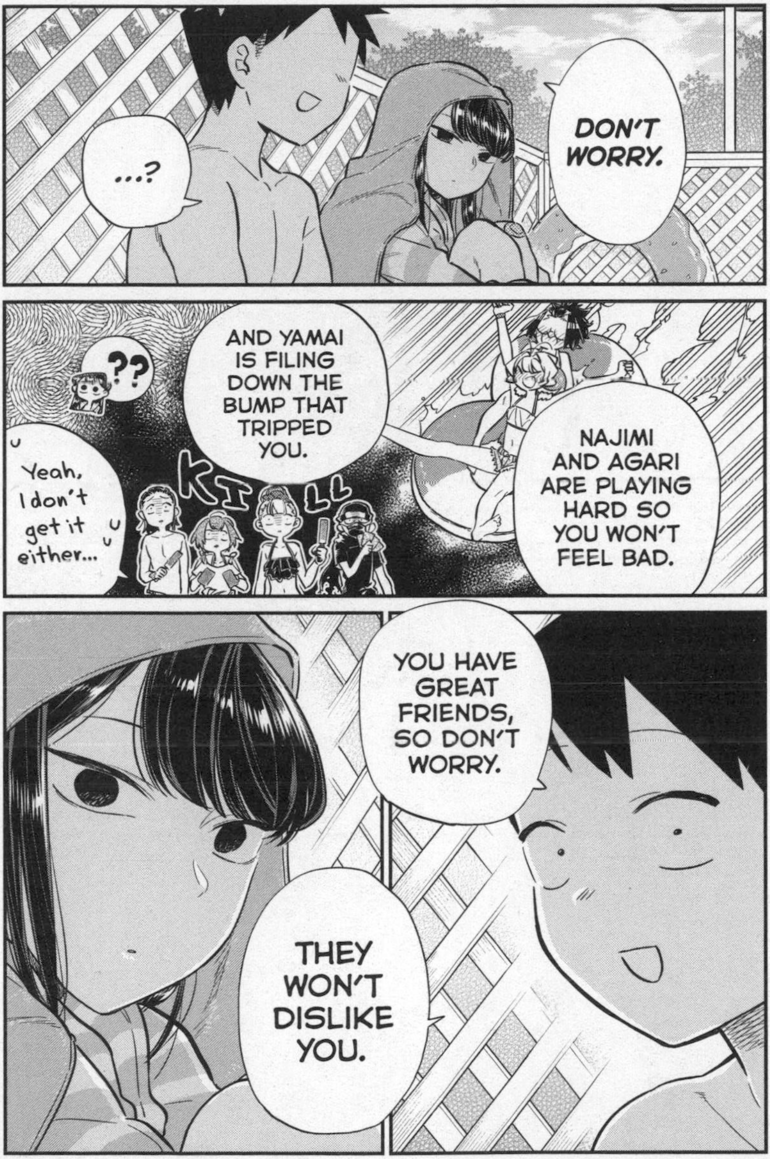
DON'T WORRY.
...?
NAJIMI AND AGARI ARE PLAYING HARD SO YOU WON'T FEEL BAD.
AND YAMAI IS FILING DOWN THE BUMP THAT TRIPPED YOU.
??
KILL
Yeah, I don't get it either...
YOU HAVE GREAT FRIENDS, SO DON'T WORRY.
THEY WON'T DISLIKE YOU.

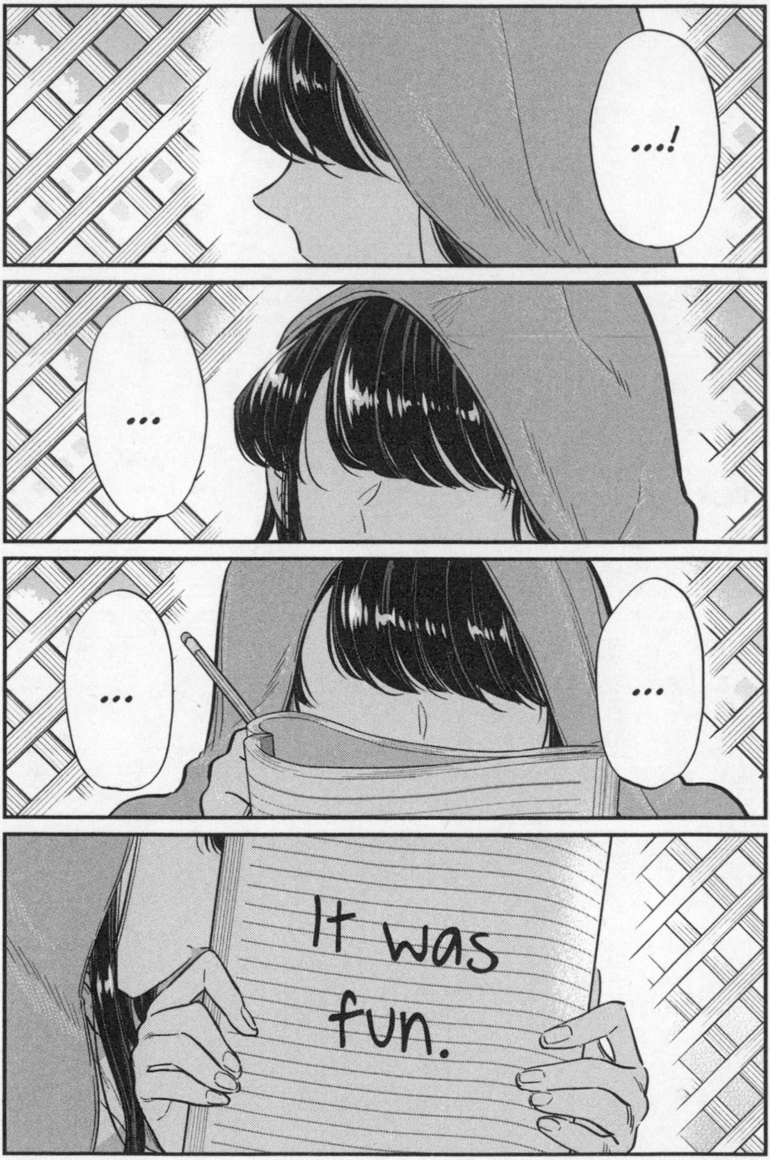
...!
...
...
...
It was fun.

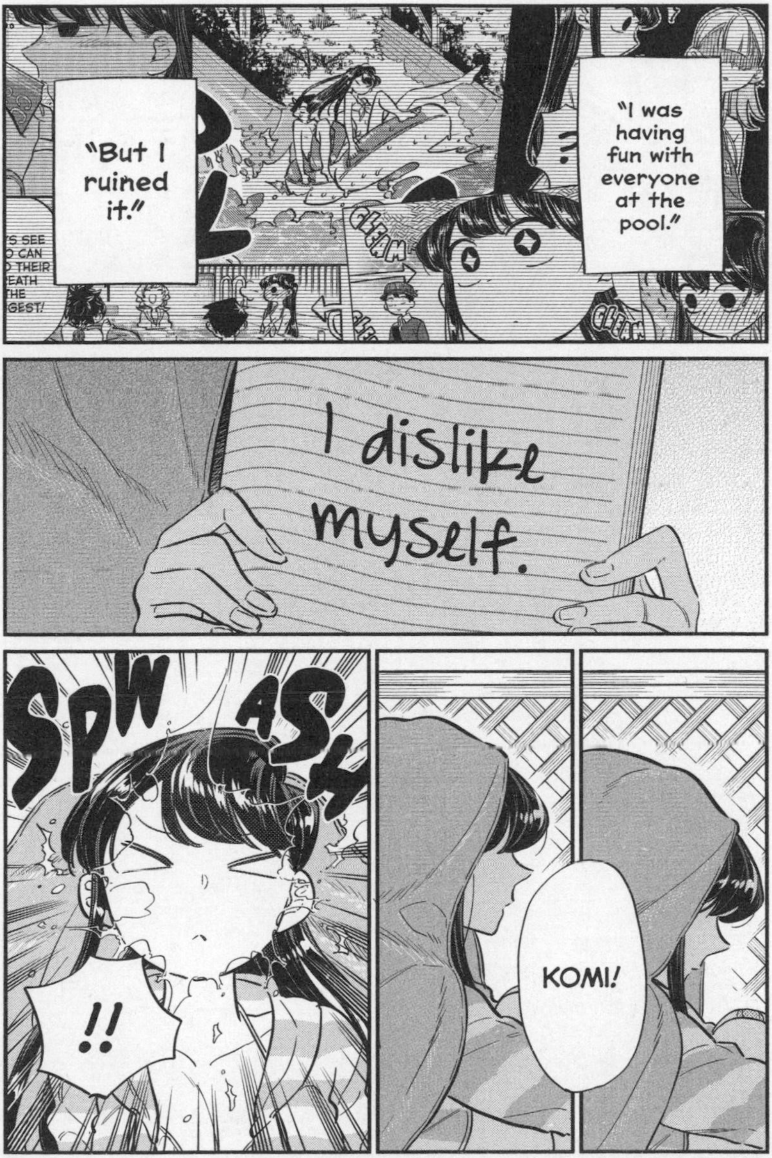
"I was having fun with everyone at the pool."
"But I ruined it."
I dislike myself.
KOMI!
SPWASH
!!

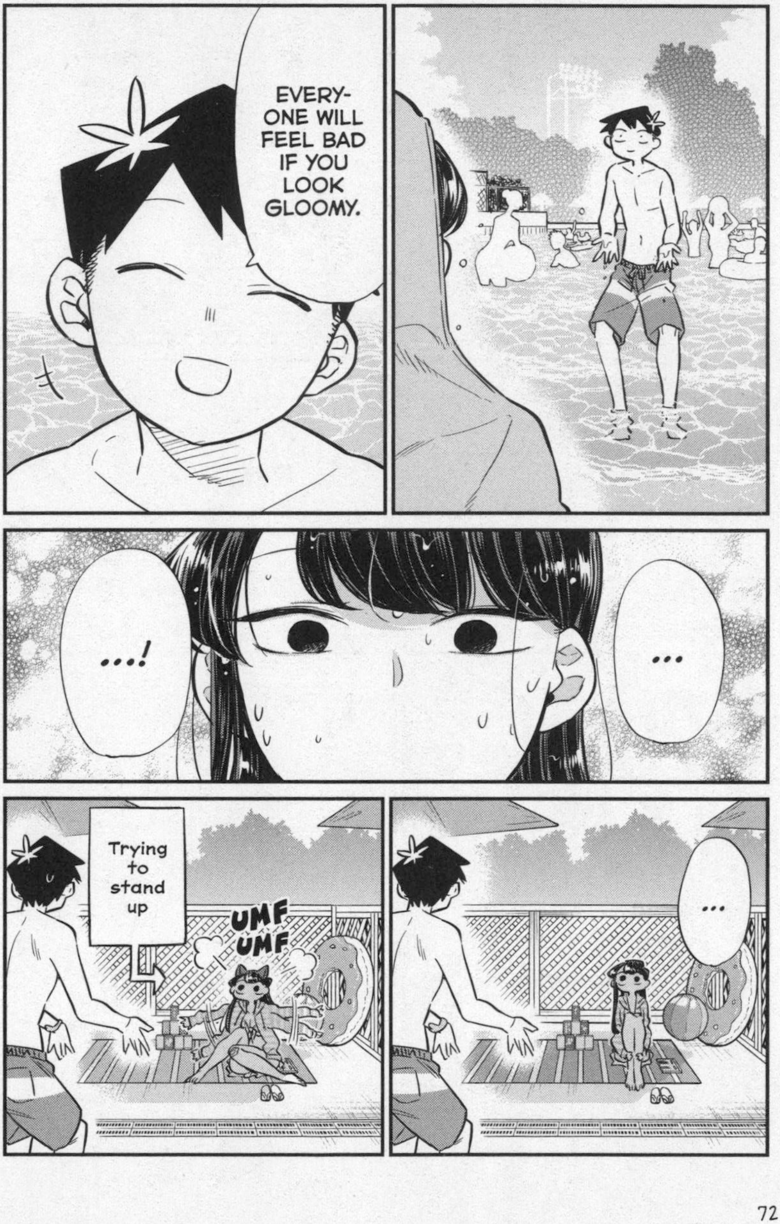
EVERY-ONE WILL FEEL BAD IF YOU LOOK GLOOMY.
...
...!
...
Trying to stand up
UMF UMF

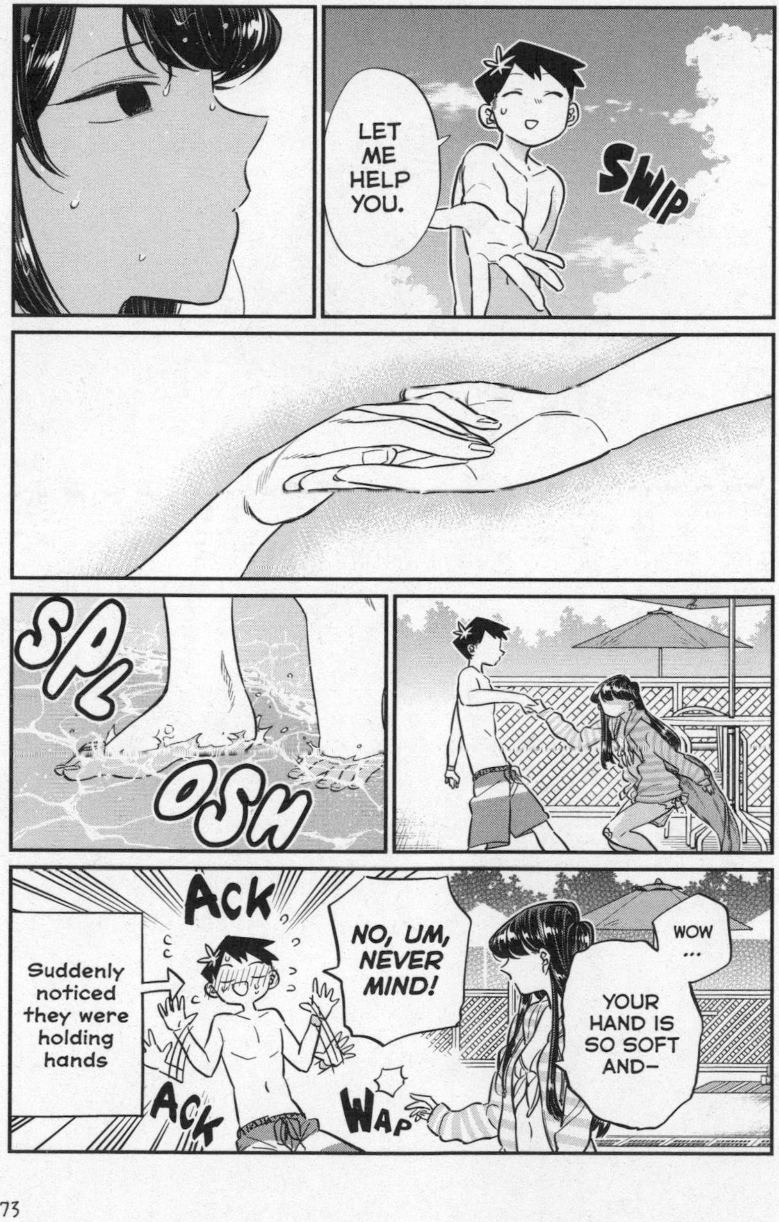
LET ME HELP YOU.
SWIP
SPLOSH
WOW ...
YOUR HAND IS SO SOFT AND—
NO, UM, NEVER MIND!
ACK
Suddenly noticed they were holding hands
WAP
ACK

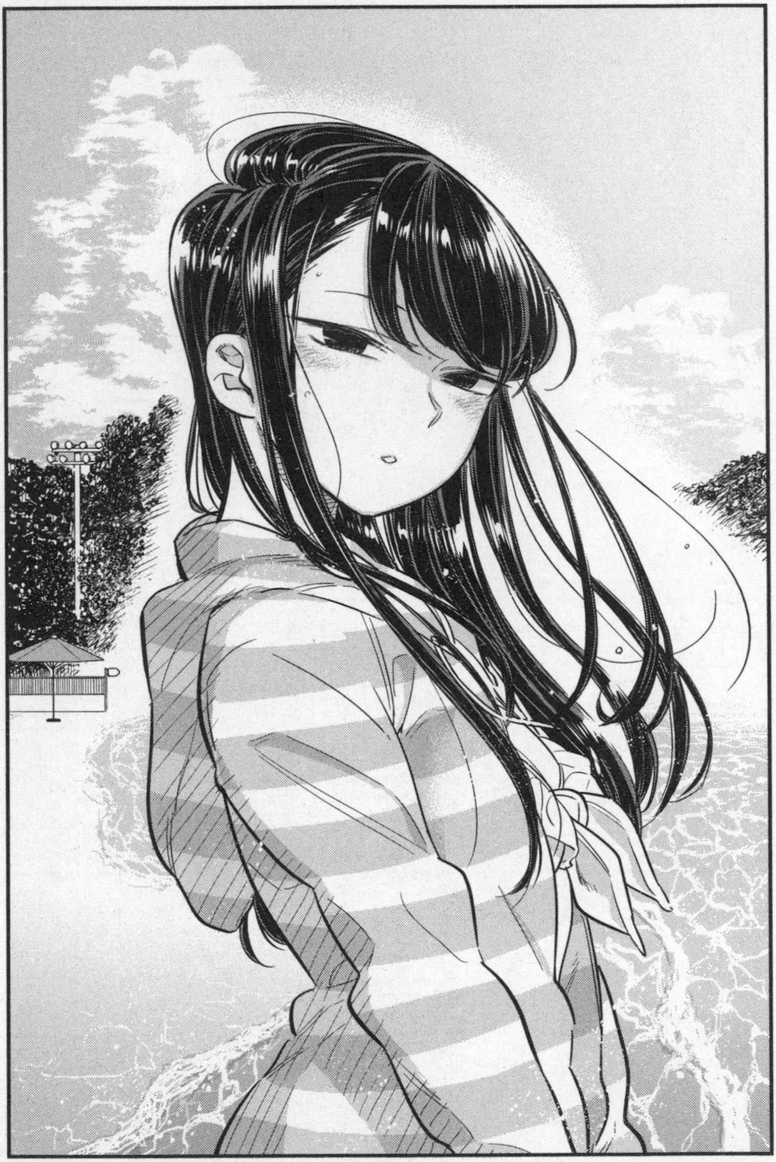

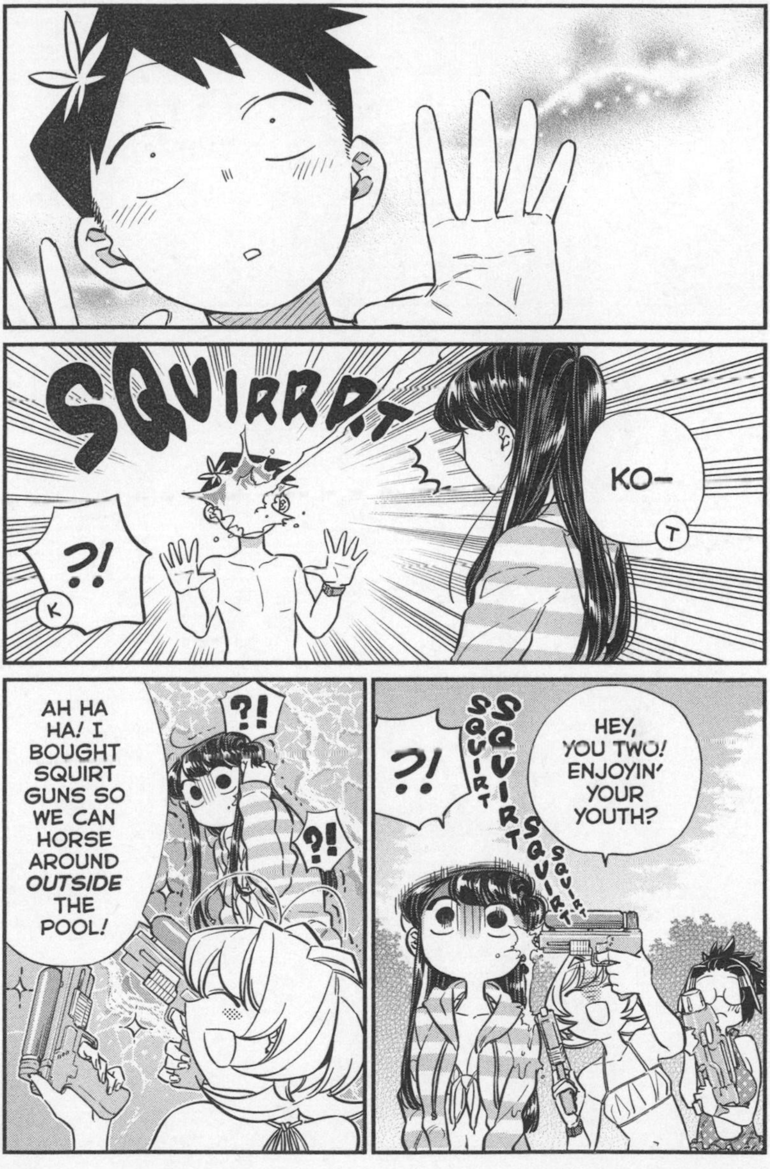
KO-
T
SQUIRRRT
?!
K
HEY, YOU TWO! ENJOYIN' YOUR YOUTH?
SQUIRT
SQUIRT
SQUIRT
SQUIRT
?!
?!
?!
AH HA HA! I BOUGHT SQUIRT GUNS SO WE CAN HORSE AROUND *OUTSIDE* THE POOL!

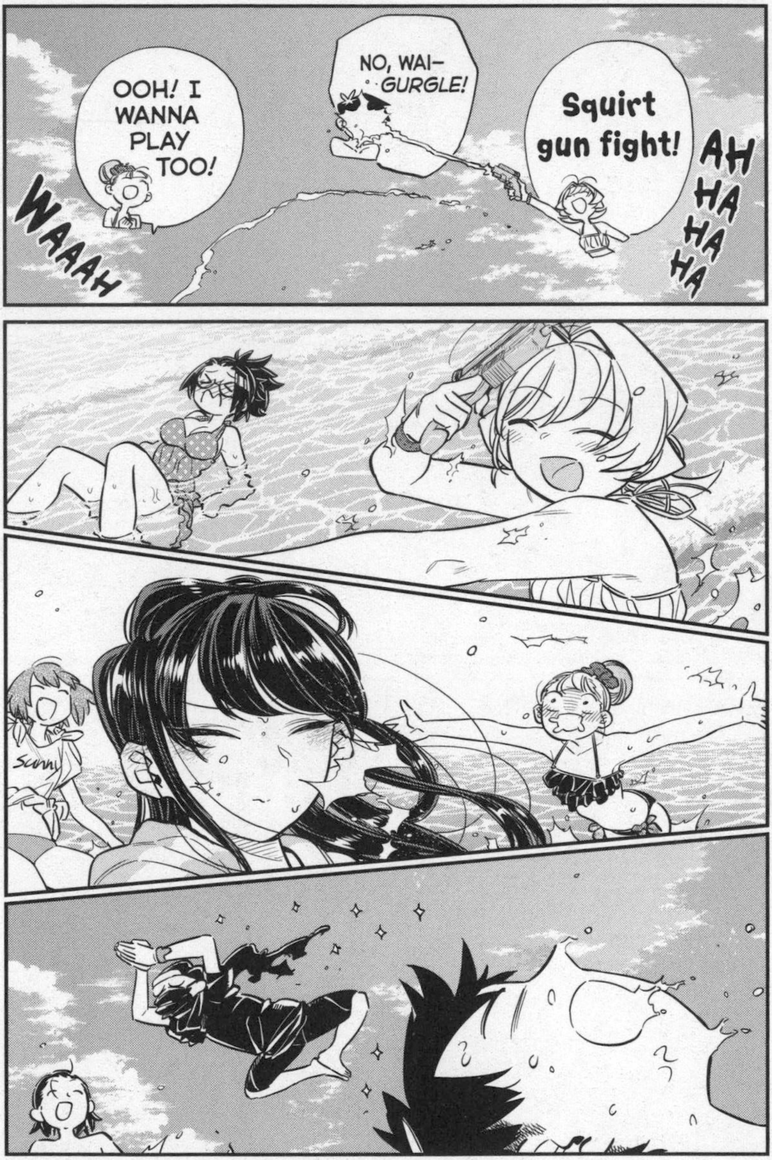
AH HA HA HA HA
Squirt gun fight!
NO, WAI- GURGLE!
OOH! I WANNA PLAY TOO!
WAAAH

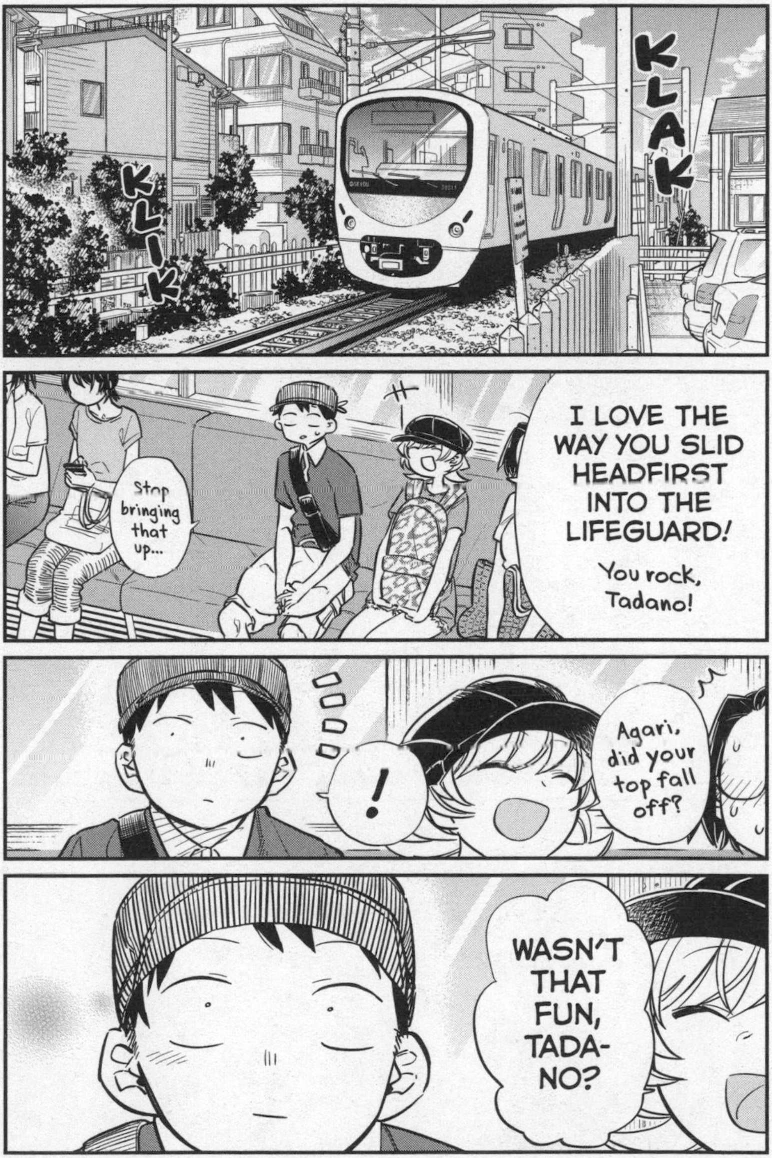
KLAK
KLIK
I LOVE THE WAY YOU SLID HEADFIRST INTO THE LIFEGUARD!
You rock, Tadano!
Stop bringing that up...
Agari, did your top fall off?
!
WASN'T THAT FUN, TADA-NO?

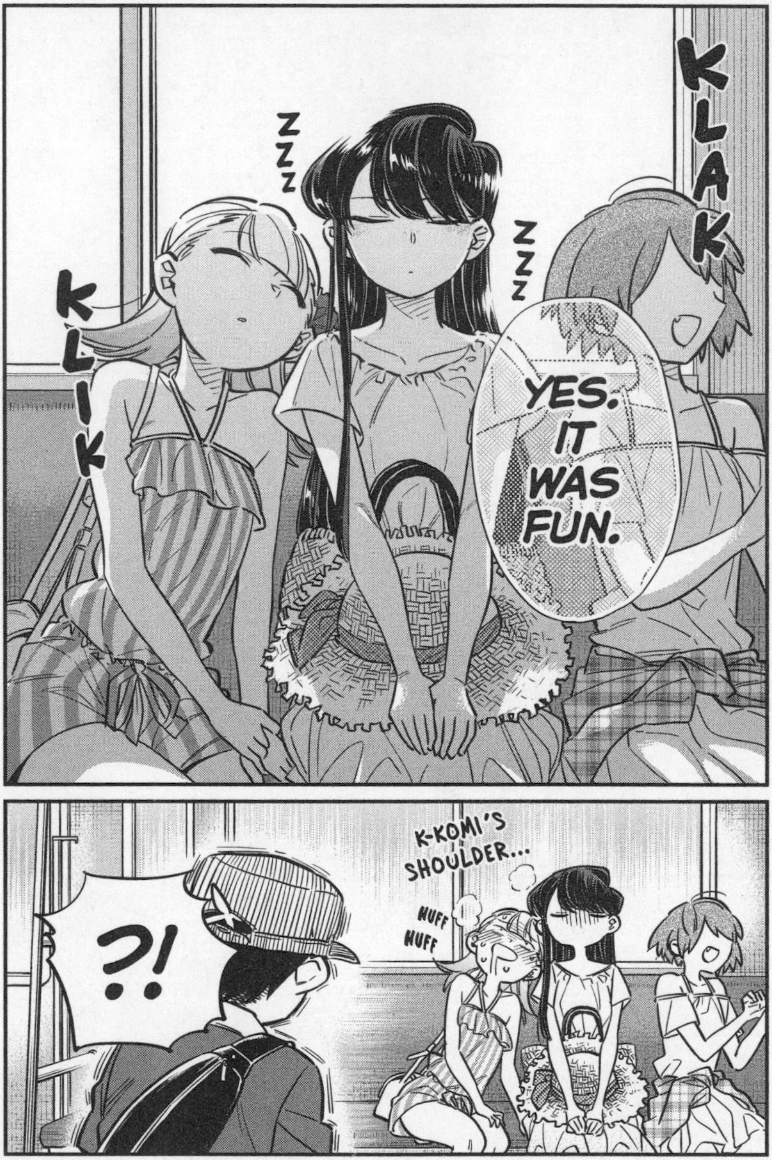
KLAK
ZZZ
YES. IT WAS FUN.
ZZZ
KLIK
K-KOMI'S SHOULDER...
HUFF HUFF
?!

Communication 40 — The End

Komi Can't Communicate

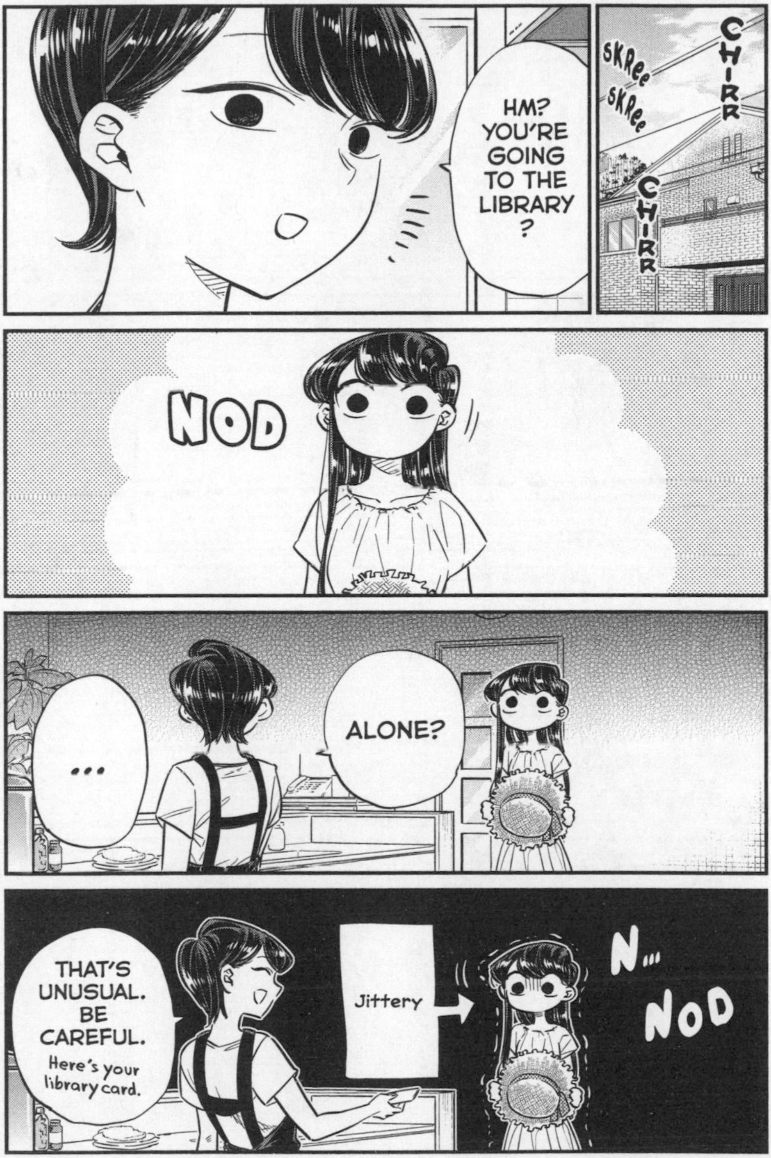
CHIRR
SKRee
SKRee
CHIRR
HM? YOU'RE GOING TO THE LIBRARY?
NOD
ALONE?
...
N...
NOD
Jittery
THAT'S UNUSUAL. BE CAREFUL.
Here's your library card.

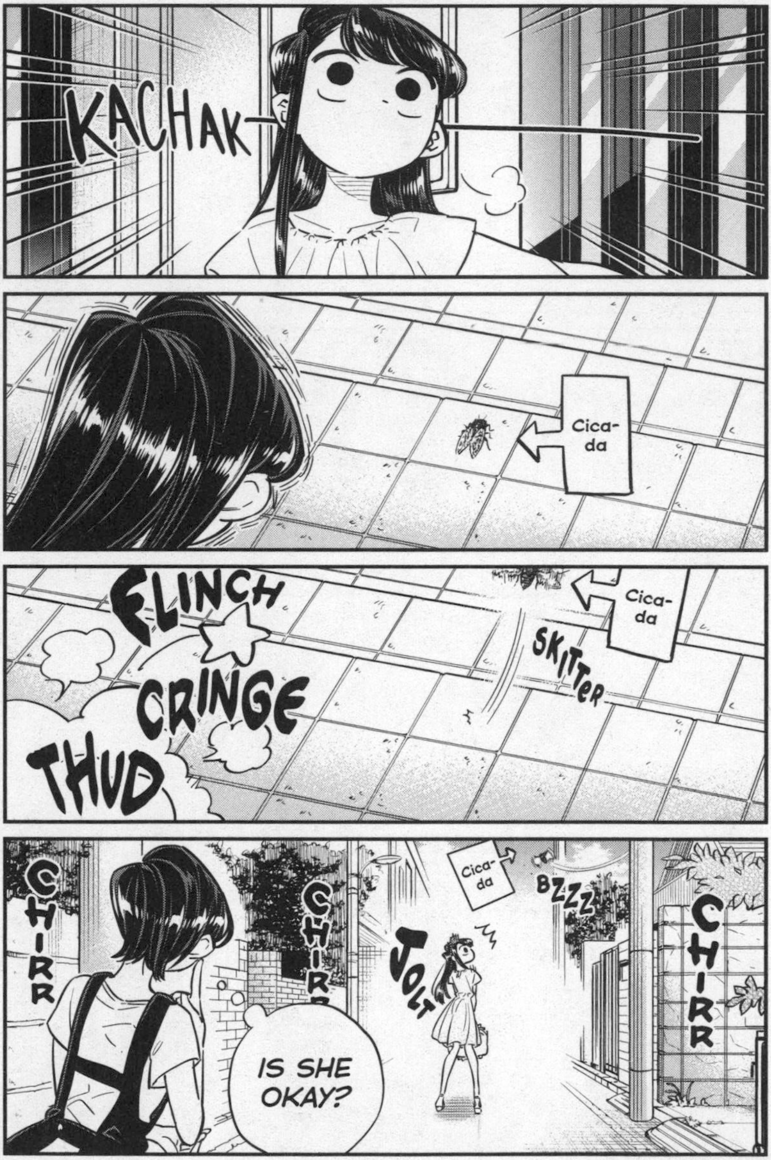
KACHAK
Cica-da
Cica-da
SKITTER
FLINCH
CRINGE
THUD
CHIRR
BZZZ
Cica-da
JOLT
CHIRR
CHIRR
IS SHE OKAY?

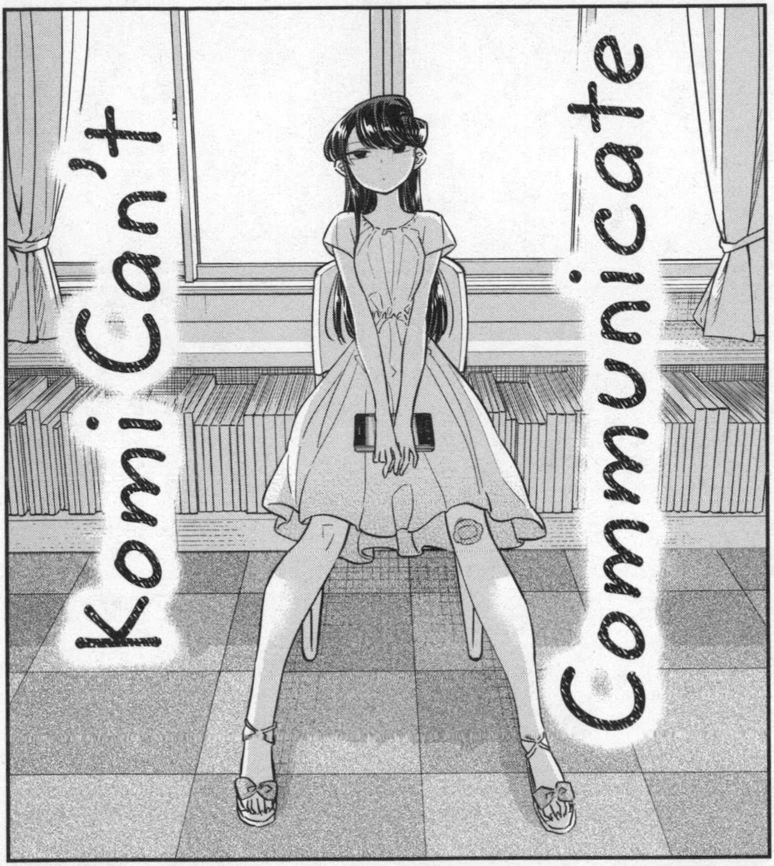
Komi Can't
Communicate

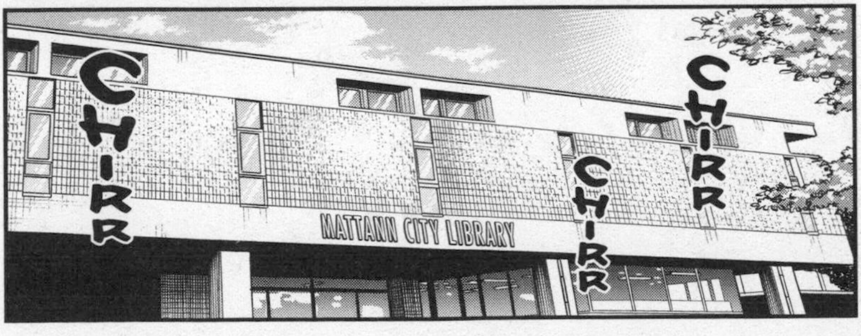
CHIRR
CHIRR
CHIRR
MATTANN CITY LIBRARY

Communication 41: The Library

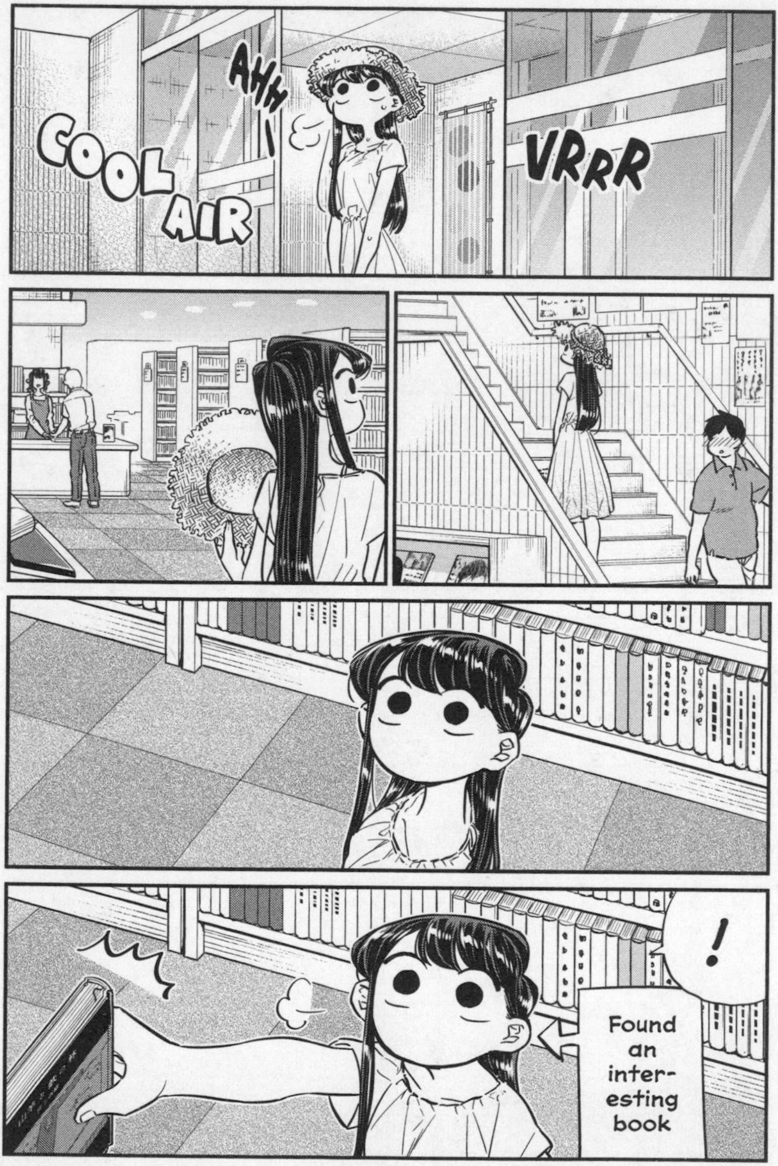
VRRR
AHH
COOL AIR
!
Found an interesting book

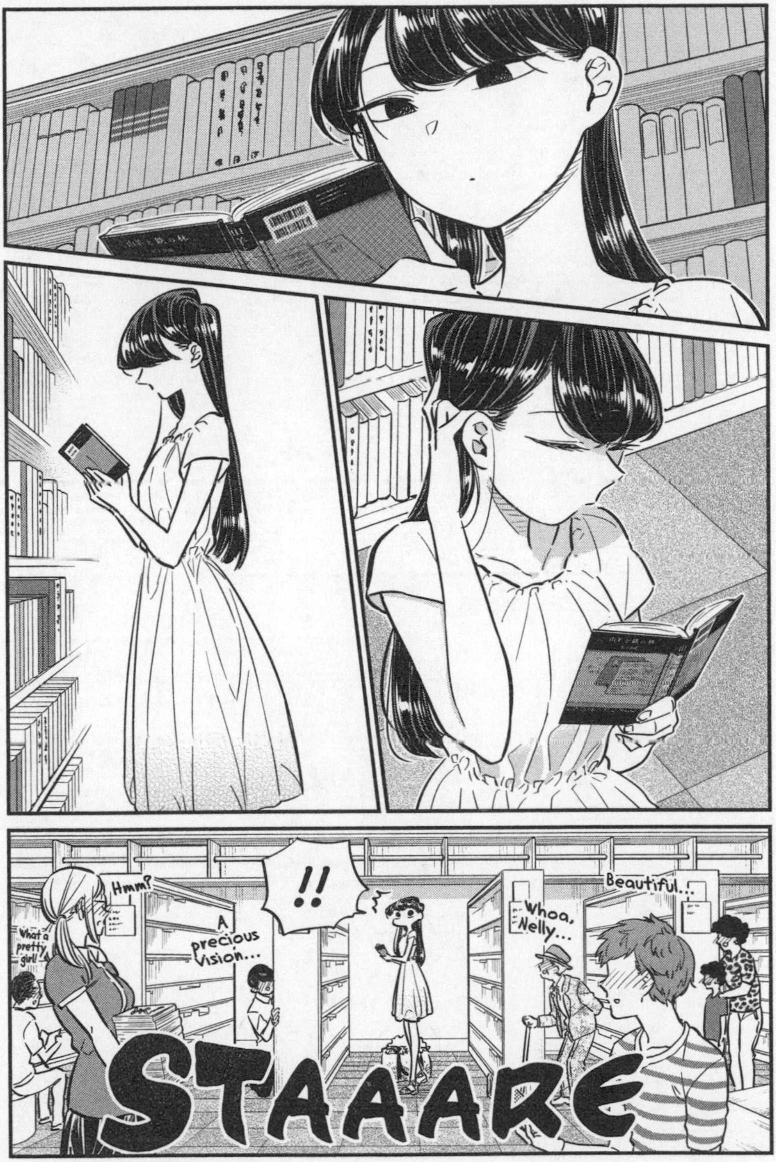
Beautiful...
Whoa, Nelly...
!!
A precious vision...
Hmm?
What a pretty girl!
STAAARE

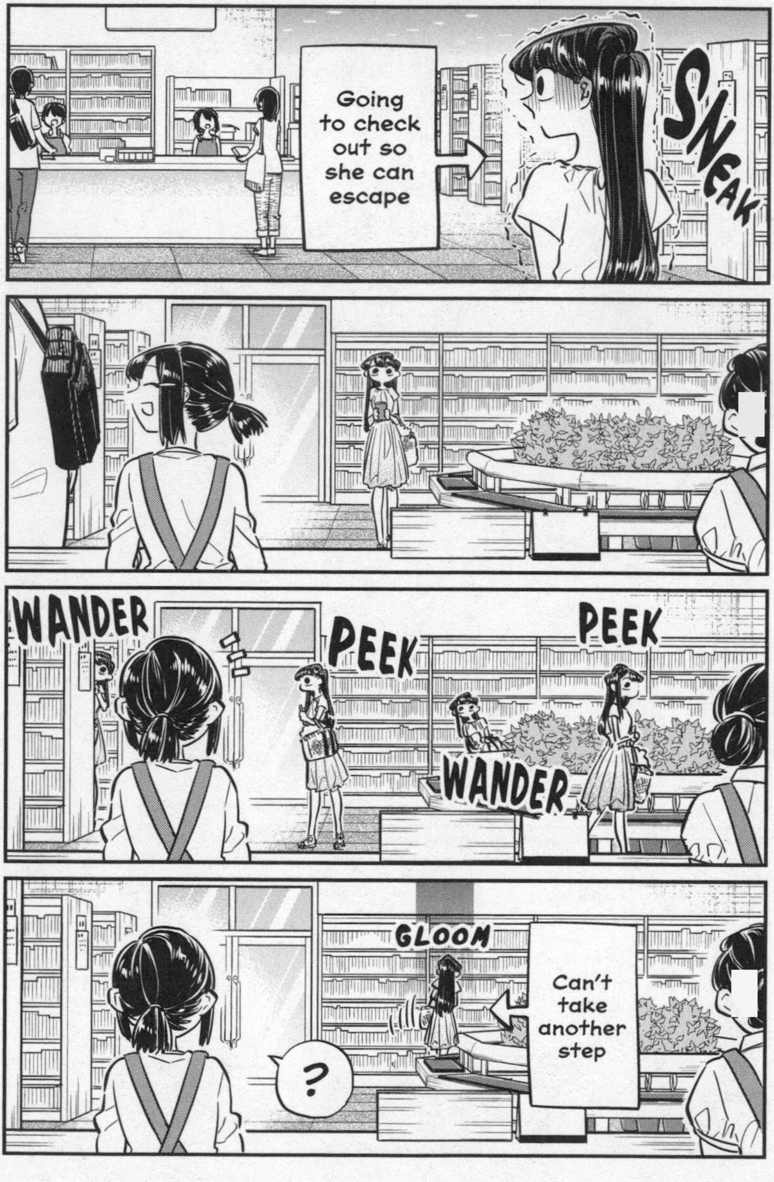
SNEAK
Going to check out so she can escape
PEEK
WANDER
PEEK
WANDER
Can't take another step
GLOOM
?

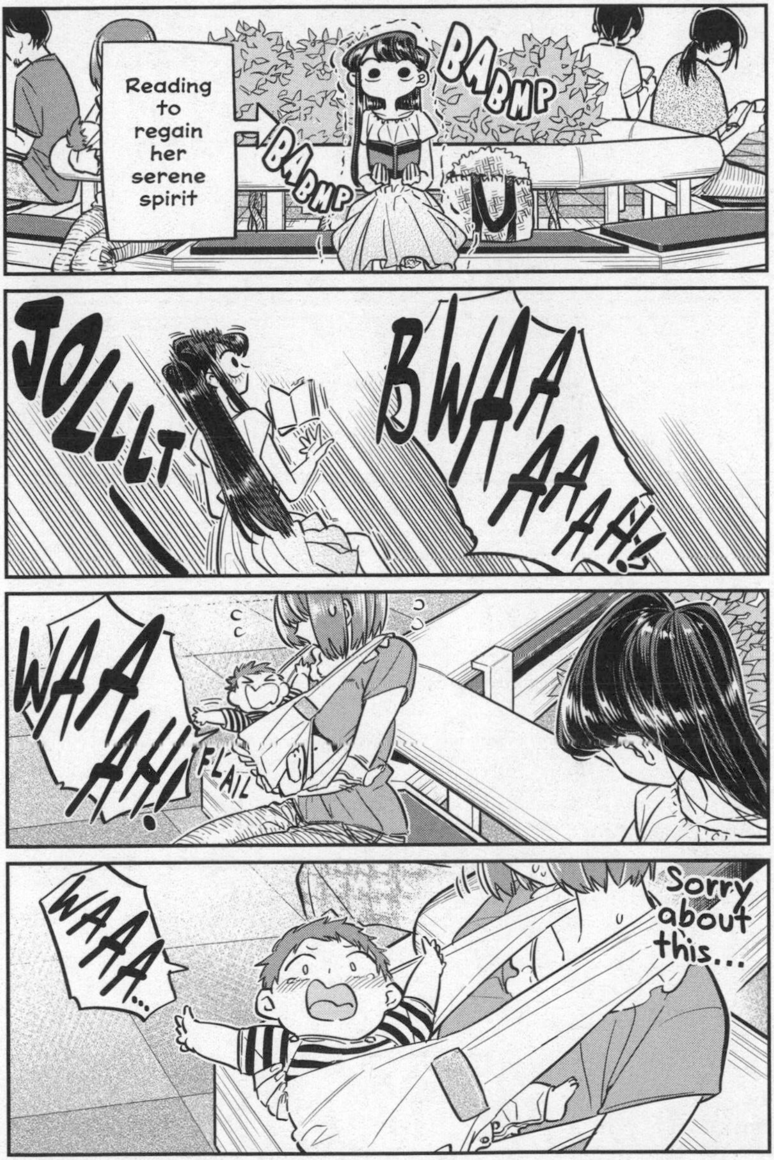
BABMP
BABMP
Reading to regain her serene spirit
BWAAAAAAH!!
JOLLLT
WAAAAH!
FLAIL
Sorry about this...
WAAAA...

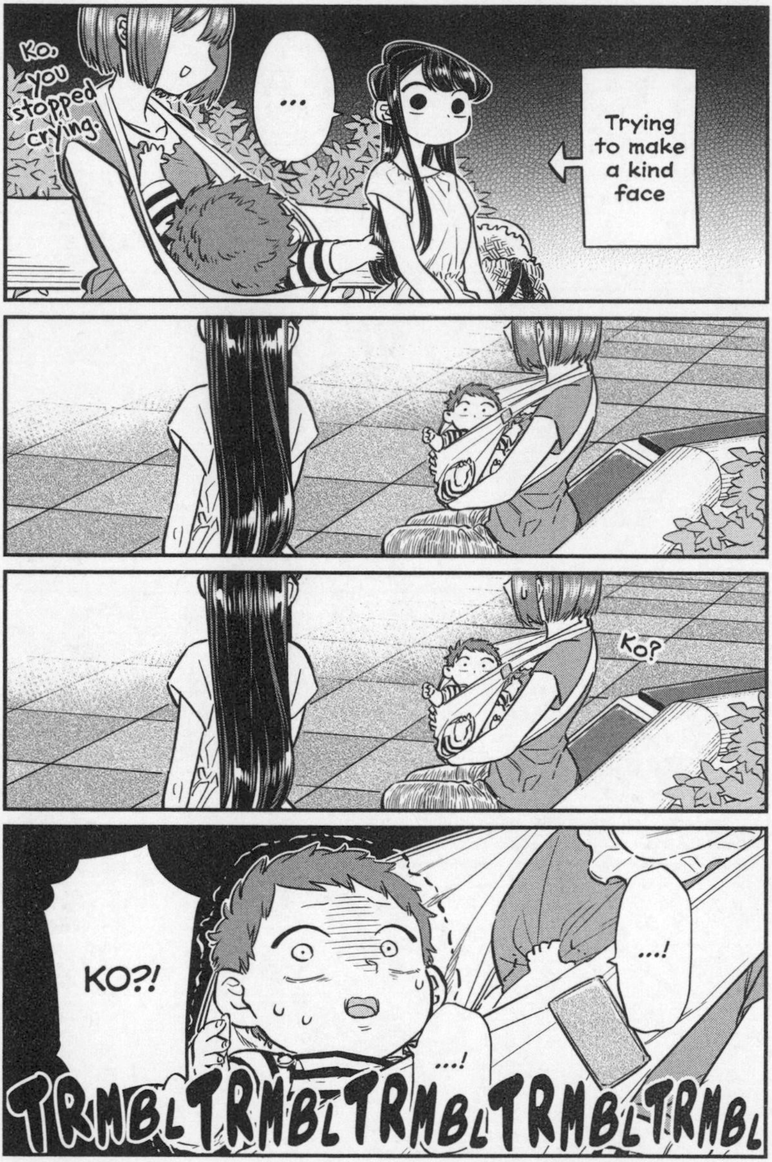
Trying to make a kind face
...
Ko, you stopped crying.
Ko?
...!
KO?!
...!
TRMBL TRMBL TRMBL TRMBL TRMBL

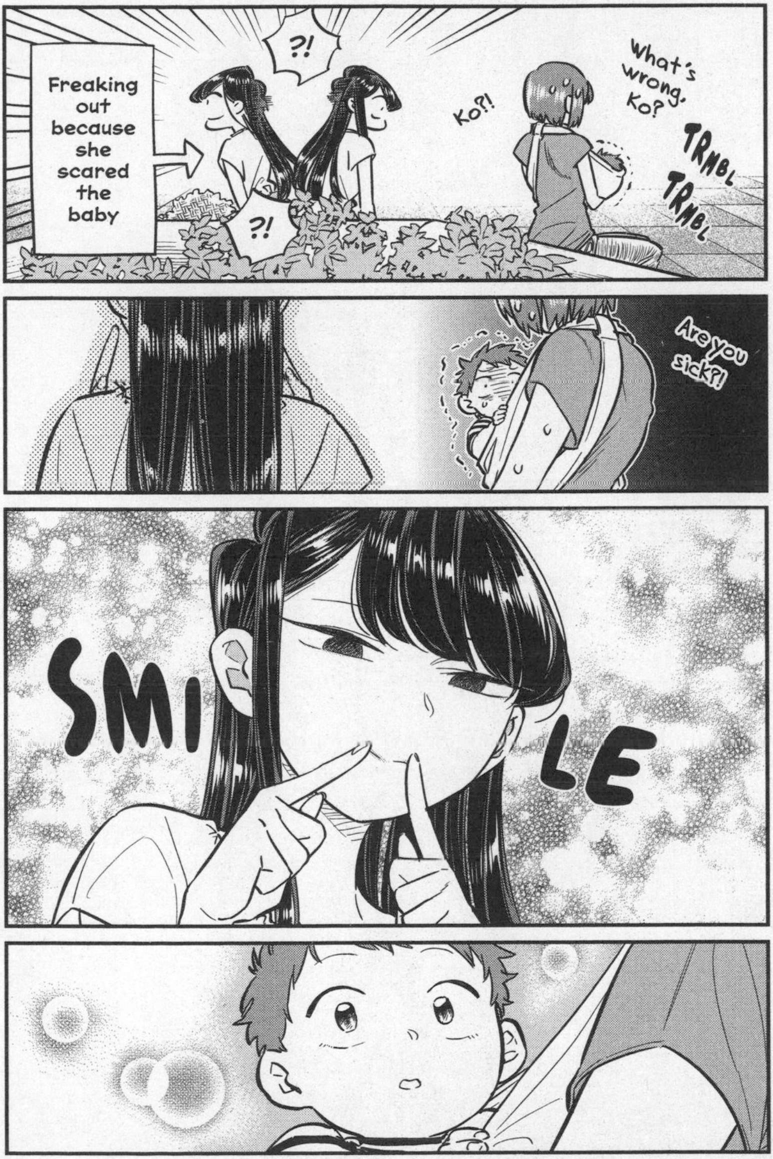
What's wrong, Ko?
Ko?!
TRMBL TRMBL
?!
?!
Freaking out because she scared the baby
Are you sick?!
SMI LE

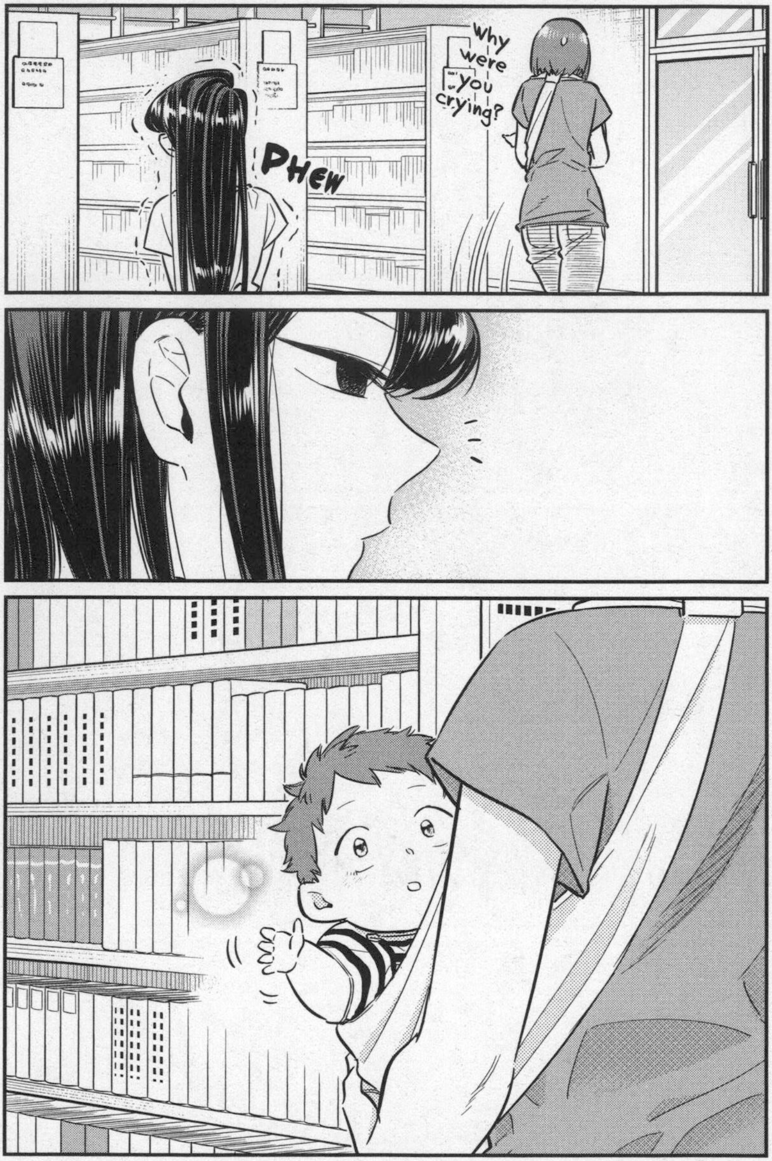
Why were you crying?
PHEW

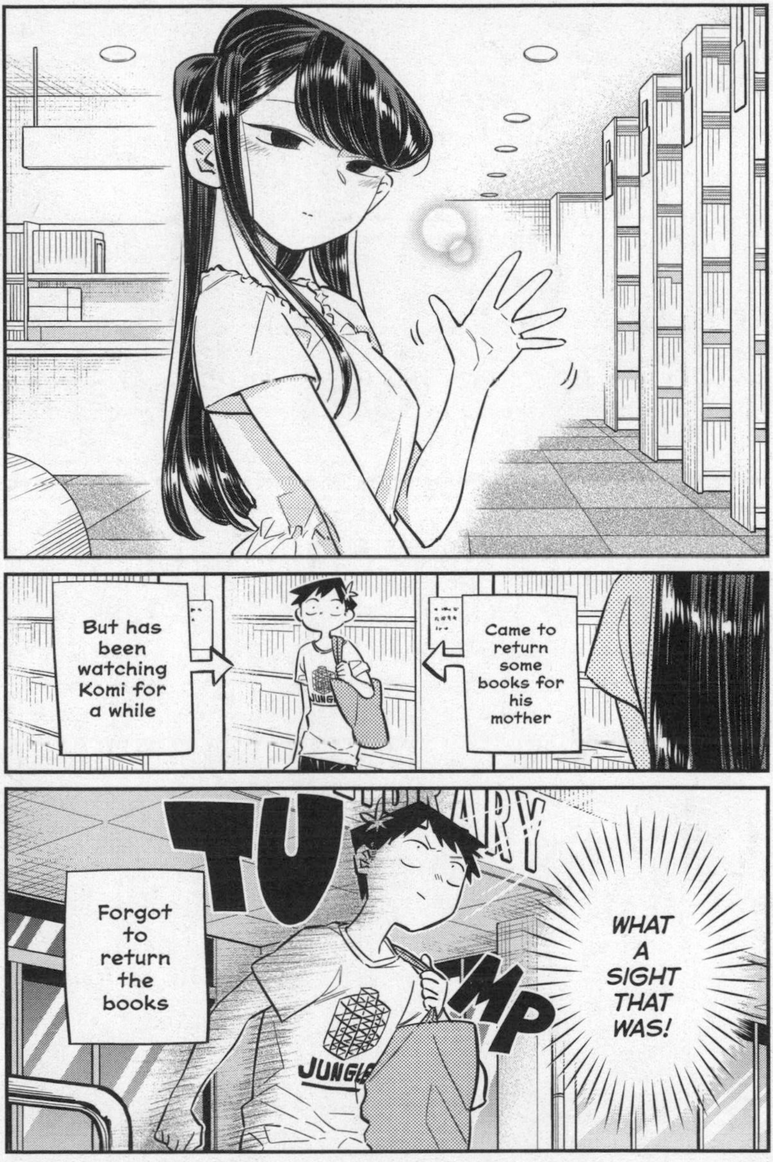
Came to return some books for his mother
But has been watching Komi for a while
WHAT A SIGHT THAT WAS!
TUMP
Forgot to return the books

Communication 41 – The End

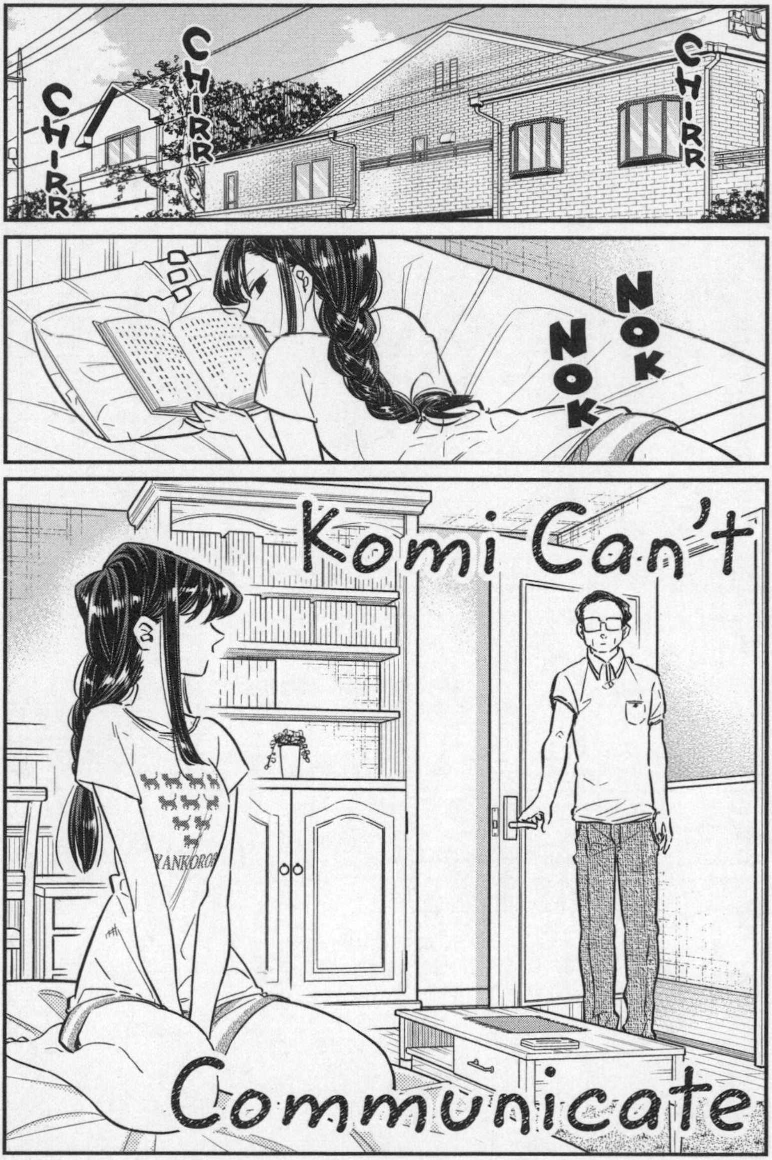
CHIRR
CHIRR
CHIRR
NOK
NOK
Komi Can't
Communicate

Communication 42: Shaved Ice

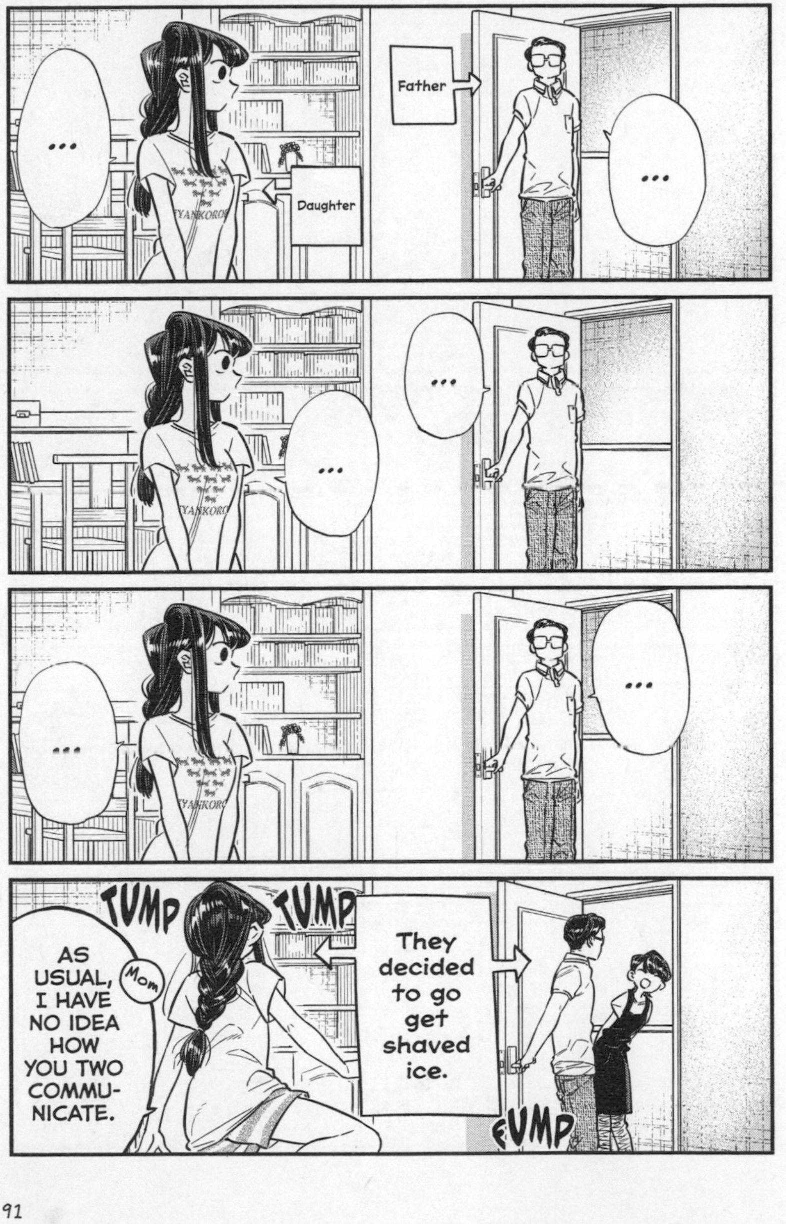

Father
...
...
Daughter
...
...
...
...
TUMP
TUMP
They decided to go get shaved ice.
FUMP
Mom
AS USUAL, I HAVE NO IDEA HOW YOU TWO COMMU-NICATE.

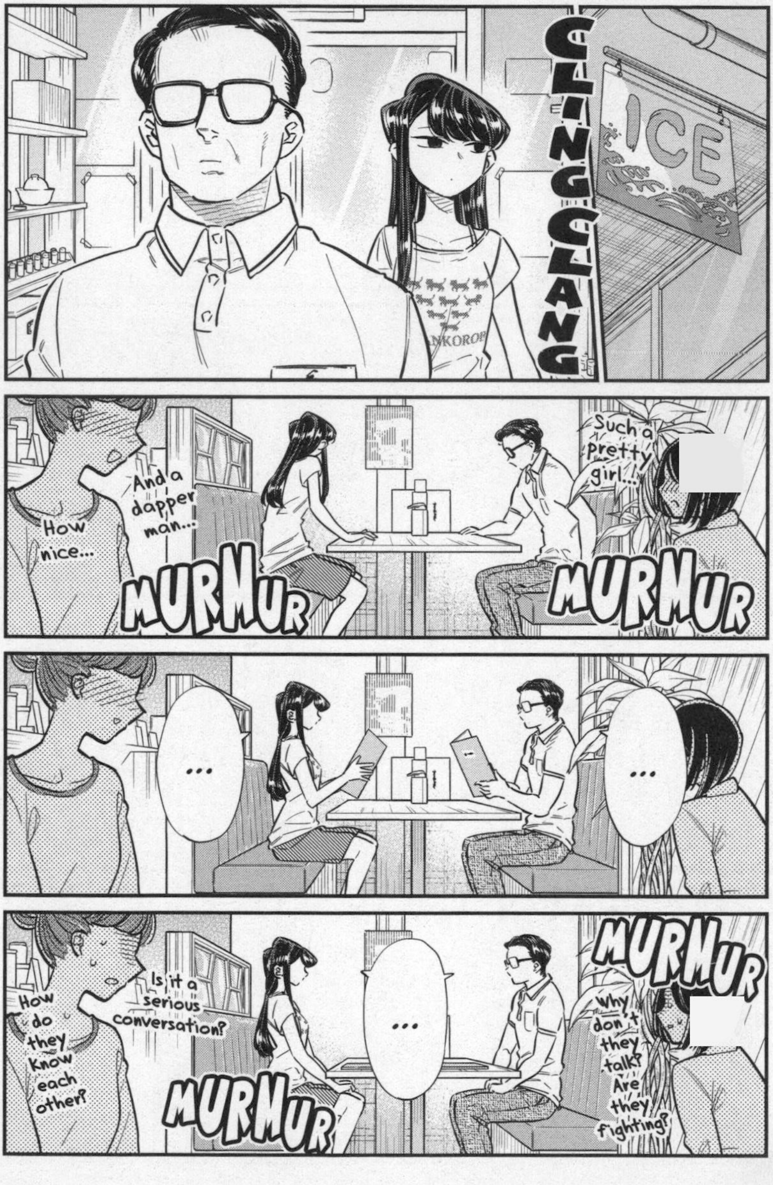
ICE
CLING CLANG
Such a pretty girl...
MURMUR
And a dapper man...
How nice...
MURMUR
...
...
MURMUR
Why don't they talk? Are they fighting?
...
Is it a serious conversation?
How do they know each other?
MURMUR

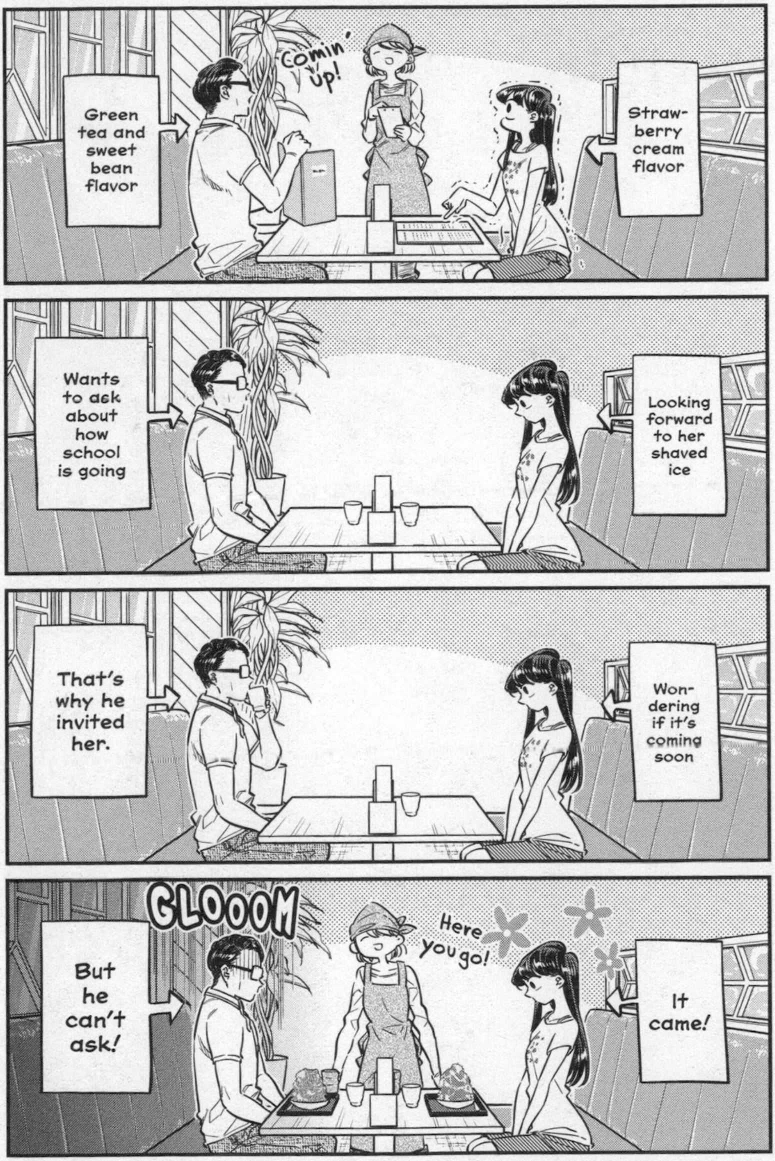
Strawberry cream flavor
Comin' up!
Green tea and sweet bean flavor
Looking forward to her shaved ice
Wants to ask about how school is going
Wondering if it's coming soon
That's why he invited her.
It came!
Here you go!
GLOOOM
But he can't ask!

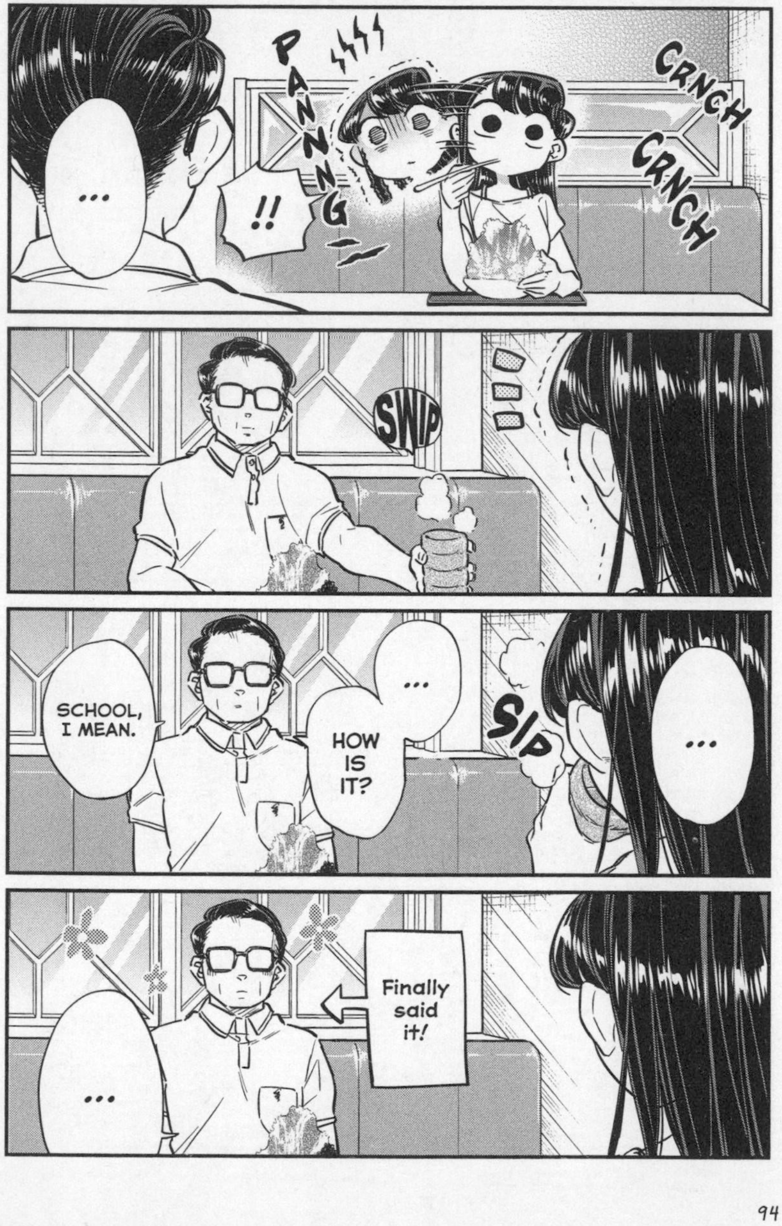
CRNCH
CRNCH
CRNCH
PANNNG
!!
...
SWIP
...
SIP
...
HOW IS IT?
SCHOOL, I MEAN.
Finally said it!
...

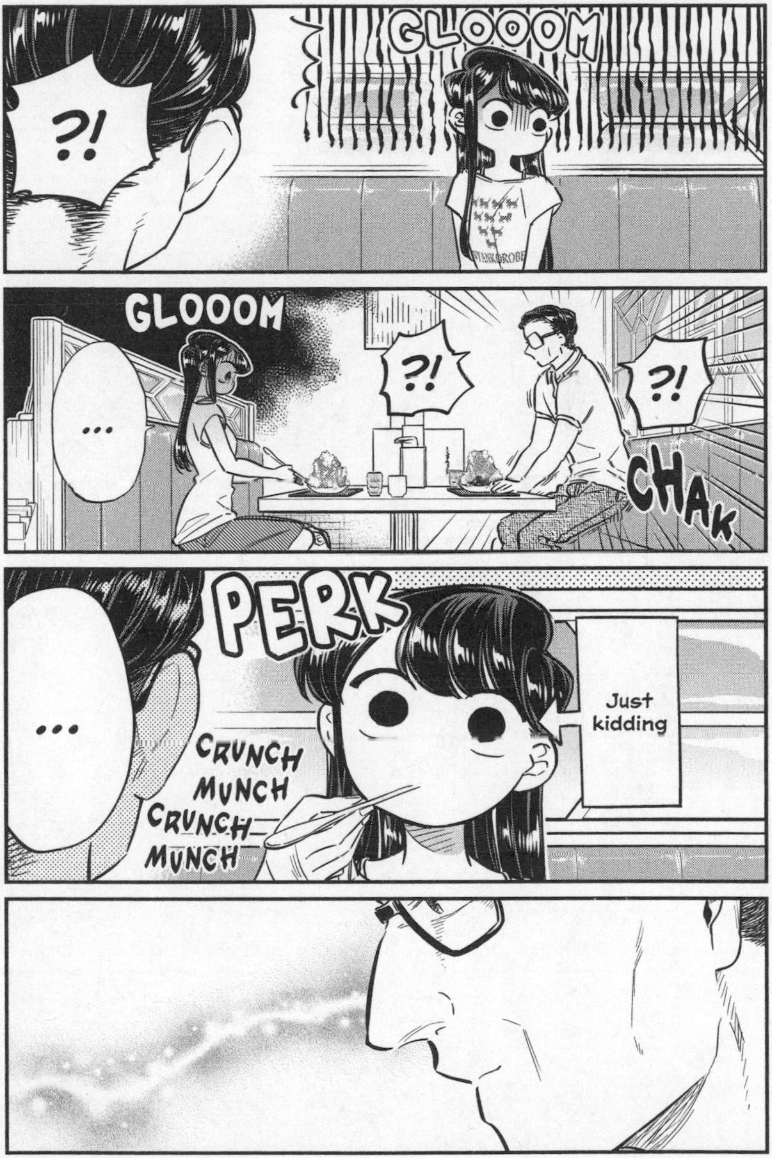
GLOOOM
?!
?!
?!
CHAK
GLOOOM
...
Just kidding
PERK
CRUNCH MUNCH CRUNCH MUNCH
...

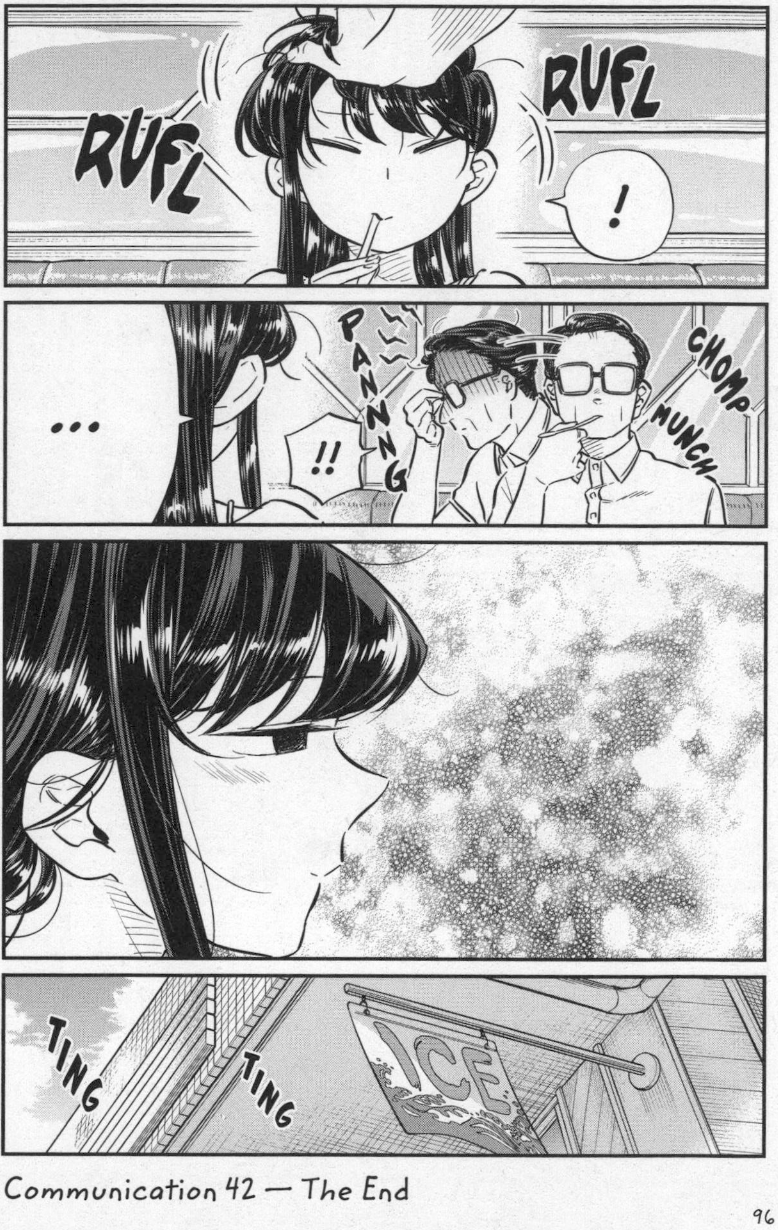
RUFL
!
RUFL
CHOMP
MUNCH
PANNNG
!!
...
TING
TING

Communication 42 — The End

Komi Can't Communicate

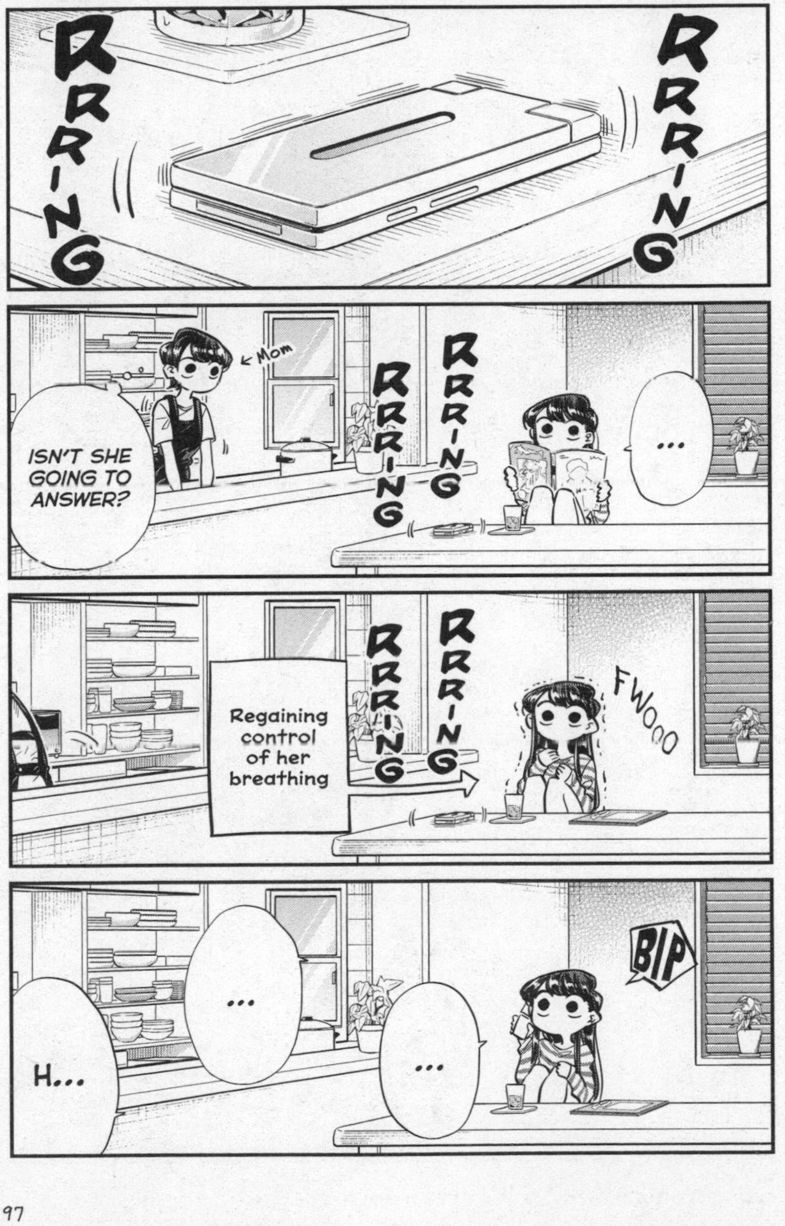
RRRING
RRRING
...
RRRING
RRRING
← Mom
ISN'T SHE GOING TO ANSWER?
FWOOO
RRRING
RRRING
Regaining control of her breathing
BIP
...
...
H...

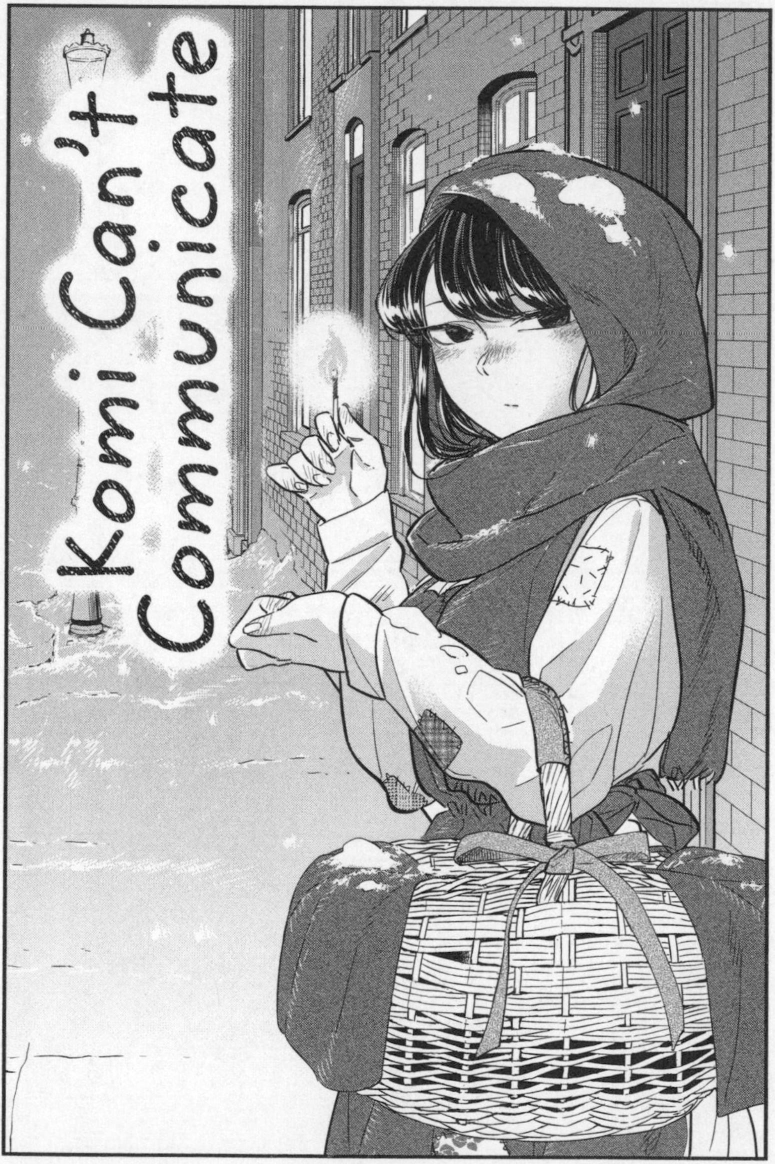
Komi Can't Communicate

Communication 43: Part-Time Job

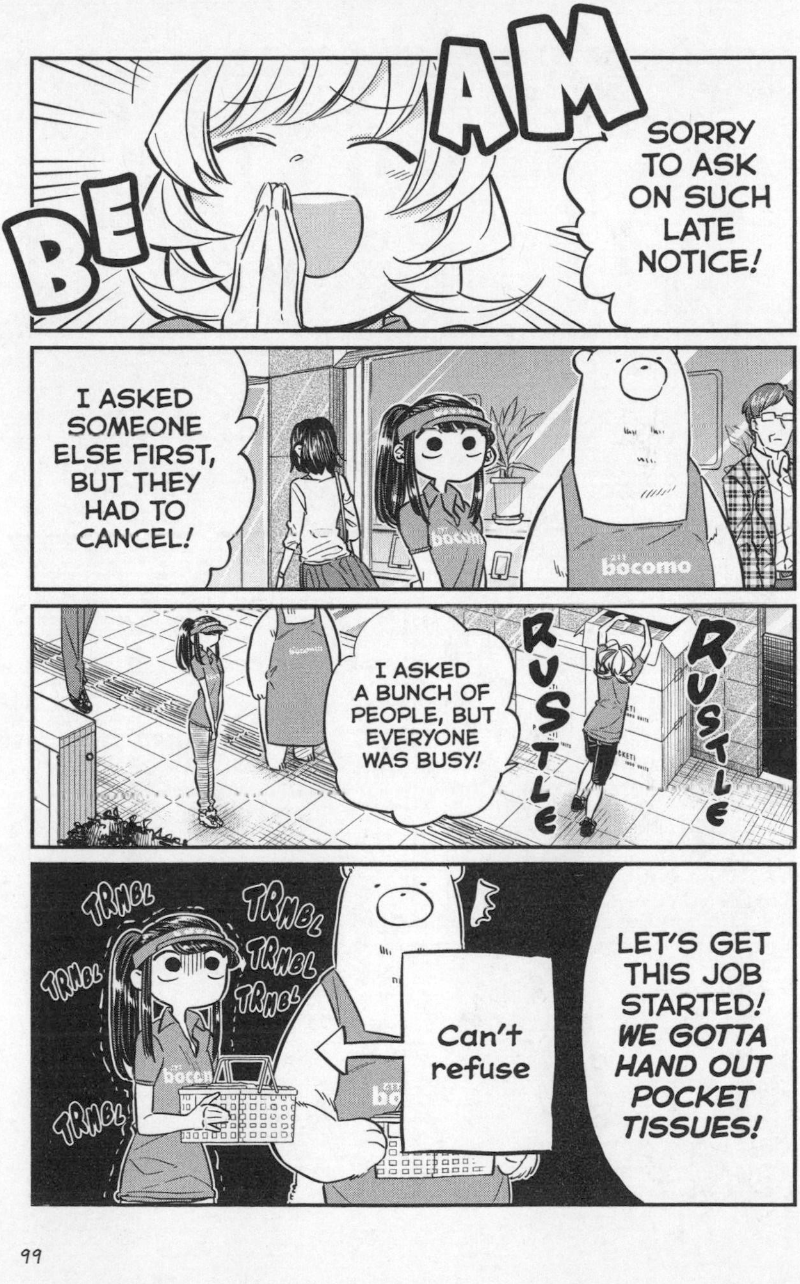
BEAM
SORRY TO ASK ON SUCH LATE NOTICE!
I ASKED SOMEONE ELSE FIRST, BUT THEY HAD TO CANCEL!
bocomo
RUSTLE
RUSTLE
I ASKED A BUNCH OF PEOPLE, BUT EVERYONE WAS BUSY!
LET'S GET THIS JOB STARTED! *WE GOTTA HAND OUT POCKET TISSUES!*
Can't refuse
TRMBL
TRMBL
TRMBL
TRMBL
TRMBL
TRMBL

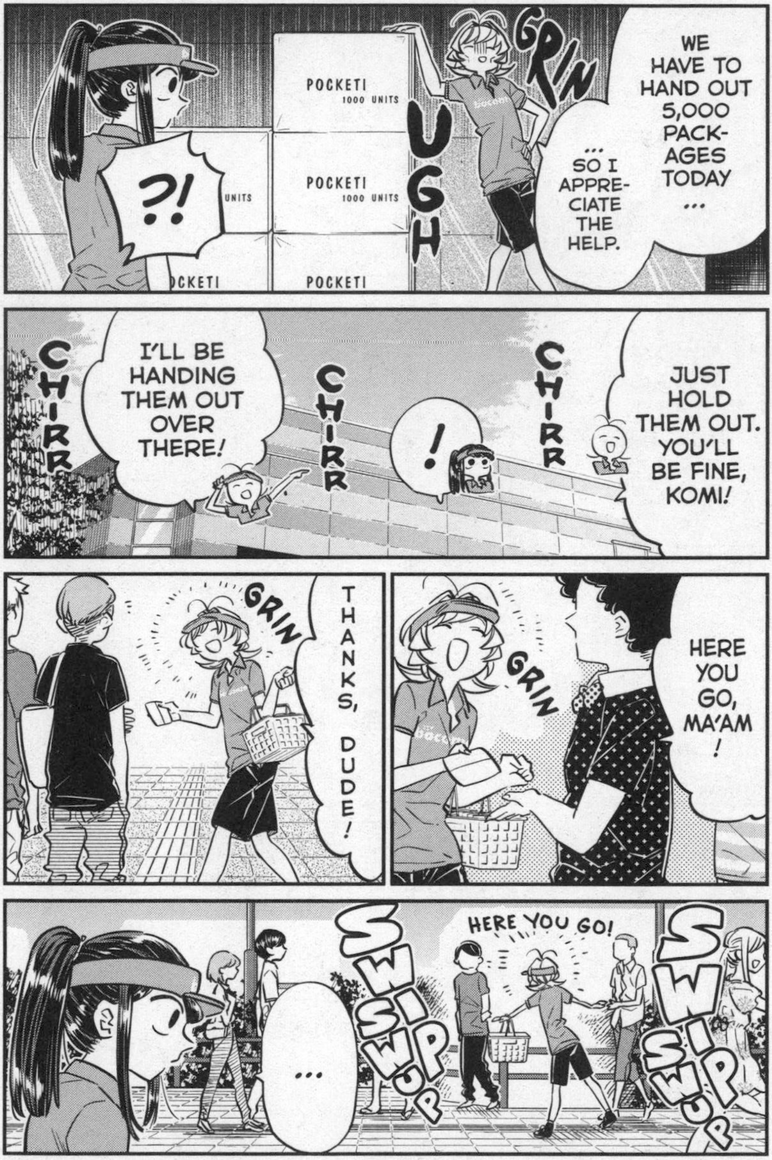
WE HAVE TO HAND OUT 5,000 PACKAGES TODAY...
GRIN
...SO I APPRECIATE THE HELP.
UGH
POCKETI 1000 UNITS
POCKETI 1000 UNITS
?!
JUST HOLD THEM OUT. YOU'LL BE FINE, KOMI!
CHIRR
!
CHIRR
I'LL BE HANDING THEM OUT OVER THERE!
CHIRR
HERE YOU GO, MA'AM!
GRIN
THANKS, DUDE!
GRIN
SWISWUP
HERE YOU GO!
SWISWUP
...

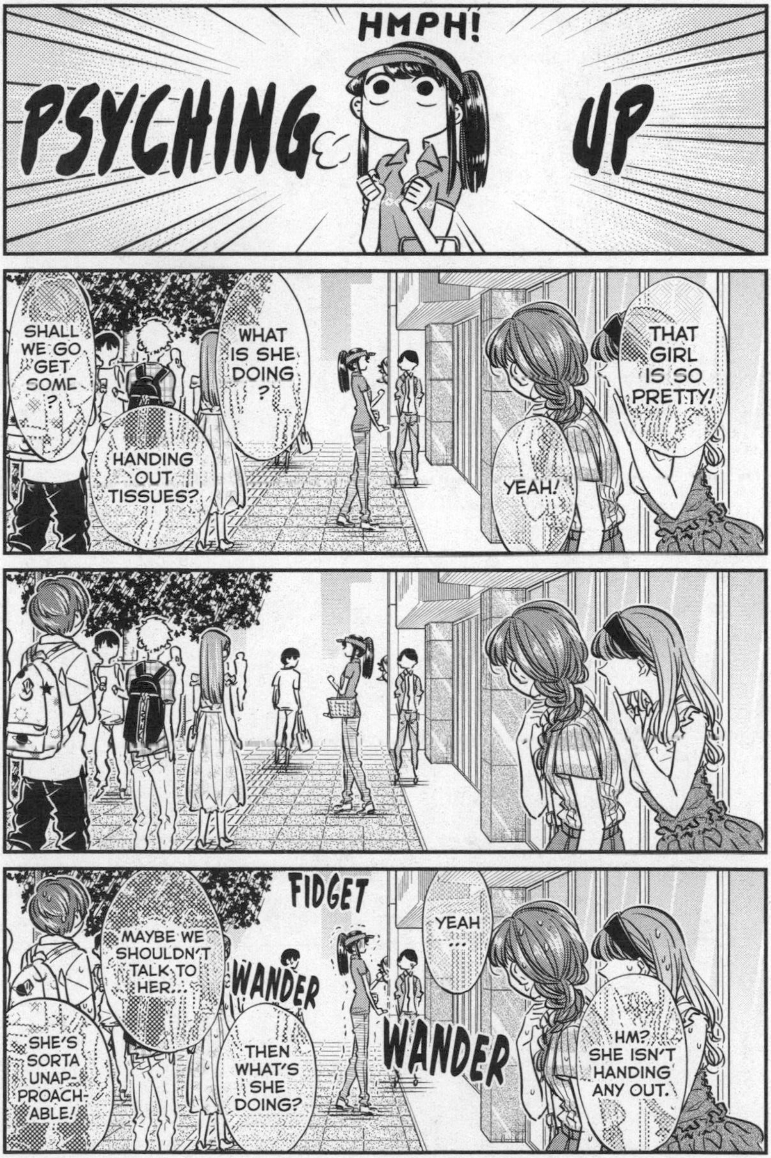
HMPH!
PSYCHING UP
THAT GIRL IS SO PRETTY!
YEAH!
WHAT IS SHE DOING?
SHALL WE GO GET SOME?
HANDING OUT TISSUES?
HM? SHE ISN'T HANDING ANY OUT.
YEAH...
FIDGET
WANDER
WANDER
MAYBE WE SHOULDN'T TALK TO HER...
THEN WHAT'S SHE DOING?
SHE'S SORTA UNAPPROACHABLE!

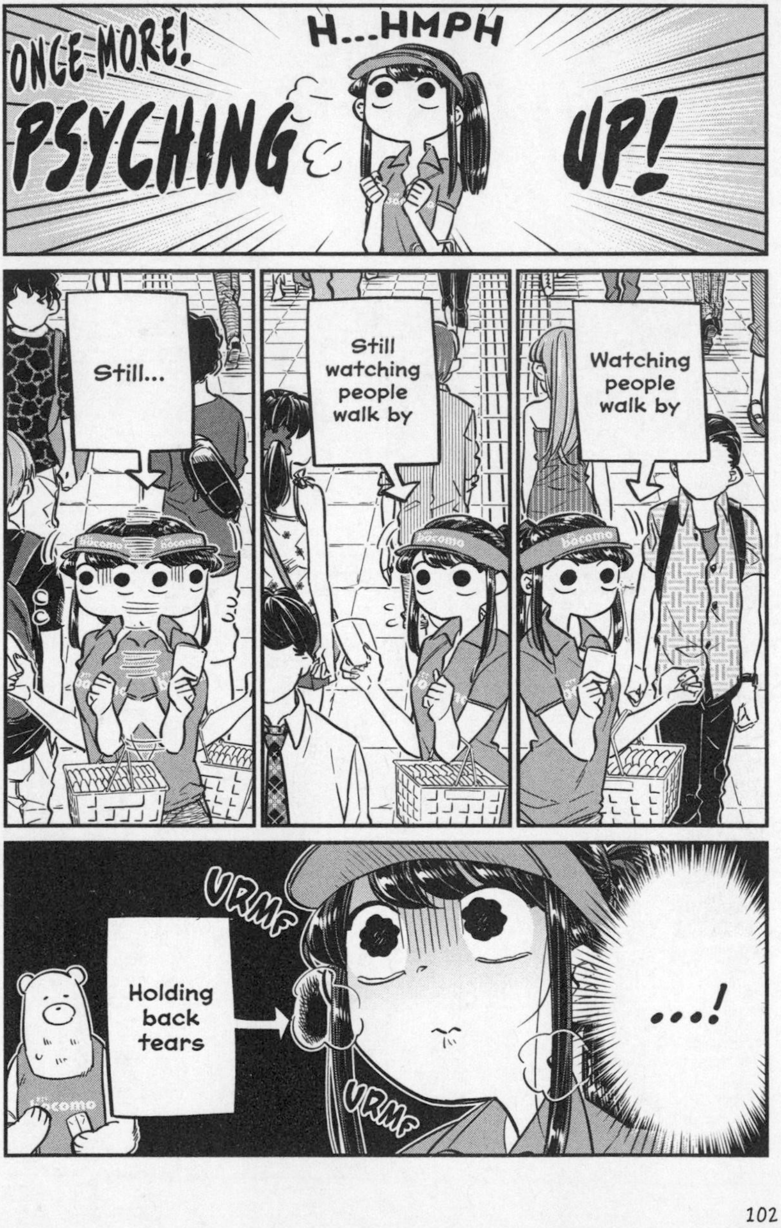
H...HMPH
ONCE MORE!
PSYCHING UP!
Watching people walk by
Still watching people walk by
Still...
URMF
...!
Holding back tears
URMF

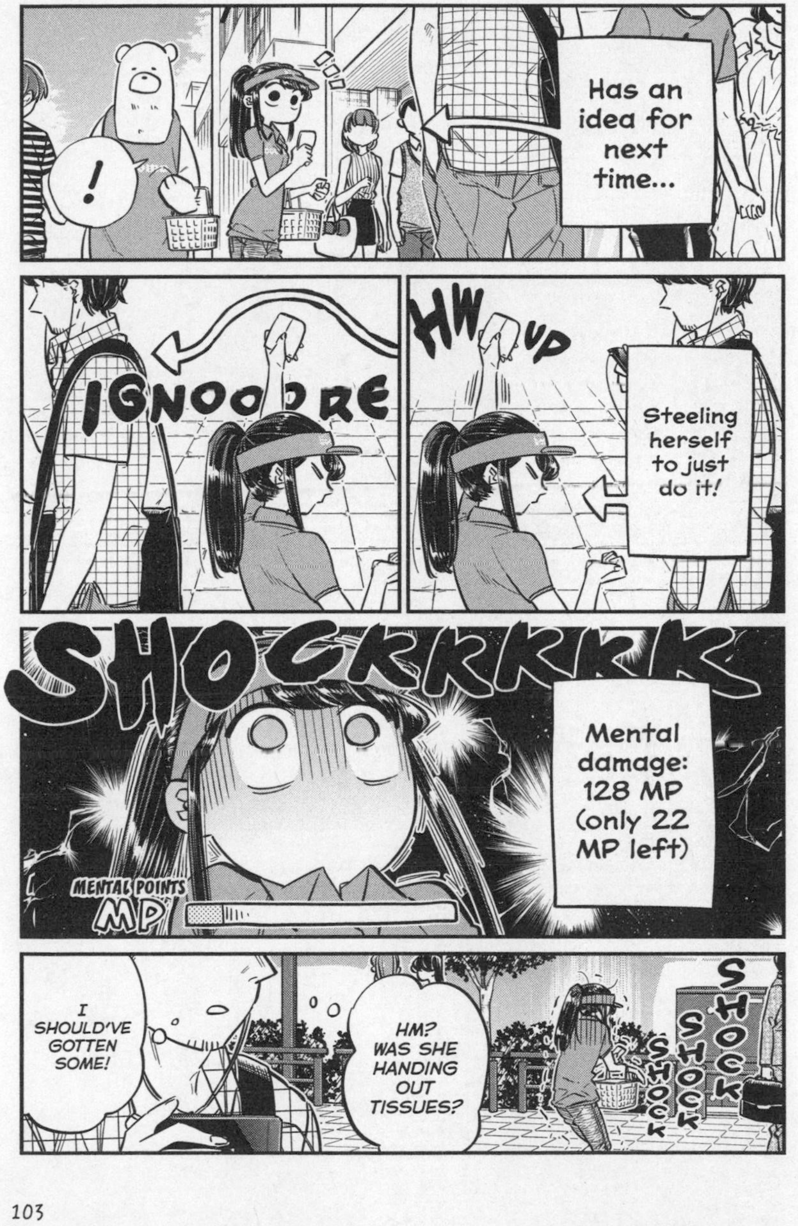
Has an idea for next time...
!
HW UP
Steeling herself to just do it!
IGNOOORE
SHOCKKKKK
Mental damage: 128 MP (only 22 MP left)
MENTAL POINTS
MP
SHOCK
SHOCK
SHOCK
HM? WAS SHE HANDING OUT TISSUES?
I SHOULD'VE GOTTEN SOME!

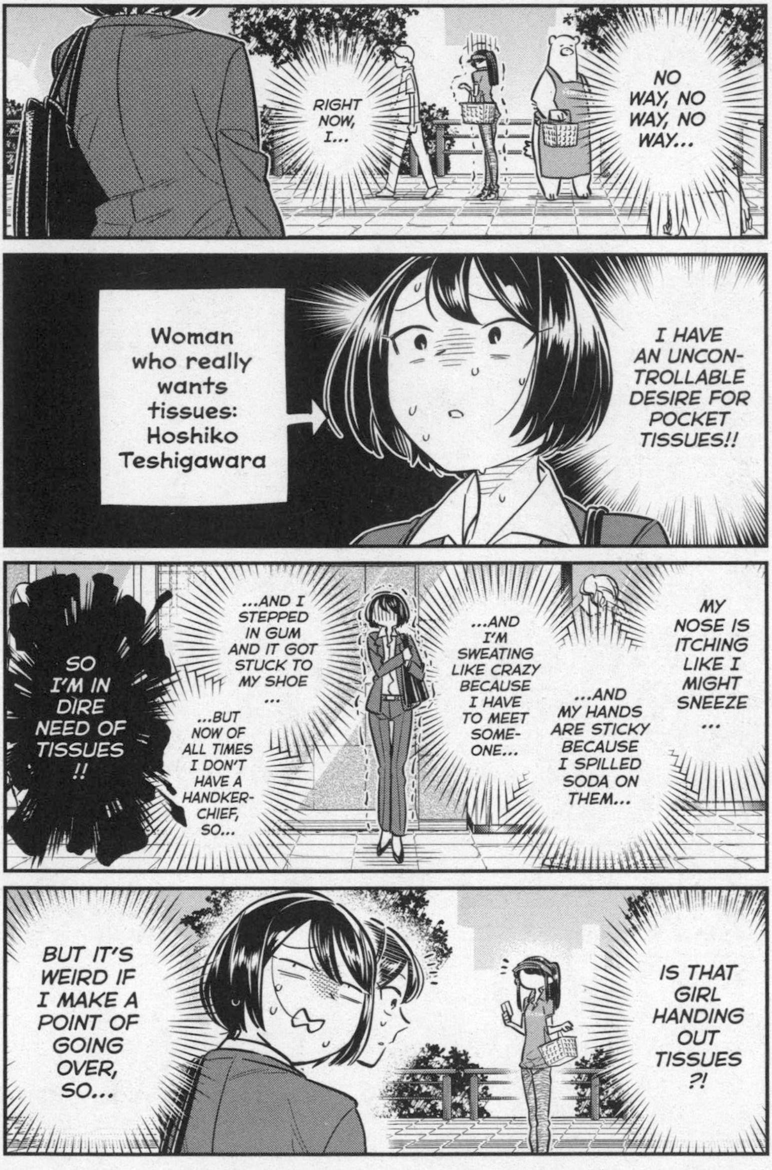
NO WAY, NO WAY, NO WAY...
RIGHT NOW, I...
I HAVE AN UNCONTROLLABLE DESIRE FOR POCKET TISSUES!!
Woman who really wants tissues: Hoshiko Teshigawara
MY NOSE IS ITCHING LIKE I MIGHT SNEEZE...
...AND MY HANDS ARE STICKY BECAUSE I SPILLED SODA ON THEM...
...AND I'M SWEATING LIKE CRAZY BECAUSE I HAVE TO MEET SOMEONE...
...AND I STEPPED IN GUM AND IT GOT STUCK TO MY SHOE...
...BUT NOW OF ALL TIMES I DON'T HAVE A HANDKERCHIEF, SO...
SO I'M IN DIRE NEED OF TISSUES!!
IS THAT GIRL HANDING OUT TISSUES?!
BUT IT'S WEIRD IF I MAKE A POINT OF GOING OVER, SO...

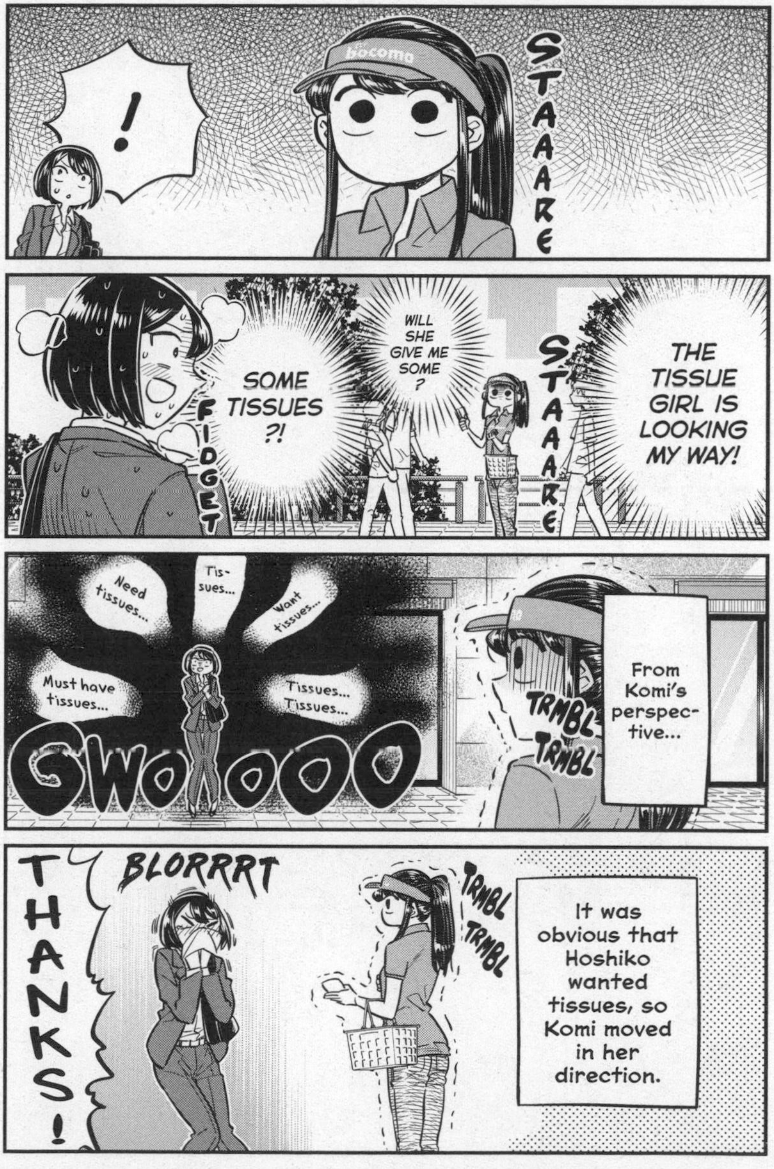
STAAARE
!
THE TISSUE GIRL IS LOOKING MY WAY!
STAAARE
WILL SHE GIVE ME SOME?
SOME TISSUES?!
FIDGET
From Komi's perspective...
TRMBL TRMBL
Tis-sues...
Want tissues...
Need tissues...
Tissues... Tissues...
Must have tissues...
GWOOOO
It was obvious that Hoshiko wanted tissues, so Komi moved in her direction.
TRMBL TRMBL
BLORRRT
THANKS!

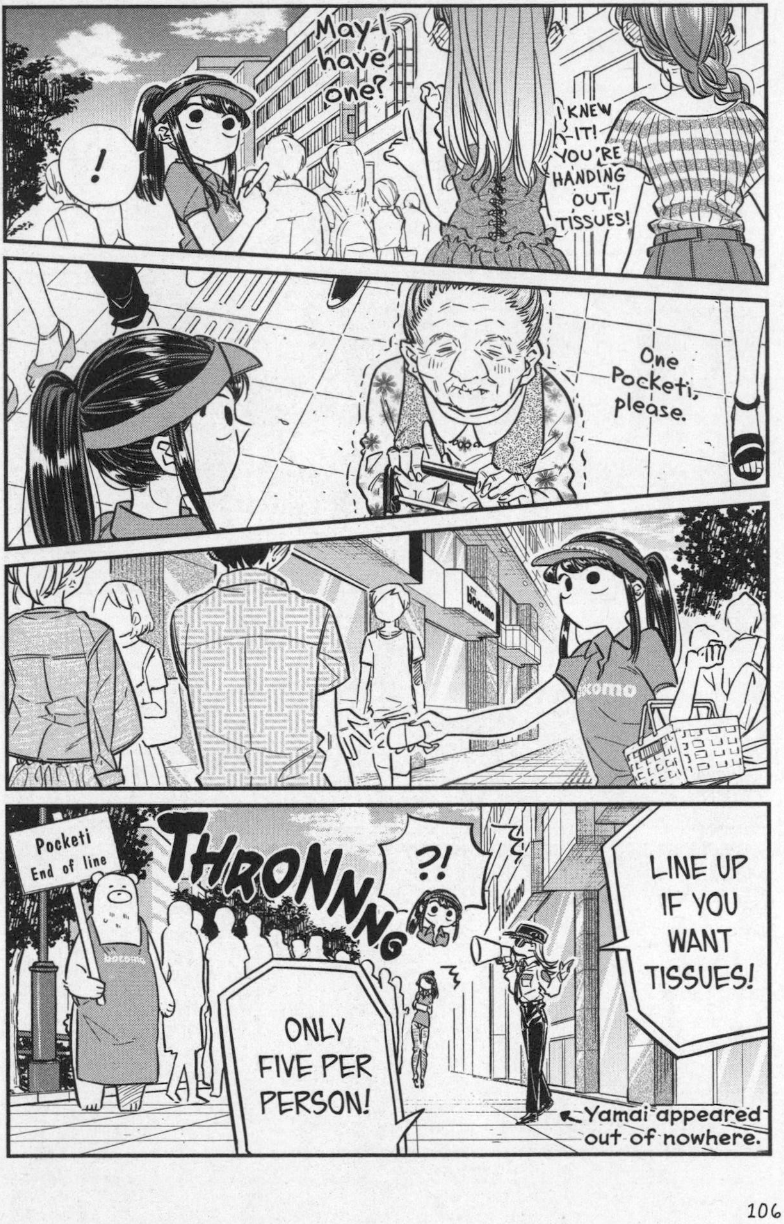
I KNEW IT! YOU'RE HANDING OUT TISSUES!
May I have one?
!
One Pocketi, please.
LINE UP IF YOU WANT TISSUES!
?!
THRONNNG
Pocketi End of line
ONLY FIVE PER PERSON!
Yamai appeared out of nowhere.

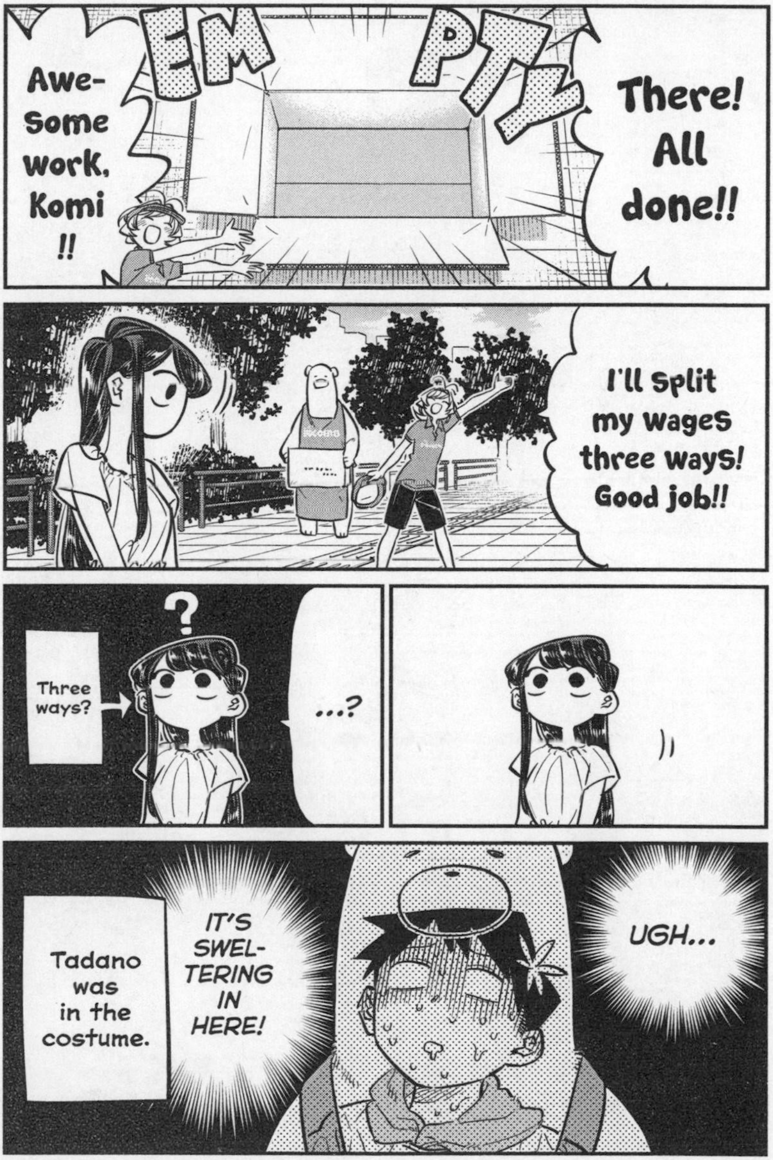
There! All done!!
EMPTY
Awesome work, Komi!!
I'll split my wages three ways! Good job!!
...?
Three ways?
UGH...
IT'S SWELTERING IN HERE!
Tadano was in the costume.

Communication 43 — The End

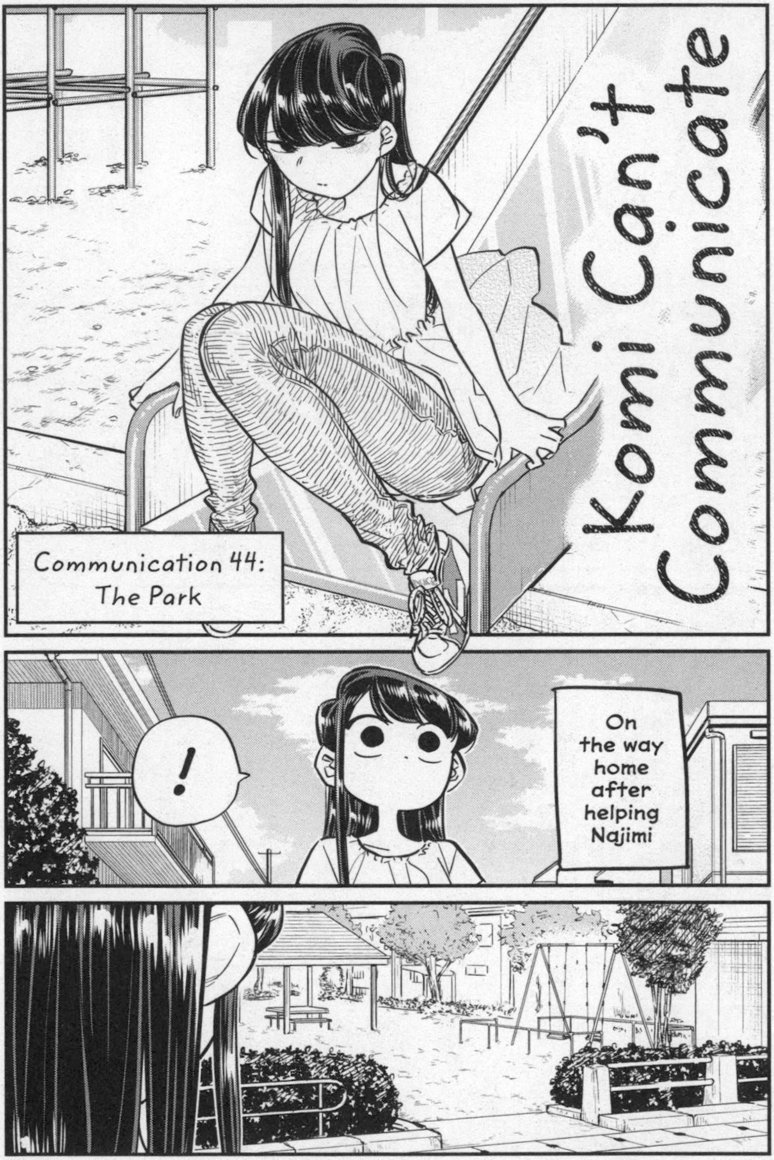
Komi Can't Communicate
Communication 44: The Park
On the way home after helping Najimi
!

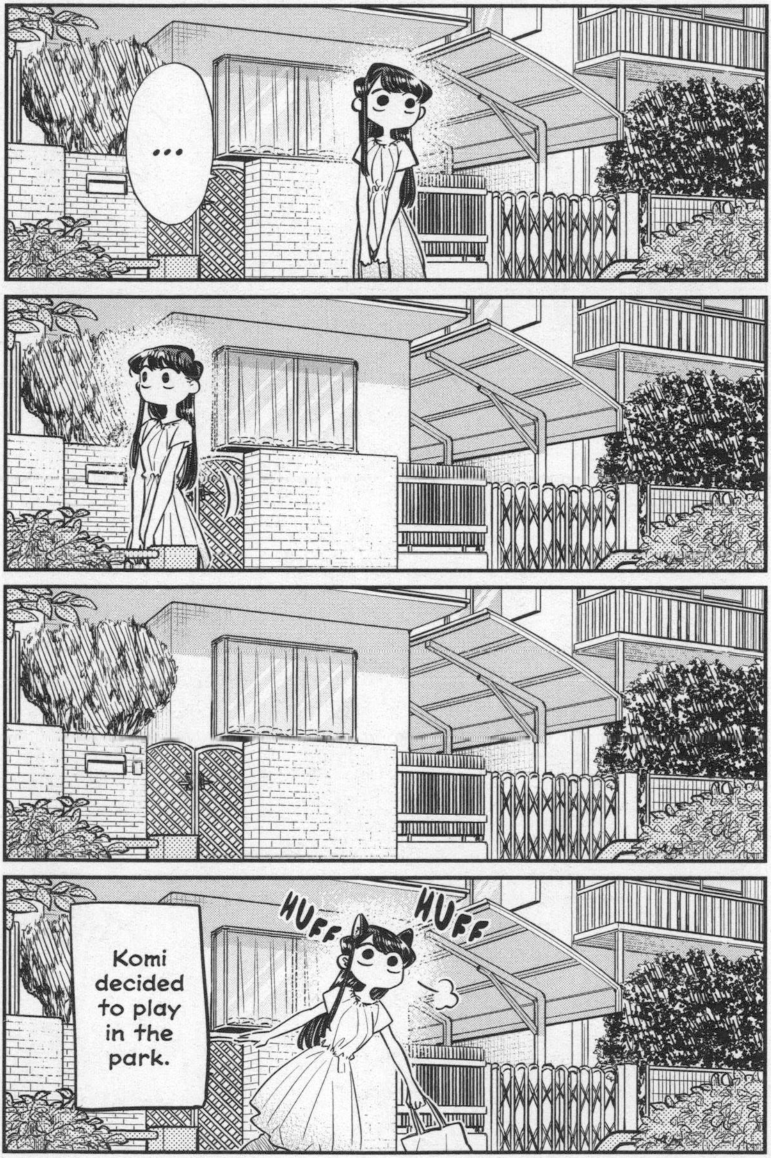
...
HUFF
HUFF
Komi decided to play in the park.

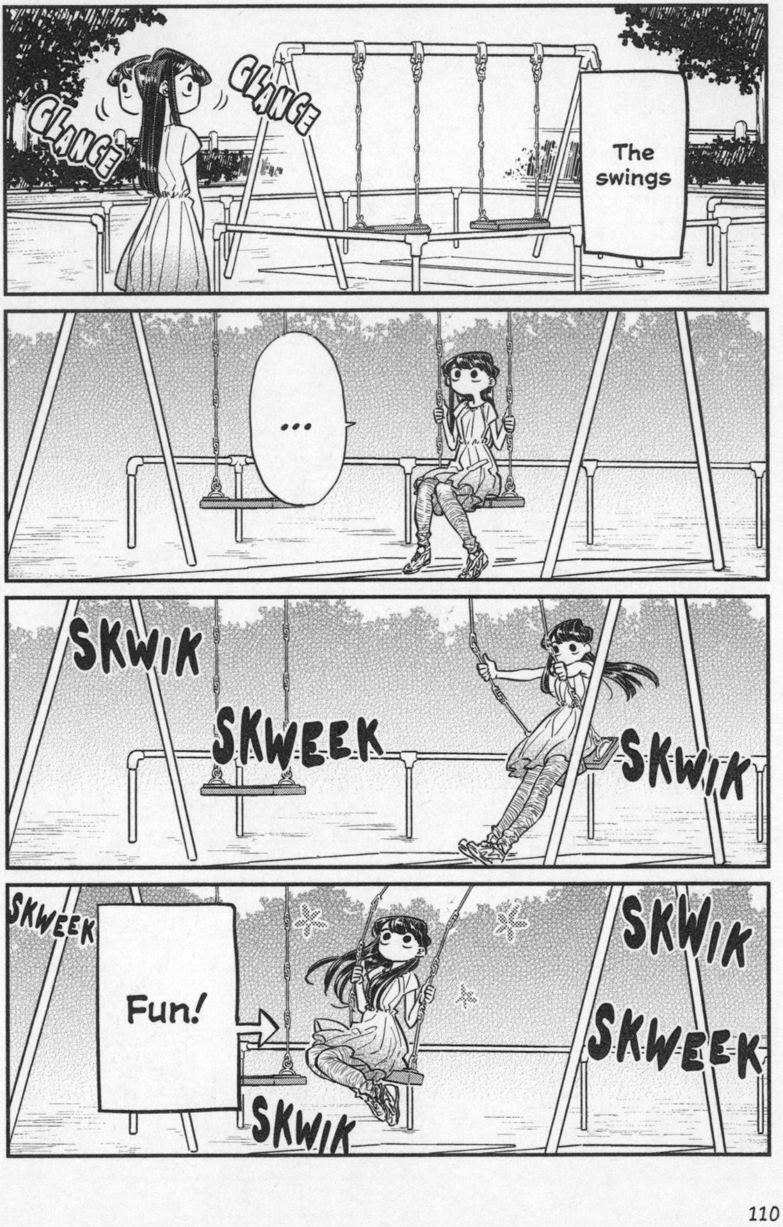
GLANCE
GLANCE
The swings
...
SKWIK
SKWEEK
SKWIK
SKWIK
SKWEEK
SKWEEK
Fun!
SKWIK

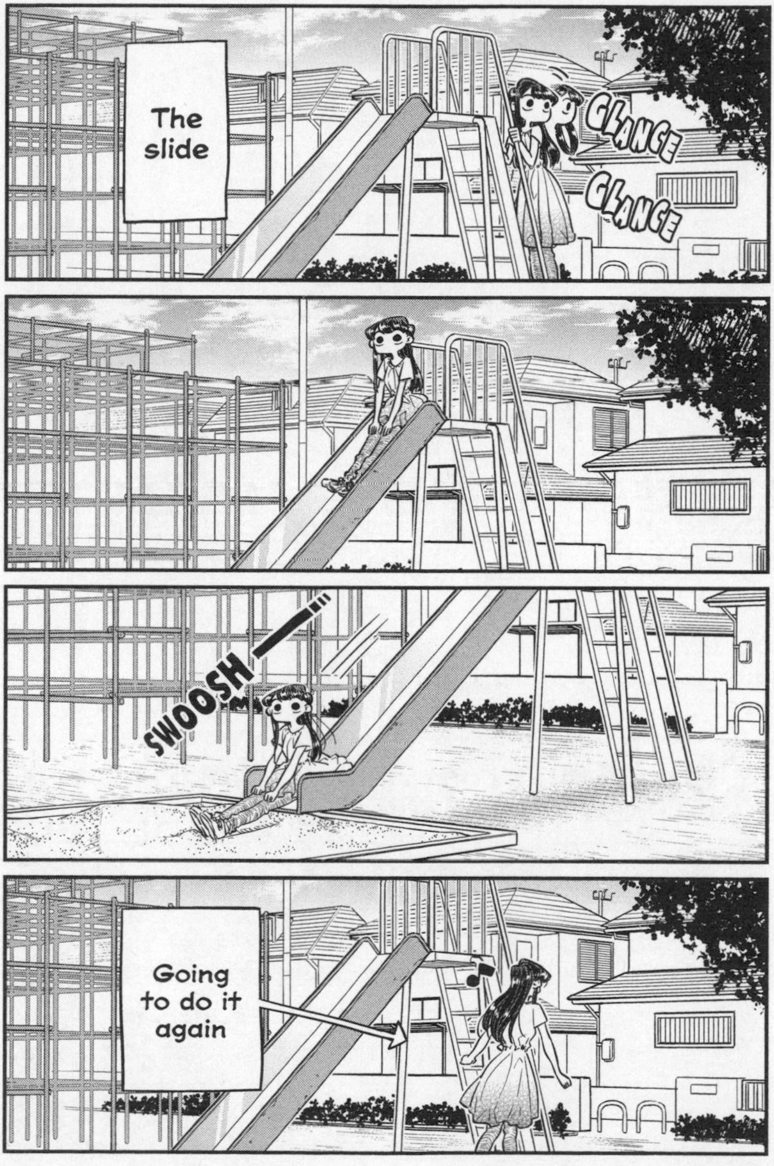
GLANCE
GLANCE
The slide
SWOOSH
Going to do it again

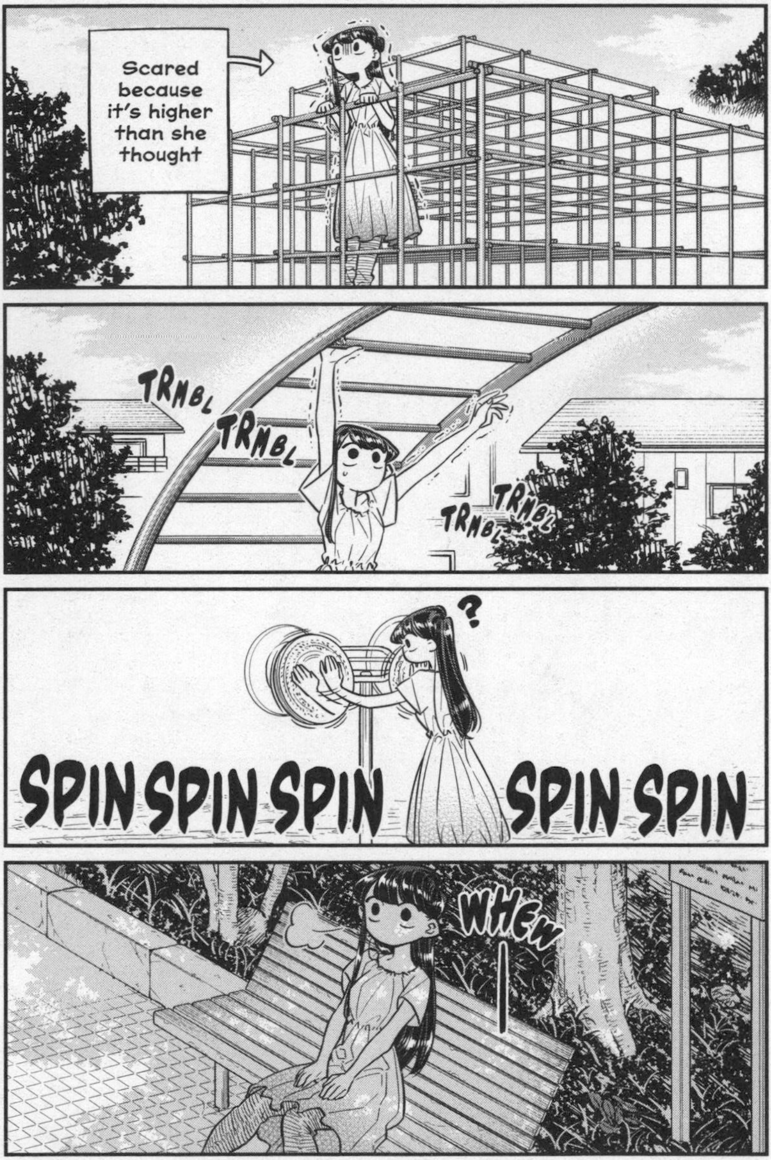
Scared because it's higher than she thought
TRMBL TRMBL
TRMBL TRMBL
?
SPIN SPIN
SPIN SPIN SPIN
WHEW

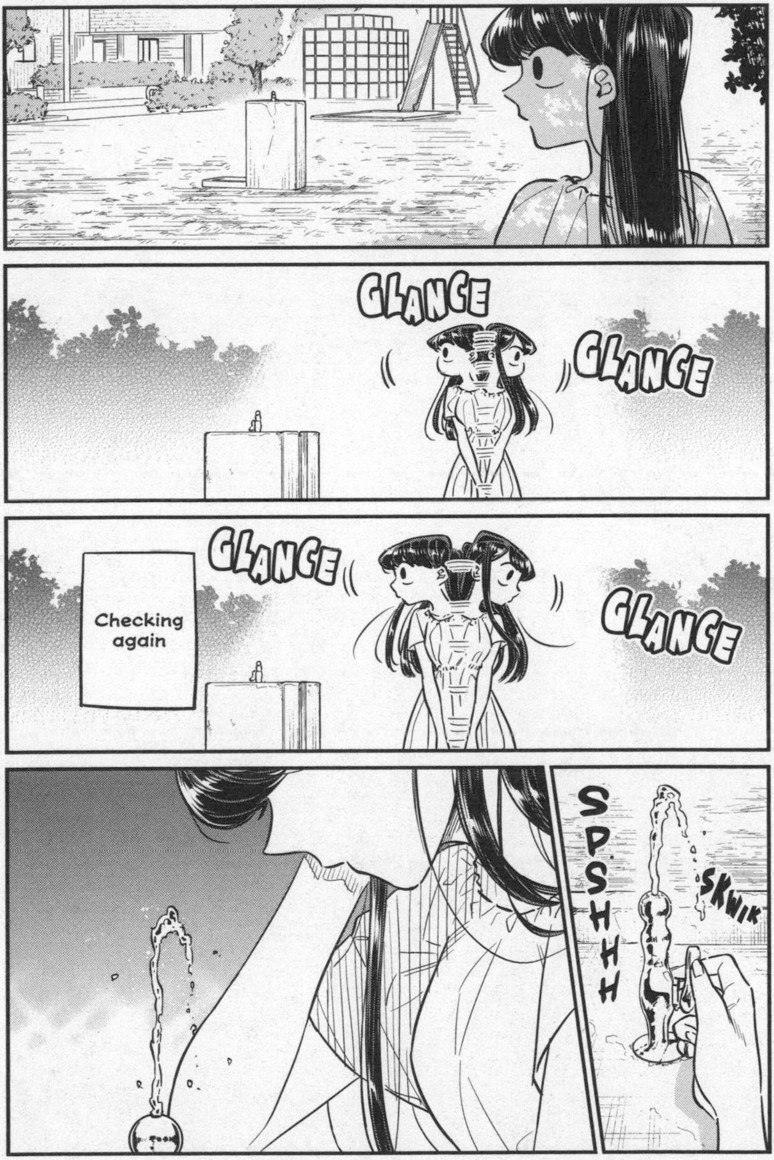
GLANCE
GLANCE
GLANCE
GLANCE
Checking again
SPSHHH
SKWIK

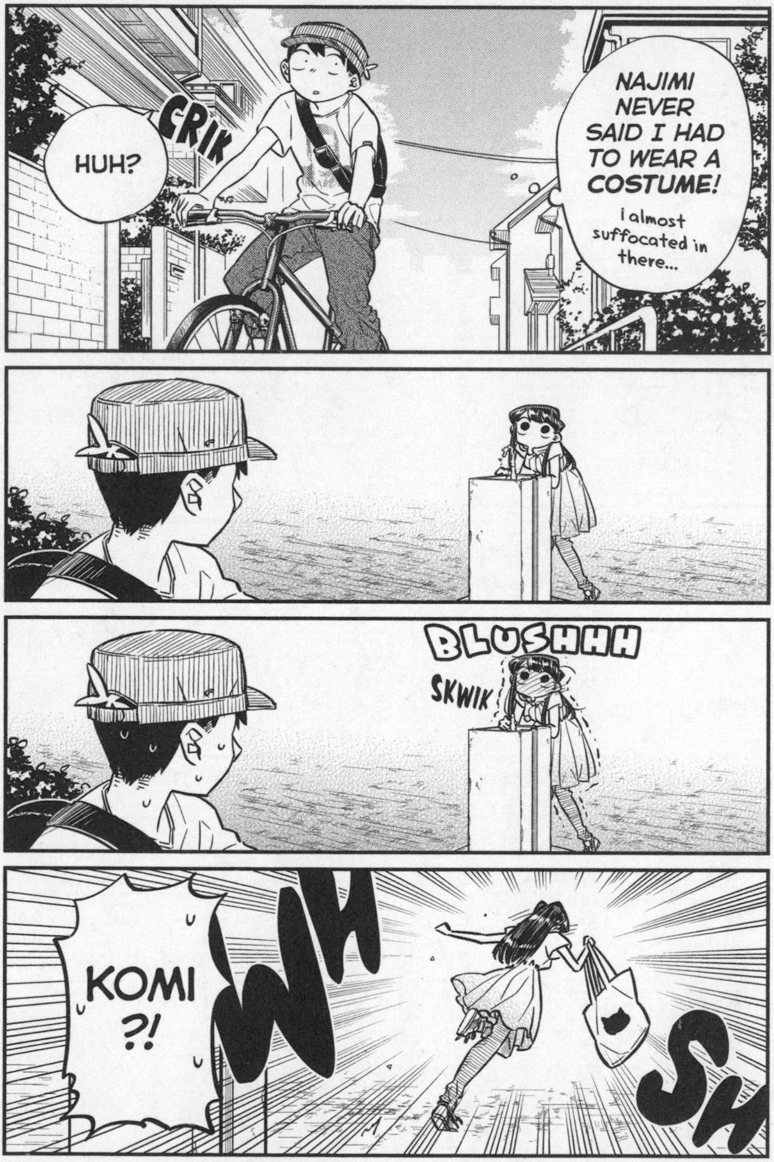
NAJIMI NEVER SAID I HAD TO WEAR A COSTUME!
i almost suffocated in there...
CRIK
HUH?
BLUSHHH
SKWIK
WHSH
KOMI ?!

Communication 44 — The End

WENT HOME AND
FLOMPED AROUND

Komi Can't
Communicate

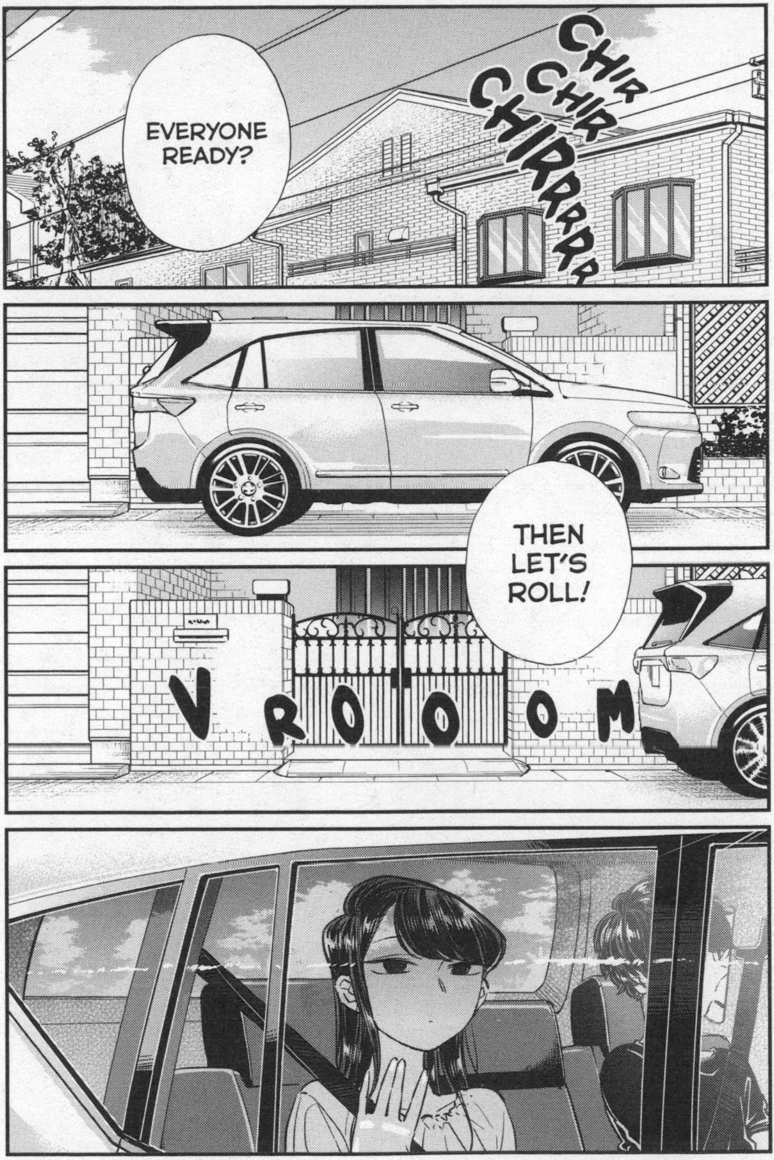
EVERYONE READY?
CHIR CHIR CHIRRRRRR
THEN LET'S ROLL!
VROOOM

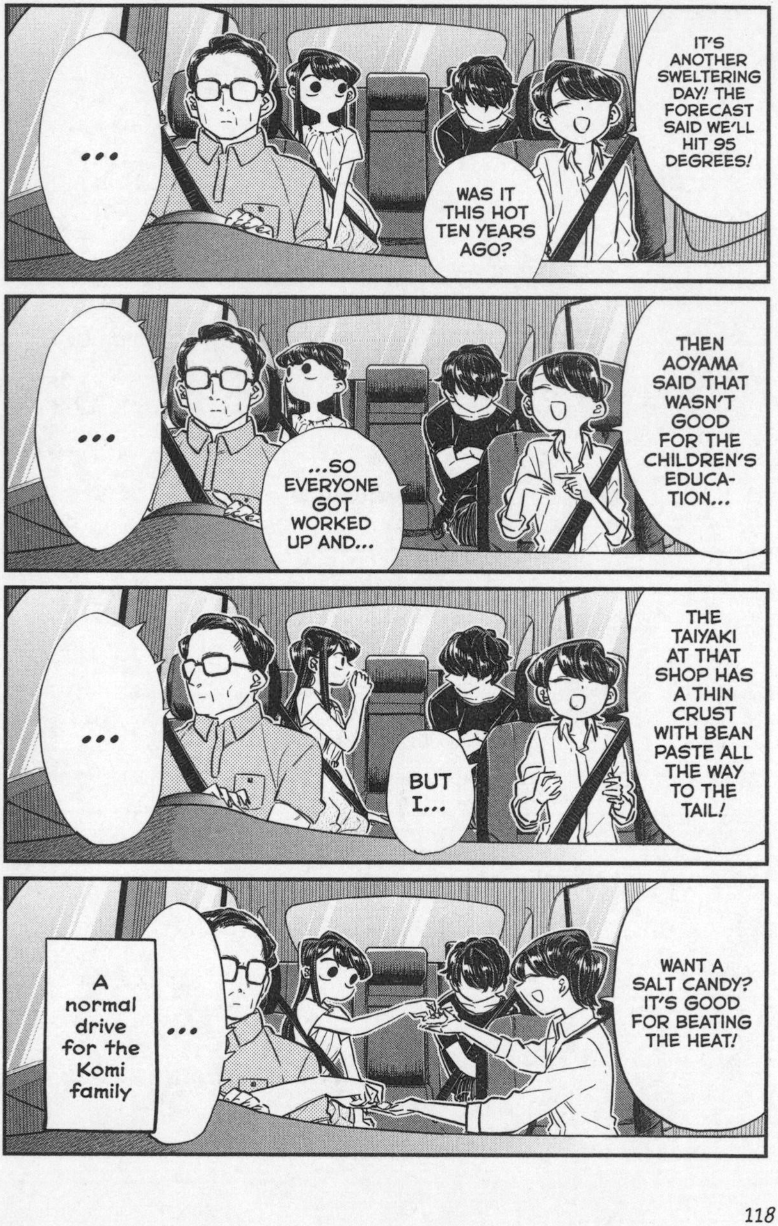
IT'S ANOTHER SWELTERING DAY! THE FORECAST SAID WE'LL HIT 95 DEGREES!
WAS IT THIS HOT TEN YEARS AGO?
...
THEN AOYAMA SAID THAT WASN'T GOOD FOR THE CHILDREN'S EDUCA-TION...
...SO EVERYONE GOT WORKED UP AND...
...
THE TAIYAKI AT THAT SHOP HAS A THIN CRUST WITH BEAN PASTE ALL THE WAY TO THE TAIL!
BUT I...
...
WANT A SALT CANDY? IT'S GOOD FOR BEATING THE HEAT!
...
A normal drive for the Komi family

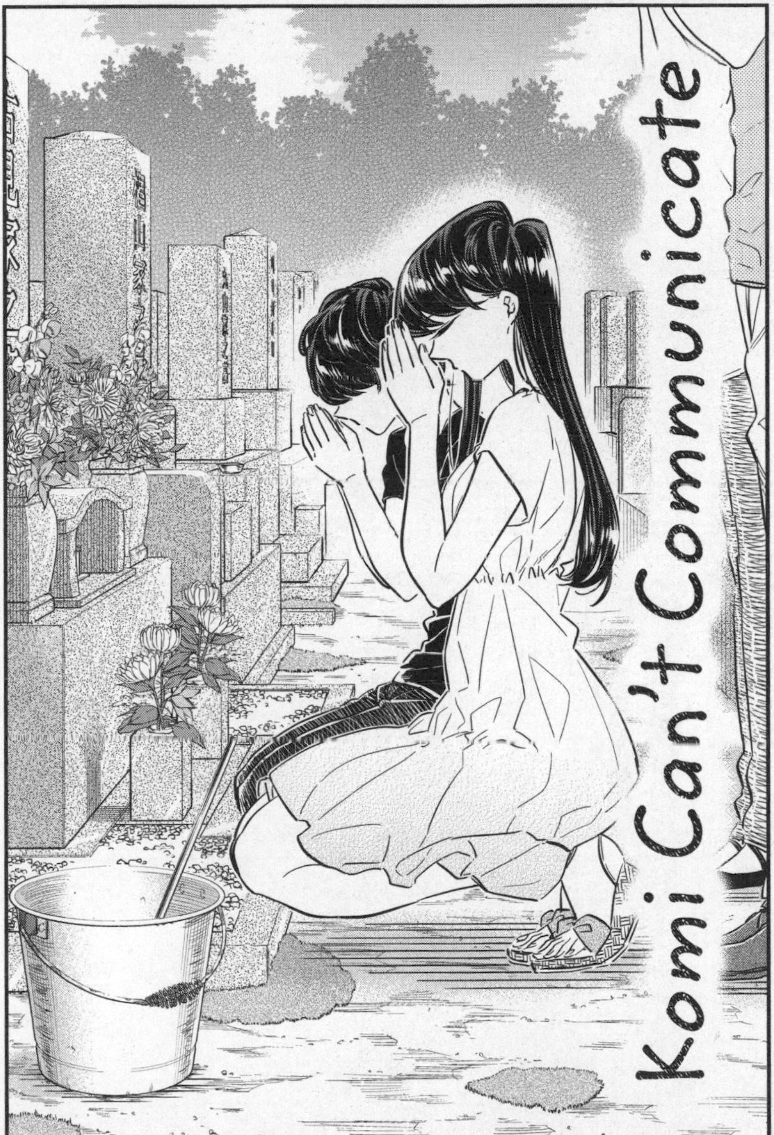
Komi Can't Communicate

Communication 45: Celebrating Obon

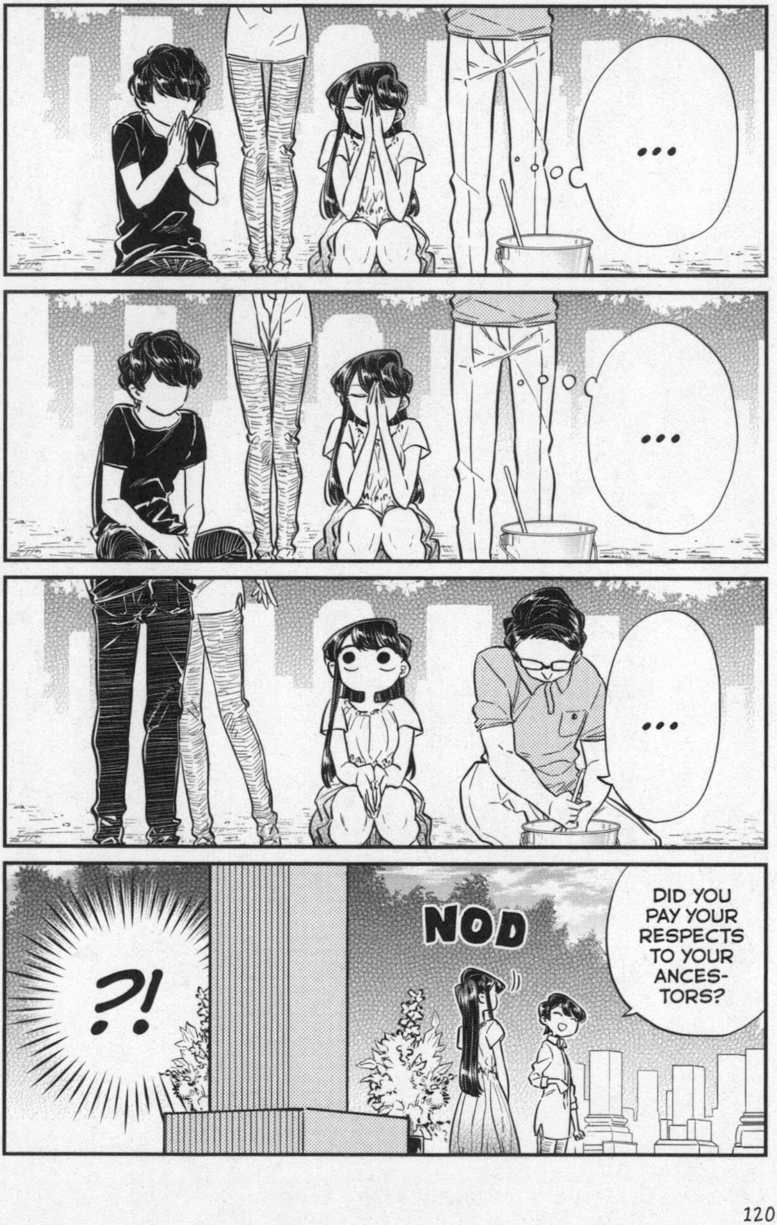
...
...
...
DID YOU PAY YOUR RESPECTS TO YOUR ANCES-TORS?
NOD
?!

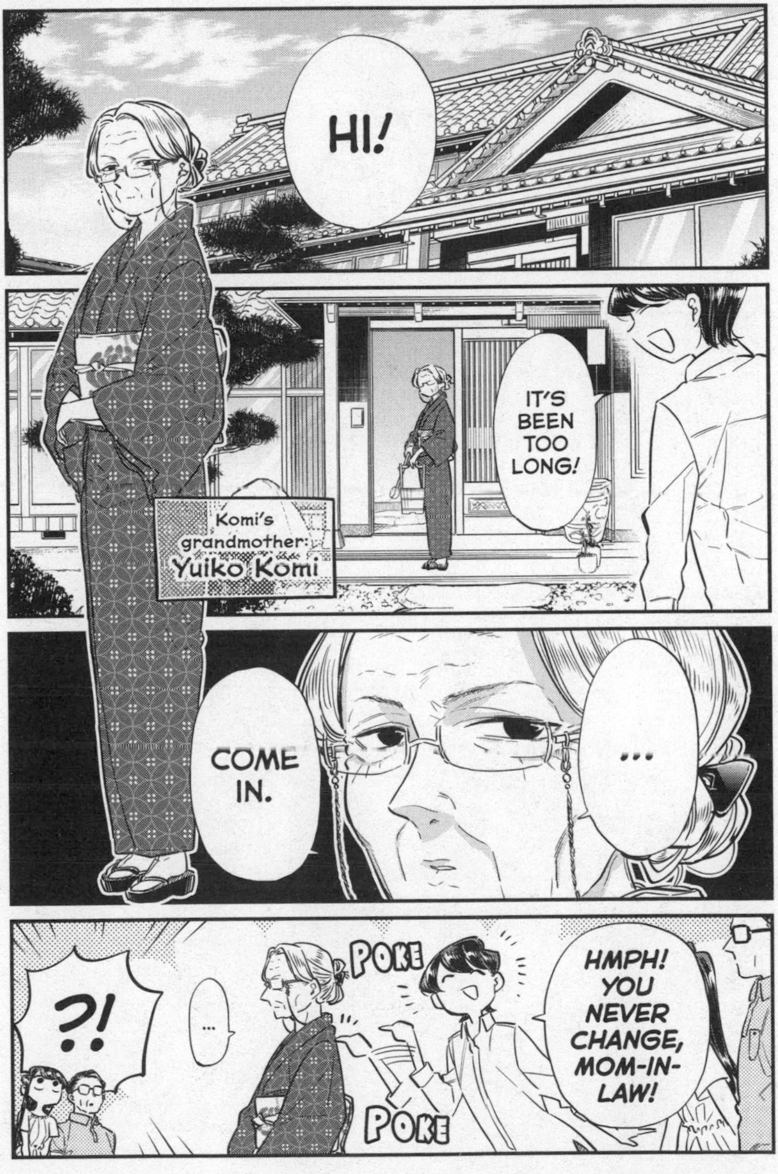
HI!
IT'S BEEN TOO LONG!
Komi's grandmother: Yuiko Komi
...
COME IN.
HMPH! YOU NEVER CHANGE, MOM-IN-LAW!
POKE
POKE
...
?!

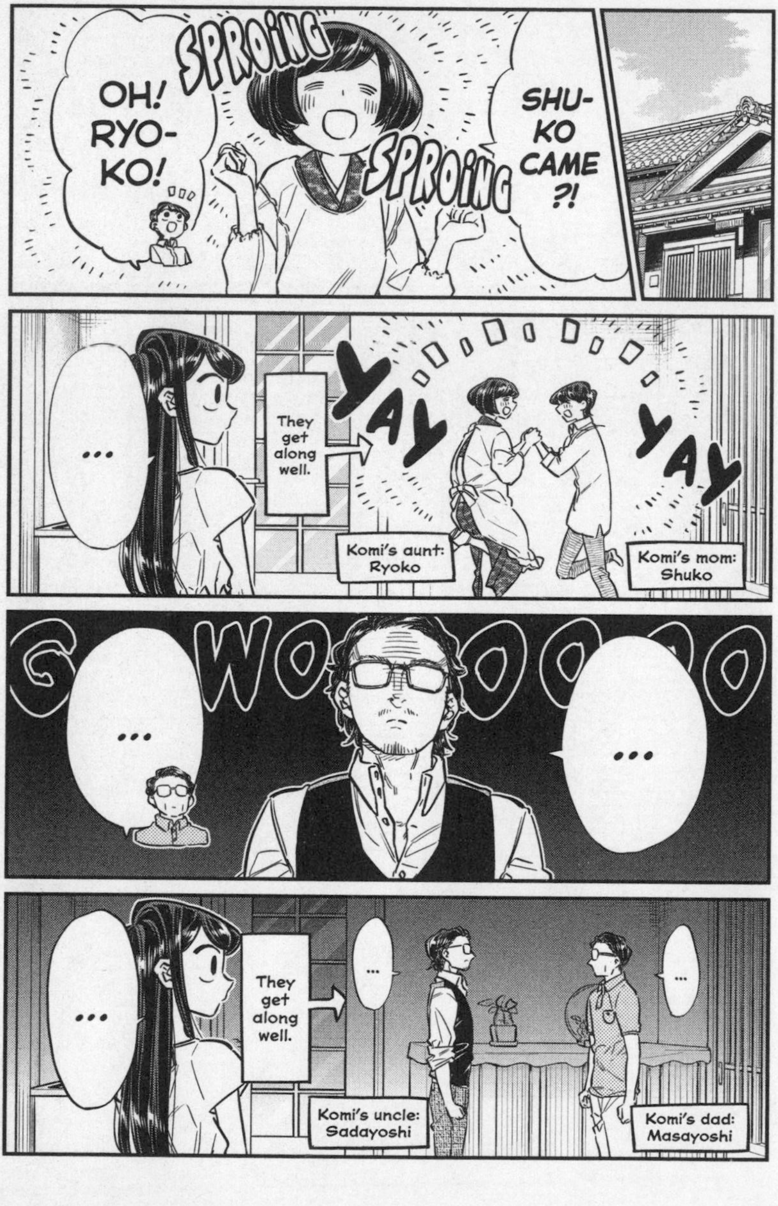
SHU-KO CAME?!
SPROING
SPROING
OH! RYO-KO!
YAY
YAY
Komi's mom: Shuko
Komi's aunt: Ryoko
They get along well.
...
...
GOWOOOOO
...
...
Komi's dad: Masayoshi
...
Komi's uncle: Sadayoshi
They get along well.
...

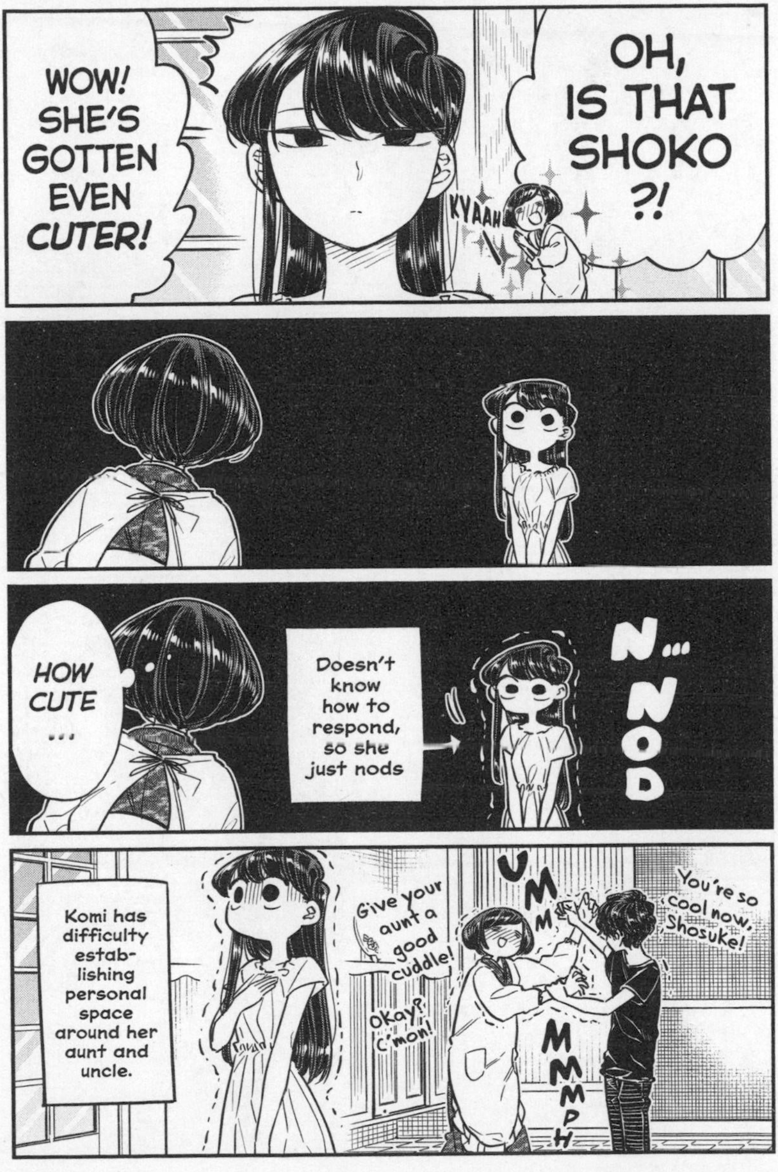
OH, IS THAT SHOKO ?!
KYAAH
WOW! SHE'S GOTTEN EVEN CUTER!
N... NOD
Doesn't know how to respond, so she just nods
HOW CUTE...
You're so cool now, Shosuke!
UMM
MMMPH
Give your aunt a good cuddle!
Okay? C'mon!
Komi has difficulty establishing personal space around her aunt and uncle.

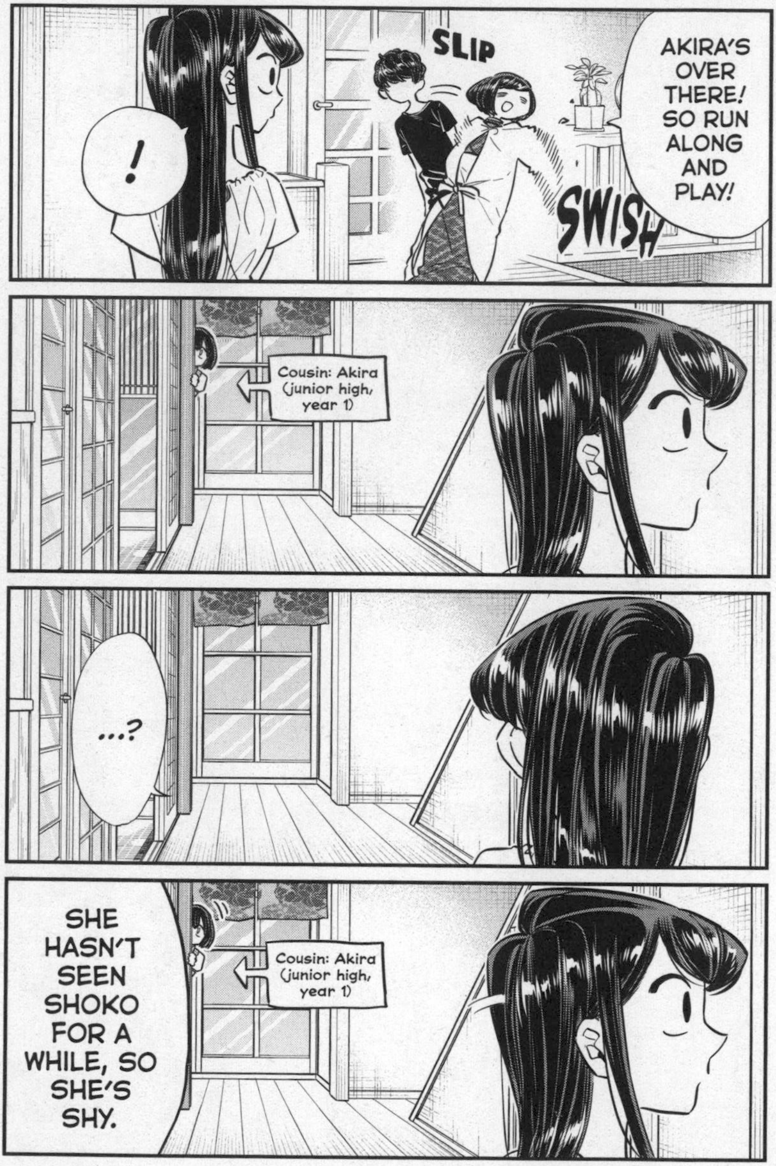
AKIRA'S OVER THERE! SO RUN ALONG AND PLAY!
SWISH
SLIP
!
Cousin: Akira (junior high, year 1)
...?
Cousin: Akira (junior high, year 1)
SHE HASN'T SEEN SHOKO FOR A WHILE, SO SHE'S SHY.

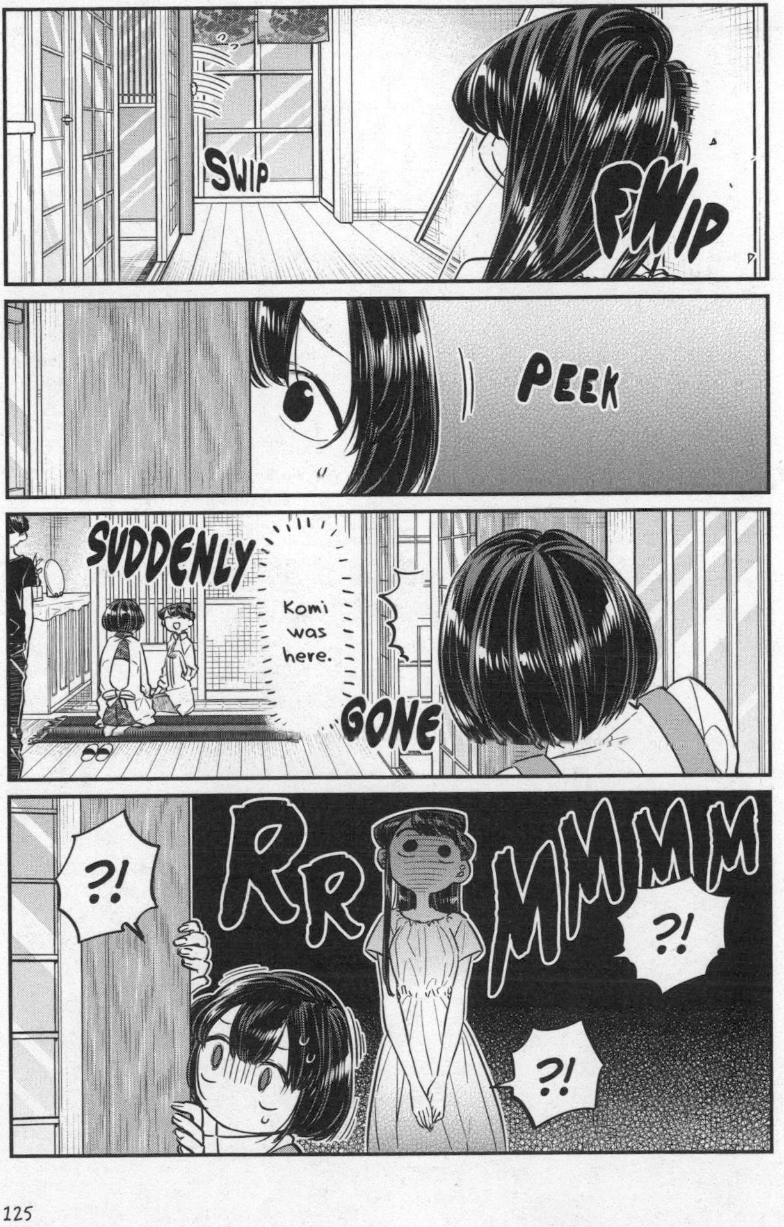
FWIP
SWIP
PEEK
Komi was here.
GONE
SUDDENLY
RRMMMMM
?!
?!
?!

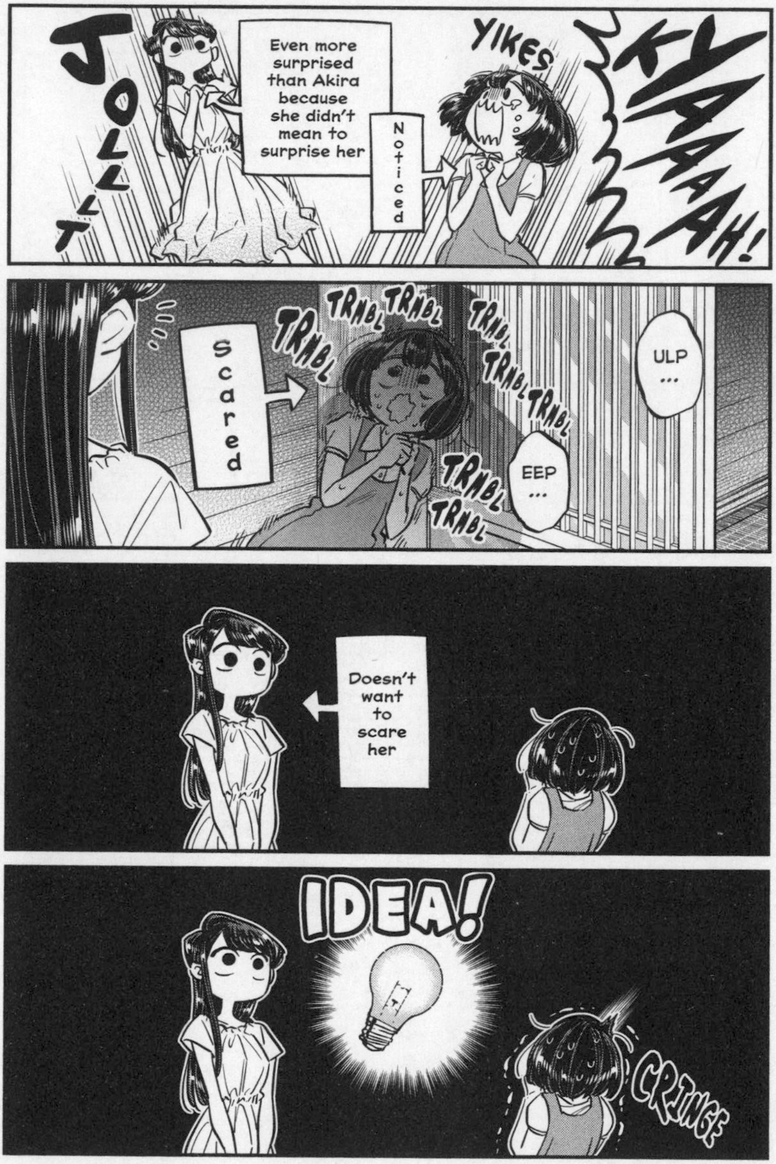
KYAAAAH!
YIKES
Noticed
Even more surprised than Akira because she didn't mean to surprise her
JOLLLT
ULP...
EEP...
TRMBL TRMBL TRMBL TRMBL TRMBL TRMBL TRMBL TRMBL
Scared
Doesn't want to scare her
IDEA!
CRINGE

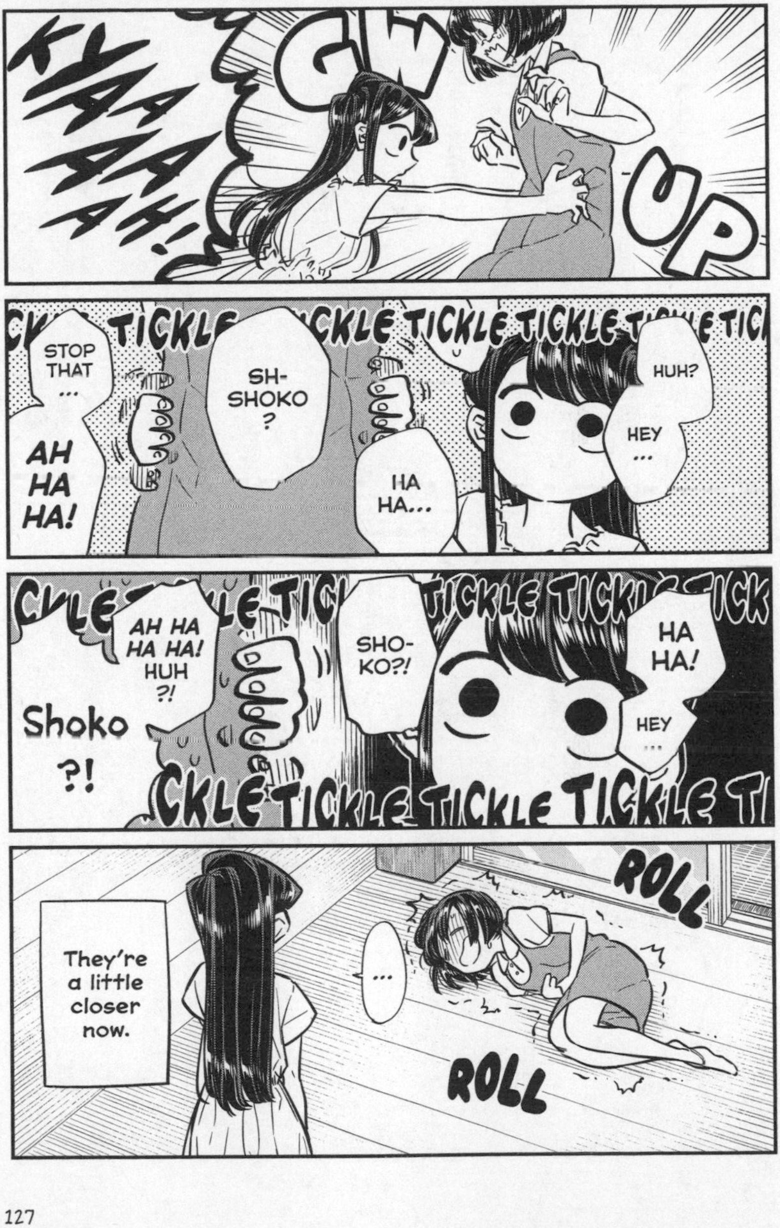
GW
UP
KYAAAAAH!
TICKLE TICKLE TICKLE TICKLE
HUH?
HEY ...
HA HA...
SH-SHOKO?
STOP THAT ...
AH HA HA!
TICKLE TICKLE TICKLE
HA HA!
HEY ...
SHO-KO?!
AH HA HA HA! HUH?!
Shoko ?!
CKLE TICKLE TICKLE TICKLE
ROLL
...
They're a little closer now.
ROLL

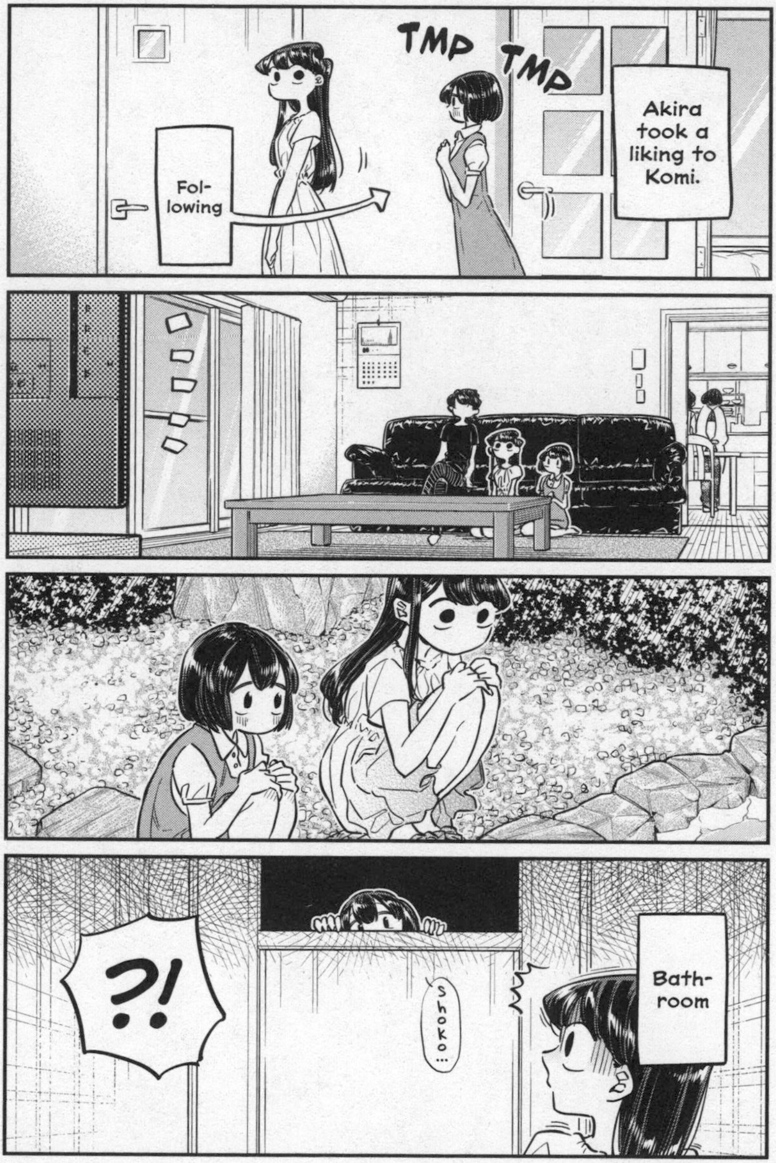
Akira took a liking to Komi.
TMP TMP
Fol-lowing
Bath-room
Shoko...
?!

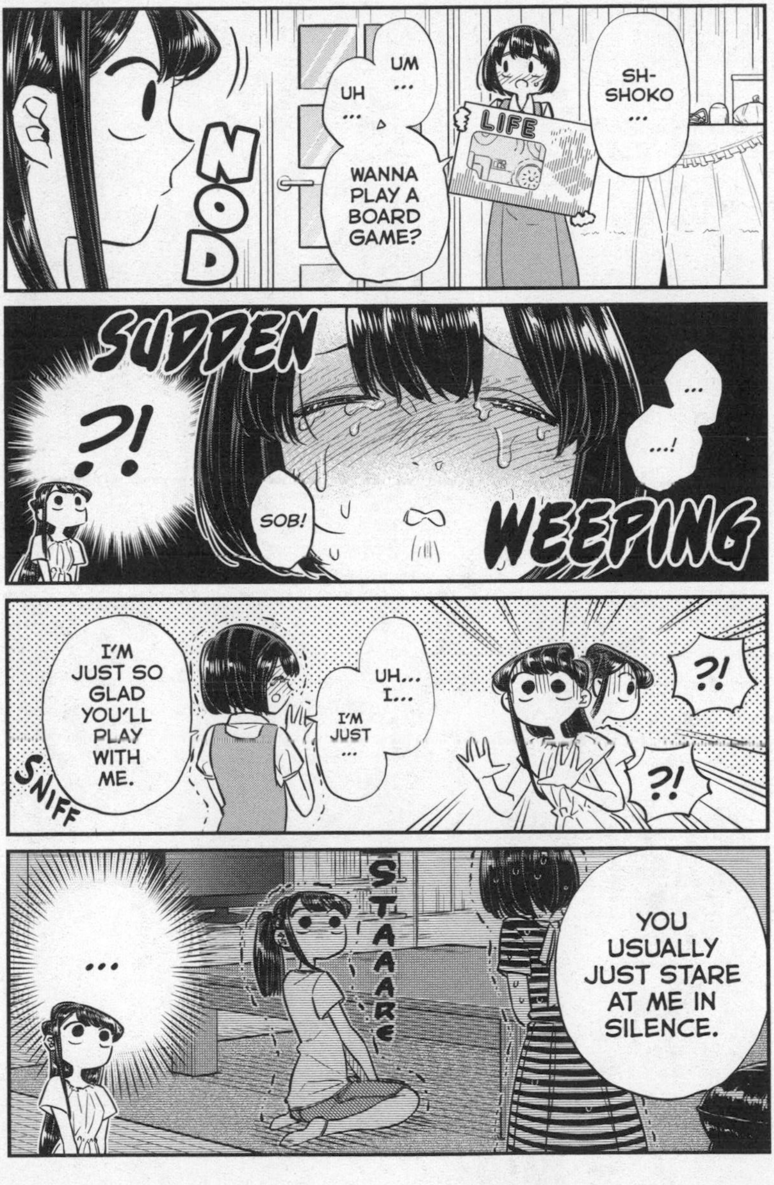
SH-SHOKO ...
UM ... UH ...
LIFE
WANNA PLAY A BOARD GAME?
NOD
... ...!
SUDDEN
?!
WEEPING
SOB!
?!
?!
UH... I... I'M JUST ...
I'M JUST SO GLAD YOU'LL PLAY WITH ME.
SNIFF
YOU USUALLY JUST STARE AT ME IN SILENCE.
STAAAARE
...

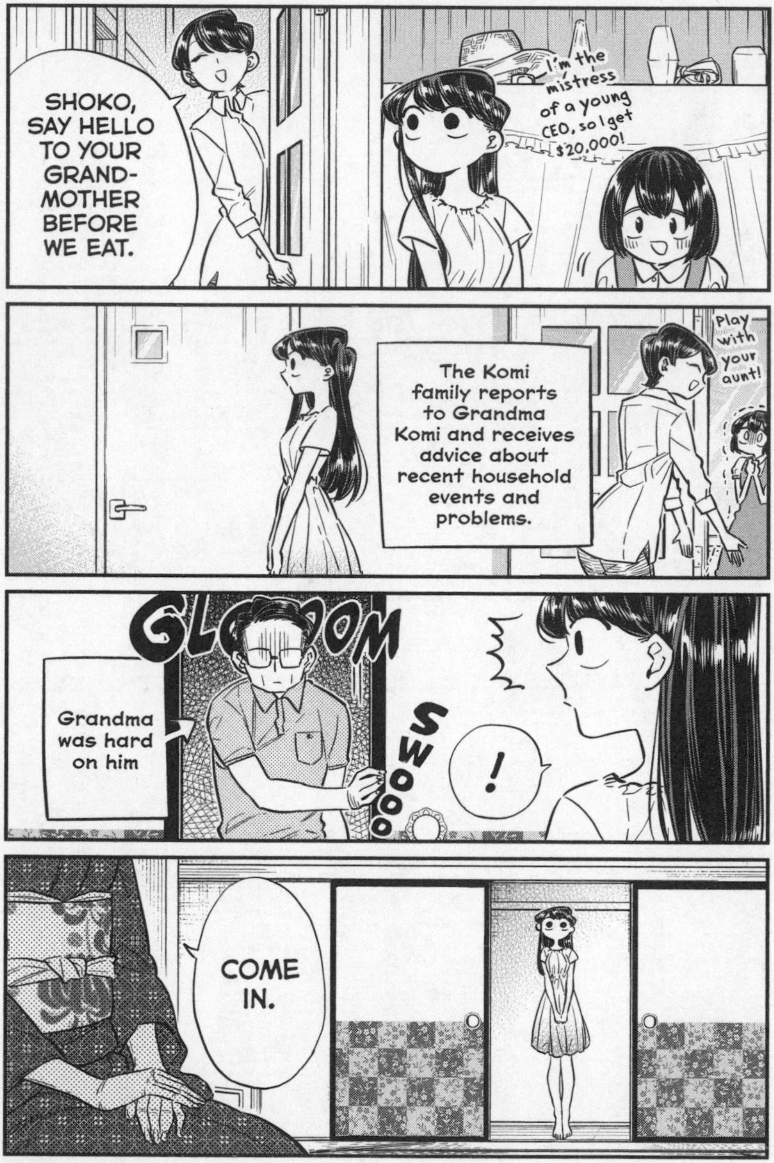
I'm the mistress of a young CEO, so I get $20,000!
SHOKO, SAY HELLO TO YOUR GRAND-MOTHER BEFORE WE EAT.
Play with your aunt!
The Komi family reports to Grandma Komi and receives advice about recent household events and problems.
!
SWOOO
GLOOM
Grandma was hard on him
COME IN.

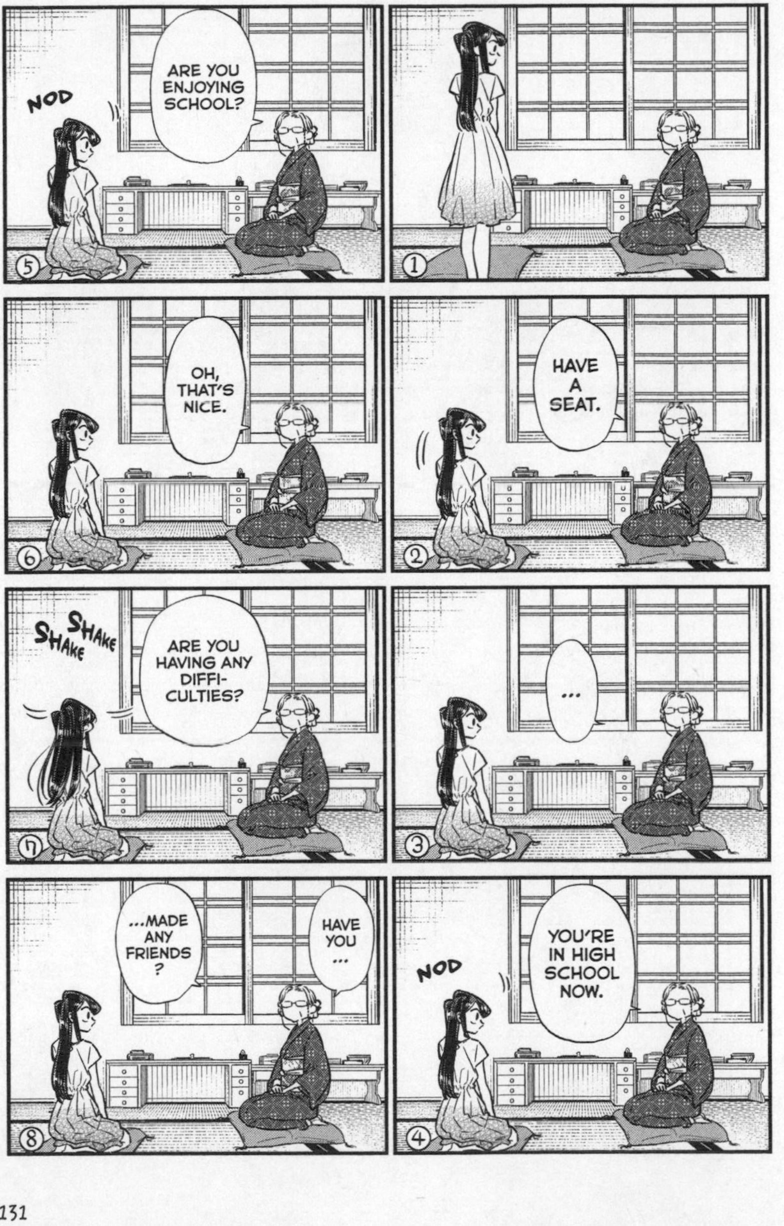
HAVE A SEAT.
...
YOU'RE IN HIGH SCHOOL NOW.
NOD
ARE YOU ENJOYING SCHOOL?
NOD
OH, THAT'S NICE.
ARE YOU HAVING ANY DIFFI-CULTIES?
SHAKE SHAKE
HAVE YOU...
...MADE ANY FRIENDS?

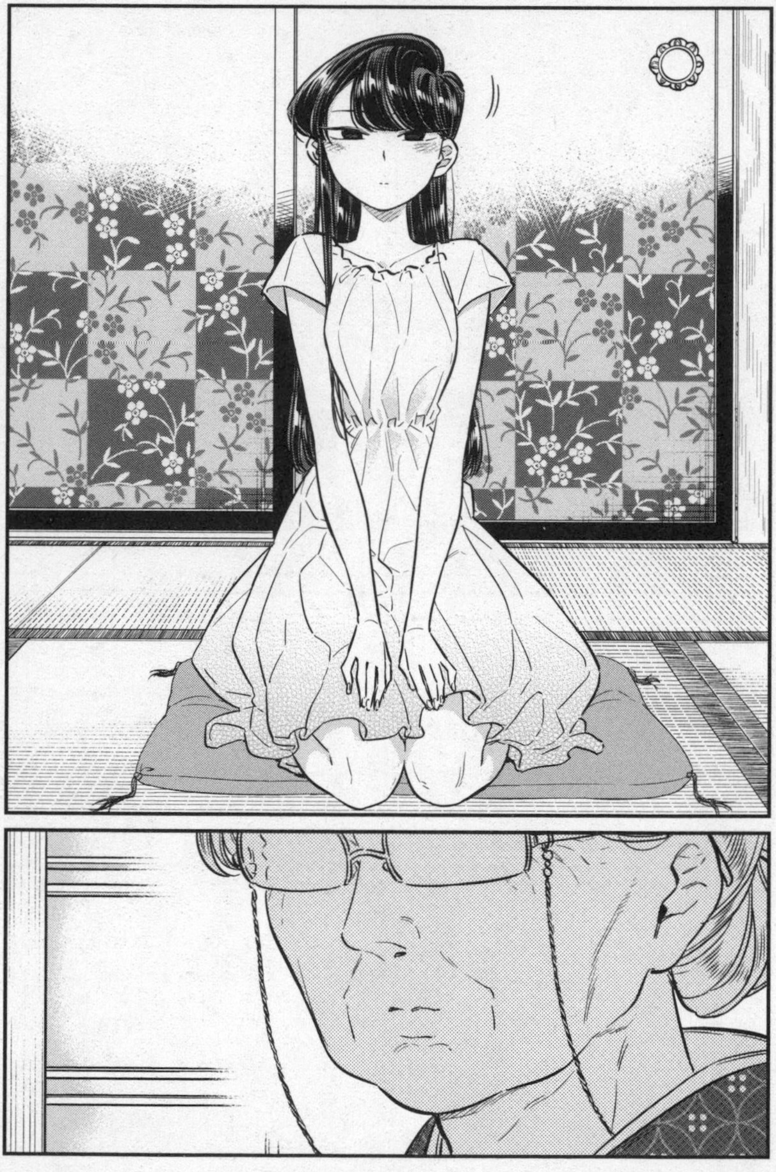

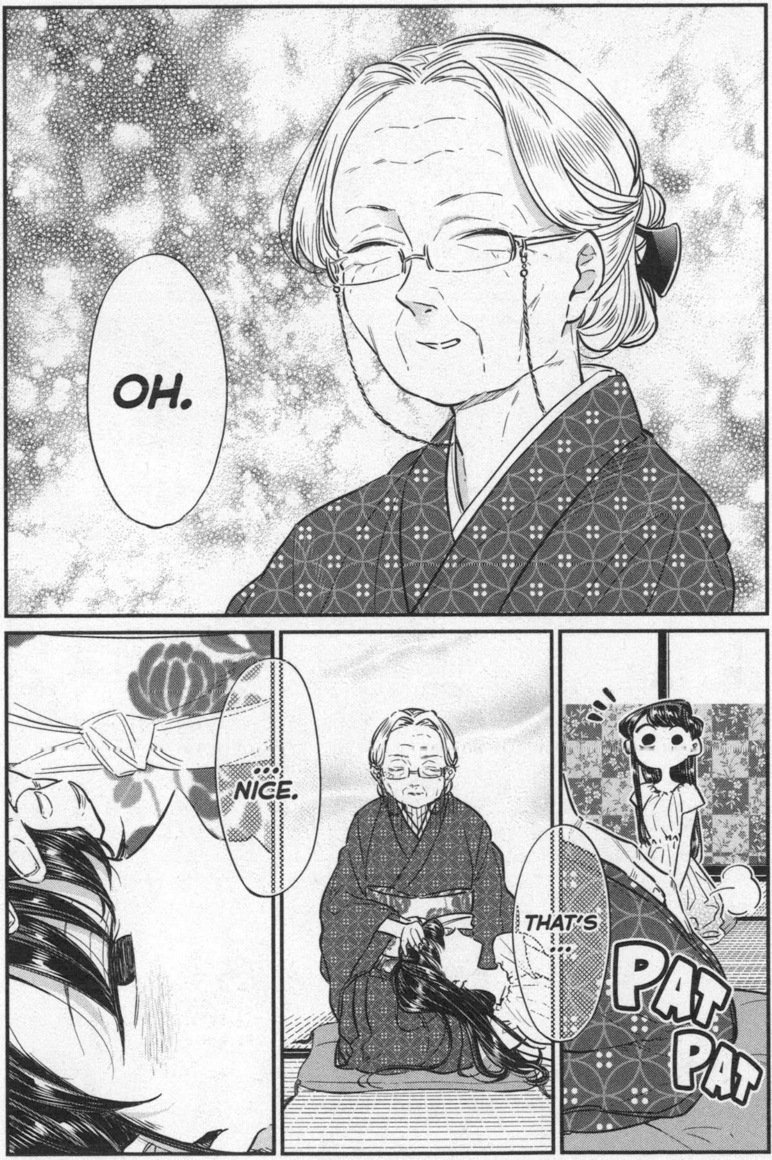
OH.
PAT PAT
THAT'S...
...NICE.

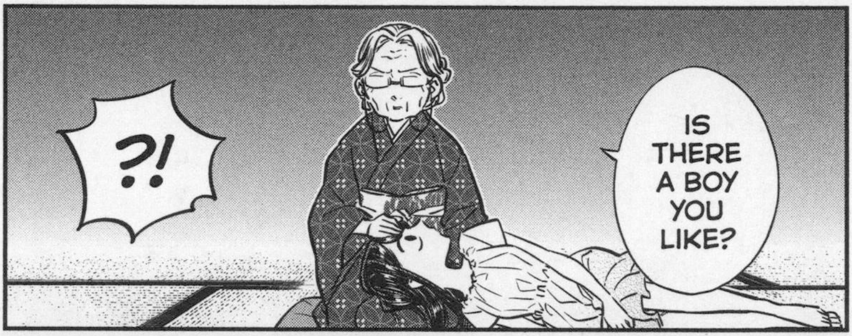
IS THERE A BOY YOU LIKE?
?!

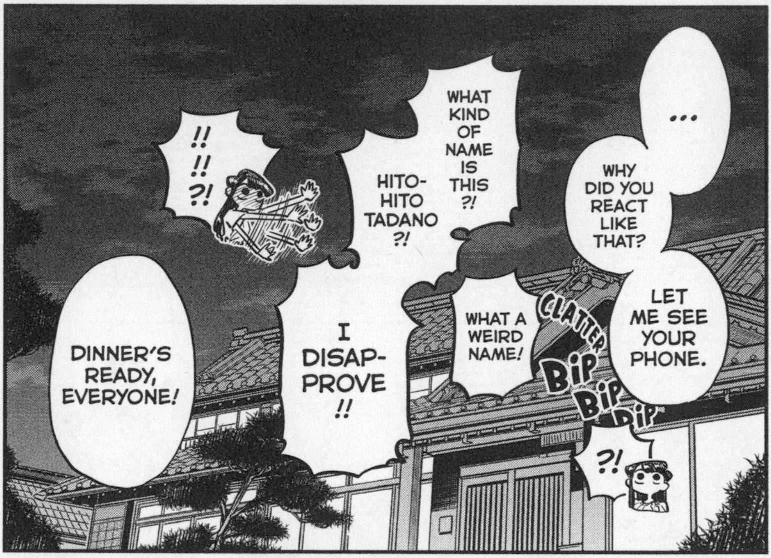
...
WHY DID YOU REACT LIKE THAT?
LET ME SEE YOUR PHONE.
CLATTER
BIP BIP BIP
?!
WHAT KIND OF NAME IS THIS ?!
HITO-HITO TADANO ?!
!! !! ?!
WHAT A WEIRD NAME!
I DISAP-PROVE !!
DINNER'S READY, EVERYONE!

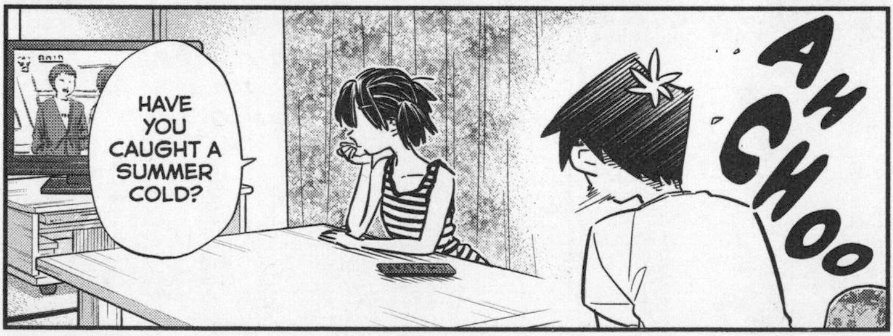
AH CHOO
HAVE YOU CAUGHT A SUMMER COLD?

Communication 45 — The End

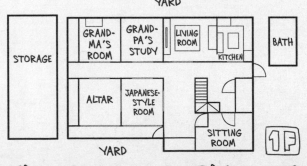

MOUNTAIN

YARD

STORAGE

GRAND-MA'S ROOM

GRAND-PA'S STUDY

LIVING ROOM

KITCHEN

BATH

ALTAR

JAPANESE-STYLE ROOM

SITTING ROOM

1F

YARD

KOMI'S GRANDMOTHER'S HOUSE

Komi Can't
Communicate

Komi Can't Communicate

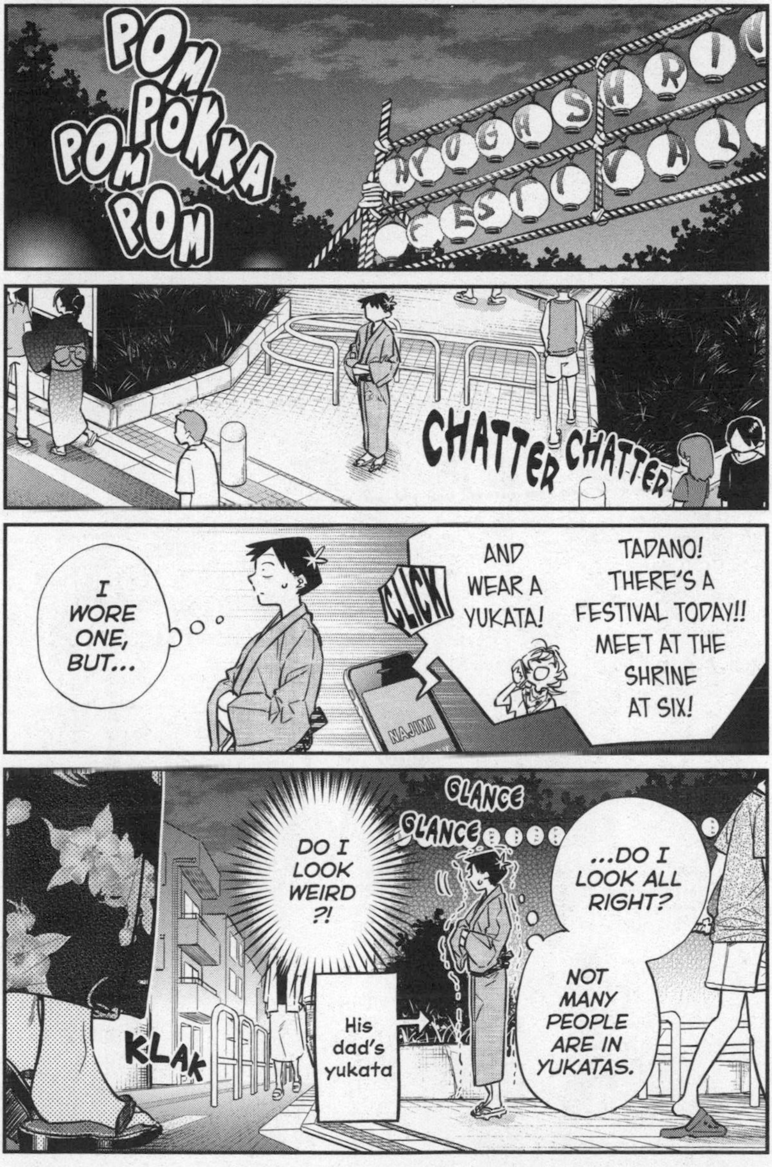
POM POKKA POM POM
CHATTER CHATTER
TADANO! THERE'S A FESTIVAL TODAY!! MEET AT THE SHRINE AT SIX!
AND WEAR A YUKATA!
CLICK
NAJIMI
I WORE ONE, BUT...
GLANCE GLANCE
...DO I LOOK ALL RIGHT?
NOT MANY PEOPLE ARE IN YUKATAS.
DO I LOOK WEIRD?!
His dad's yukata
KLAK

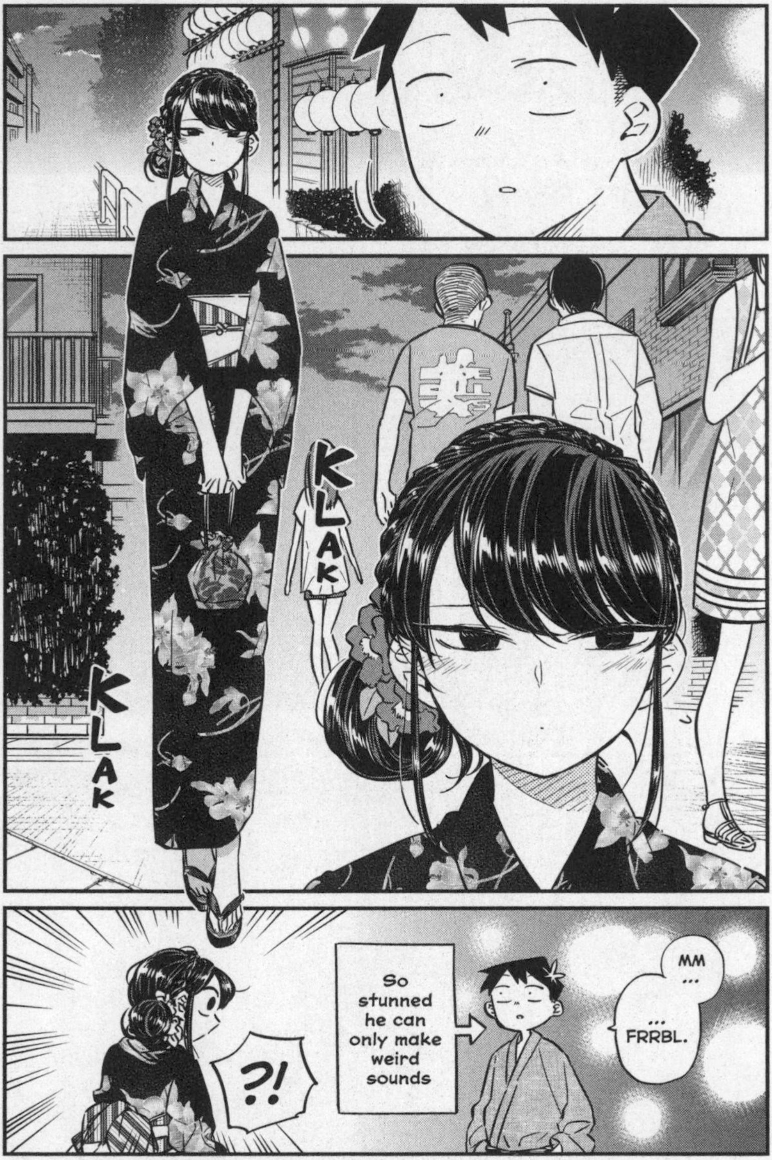
KLAK
KLAK
MM... ...FRRBL.
So stunned he can only make weird sounds
?!

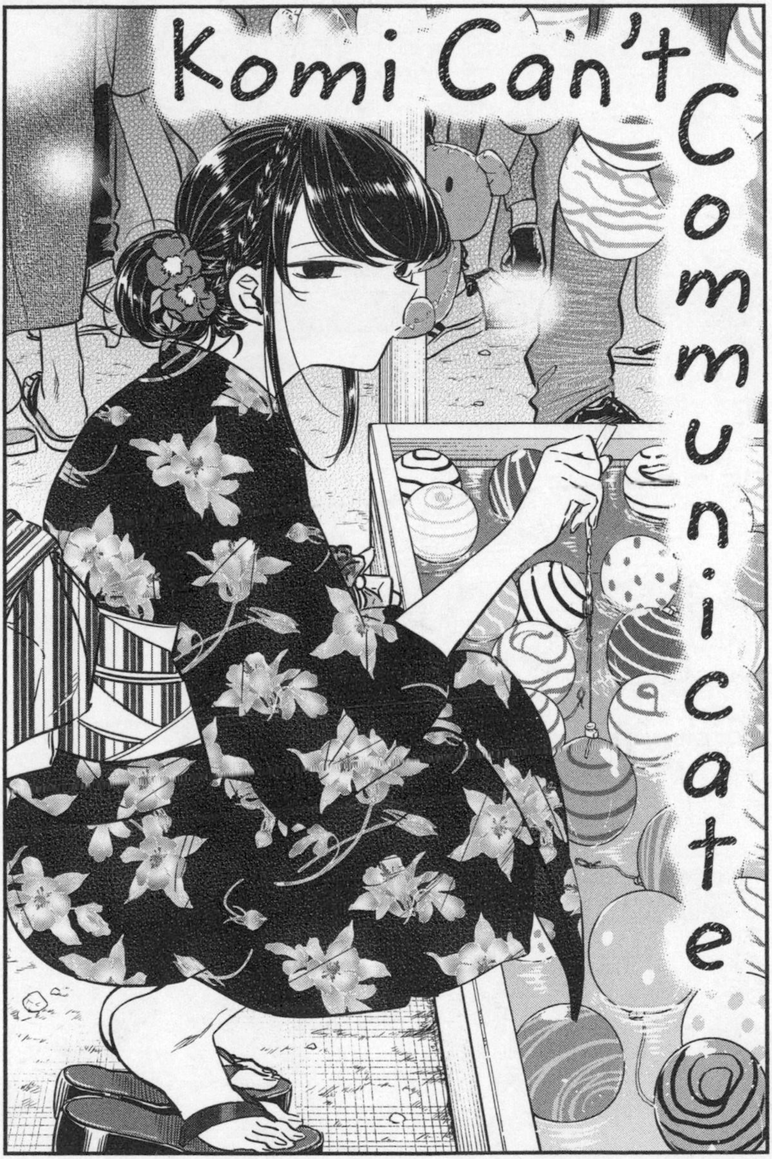
Komi Can't Communicate

Communication 46: Festival

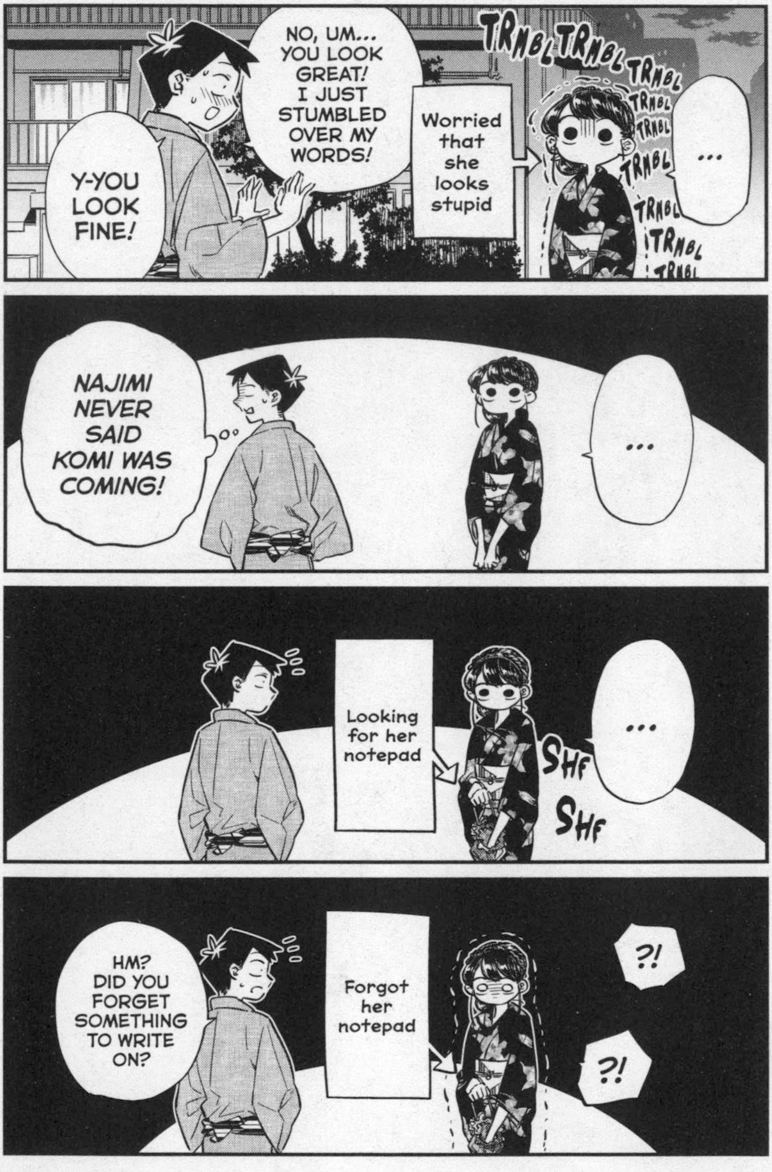
TRMBL TRMBL TRMBL TRMBL TRMBL TRMBL TRMBL TRMBL TRMBL
...
Worried that she looks stupid
NO, UM... YOU LOOK GREAT! I JUST STUMBLED OVER MY WORDS!
Y-YOU LOOK FINE!
...
NAJIMI NEVER SAID KOMI WAS COMING!
...
SHF
SHF
Looking for her notepad
?!
?!
Forgot her notepad
HM? DID YOU FORGET SOMETHING TO WRITE ON?

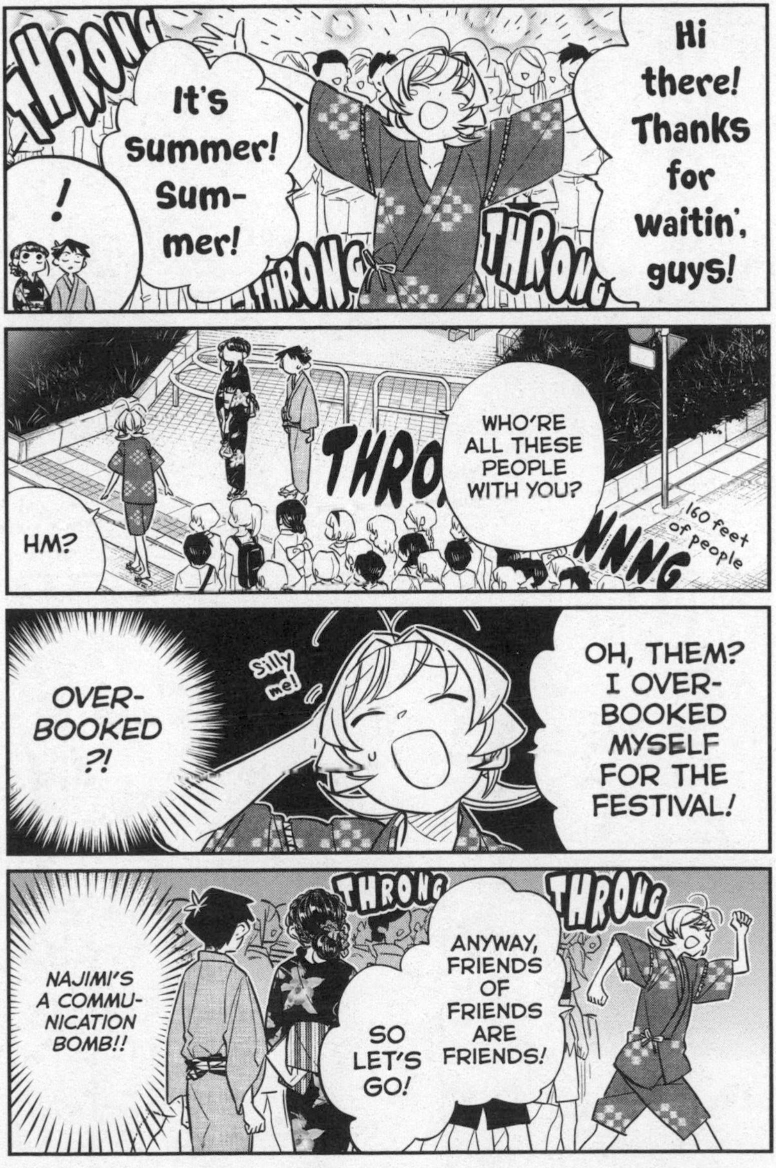
Hi there! Thanks for waitin', guys!
THRONG
THRONG
It's summer! Summer!
THRONG
!
160 feet of people
WHO'RE ALL THESE PEOPLE WITH YOU?
THRONNNG
HM?
OH, THEM? I OVER-BOOKED MYSELF FOR THE FESTIVAL!
Silly me!
OVER-BOOKED?!
THRONG
ANYWAY, FRIENDS OF FRIENDS ARE FRIENDS!
THRONG
SO LET'S GO!
NAJIMI'S A COMMUNICATION BOMB!!

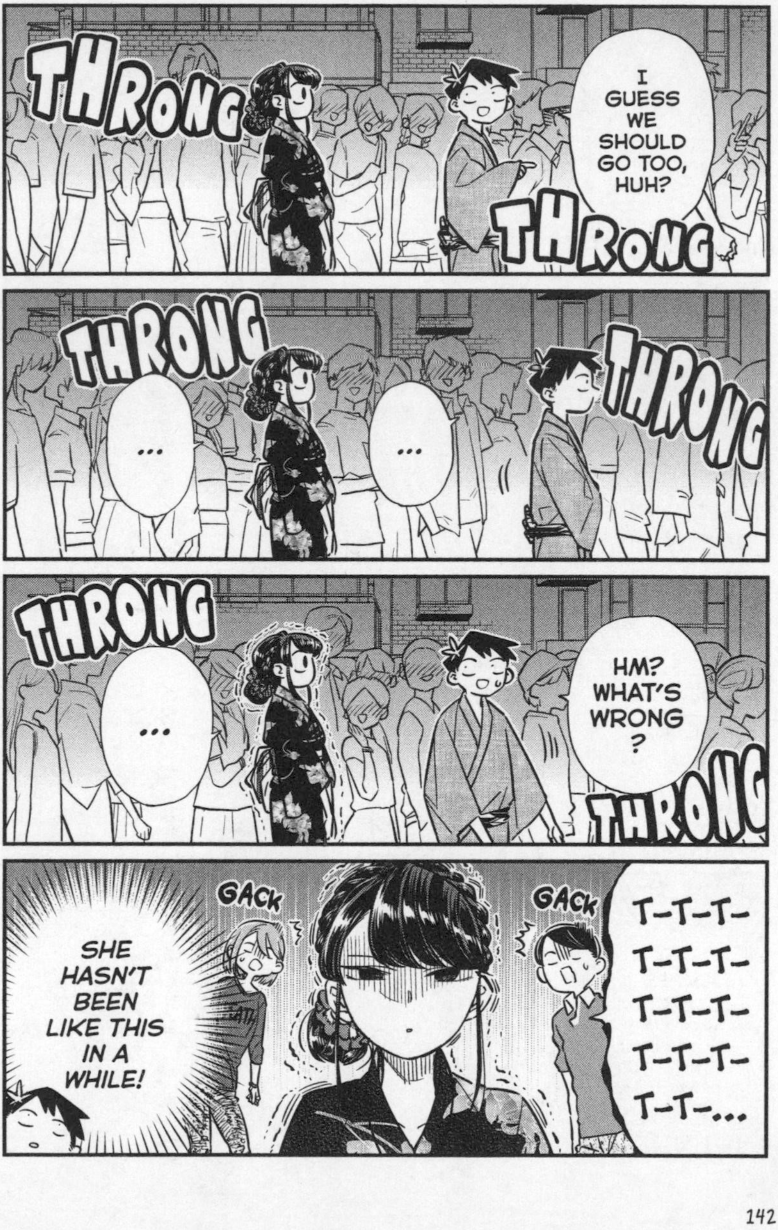

I GUESS WE SHOULD GO TOO, HUH?
THRONG
THRONG
THRONG
...
...
THRONG
HM? WHAT'S WRONG ?
THRONG
...
THRONG
T-T-T- T-T-T- T-T-T- T-T-T- T-T-...
GACK
GACK
SHE HASN'T BEEN LIKE THIS IN A WHILE!

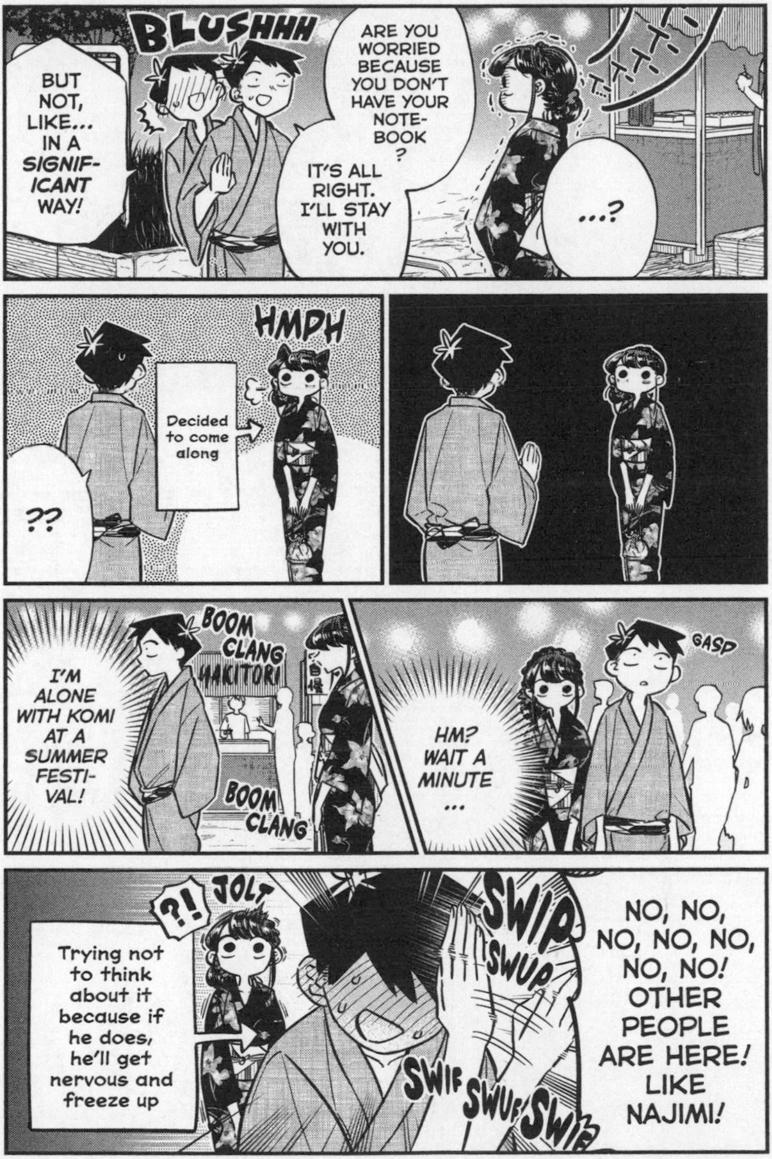
...?
ARE YOU WORRIED BECAUSE YOU DON'T HAVE YOUR NOTEBOOK?
IT'S ALL RIGHT. I'LL STAY WITH YOU.
BLUSHHH
BUT NOT, LIKE... IN A SIGNIFICANT WAY!
HMPH
Decided to come along
??
GASP
HM? WAIT A MINUTE...
BOOM CLANG
YAKITORI
BOOM CLANG
I'M ALONE WITH KOMI AT A SUMMER FESTIVAL!
NO, NO, NO, NO, NO, NO, NO! OTHER PEOPLE ARE HERE! LIKE NAJIMI!
SWIP SWUP
SWIF SWUF SWIF
?! JOLT
Trying not to think about it because if he does, he'll get nervous and freeze up

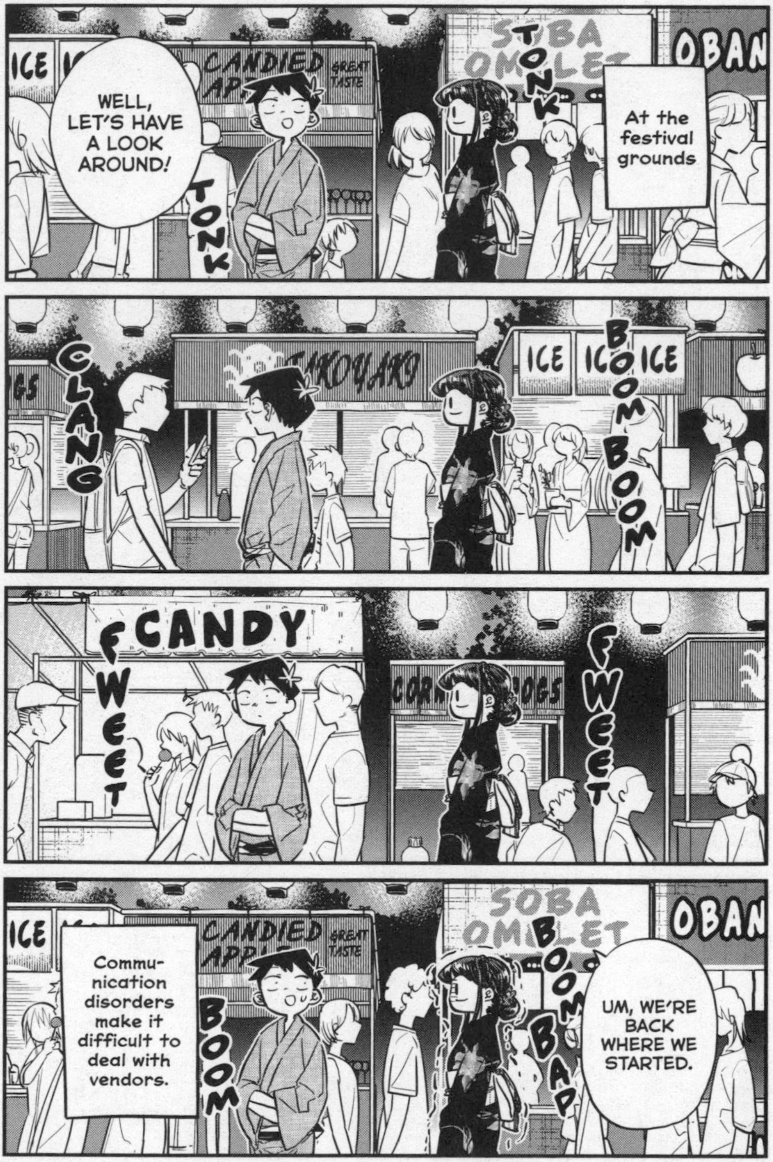
At the festival grounds
TONK
WELL, LET'S HAVE A LOOK AROUND!
GREAT TASTE
TONK
BOOM BOOM BOOM
ICE
ICE
CLANG
FWEET
CANDY
FWEET
UM, WE'RE BACK WHERE WE STARTED.
BOOM BAP
BOOM
Communication disorders make it difficult to deal with vendors.

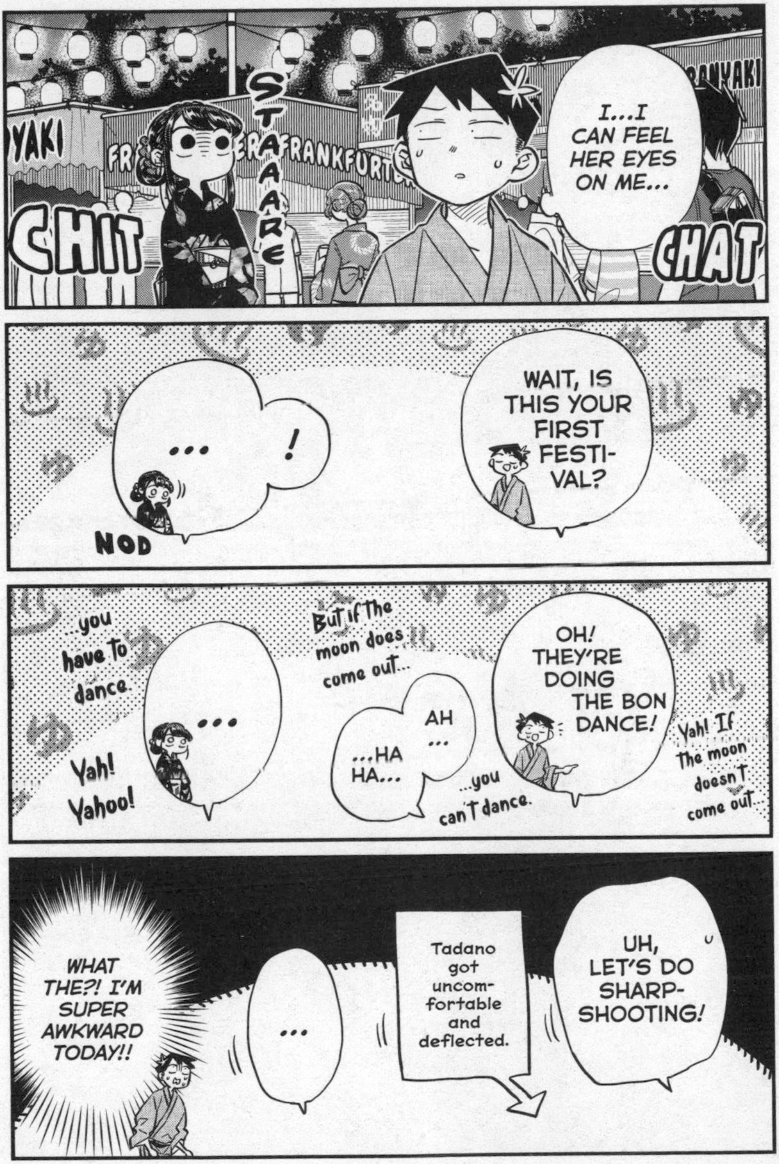
I...I CAN FEEL HER EYES ON ME...
CHAT
STAARE
CHIT
WAIT, IS THIS YOUR FIRST FESTI-VAL?
... !
NOD
Yah! If the moon doesn't come out...
OH! THEY'RE DOING THE BON DANCE!
...you can't dance.
AH... ...HA HA...
But if the moon does come out...
...you have to dance.
...
Yah! Yahoo!
UH, LET'S DO SHARP-SHOOTING!
Tadano got uncomfortable and deflected.
...
WHAT THE?! I'M SUPER AWKWARD TODAY!!

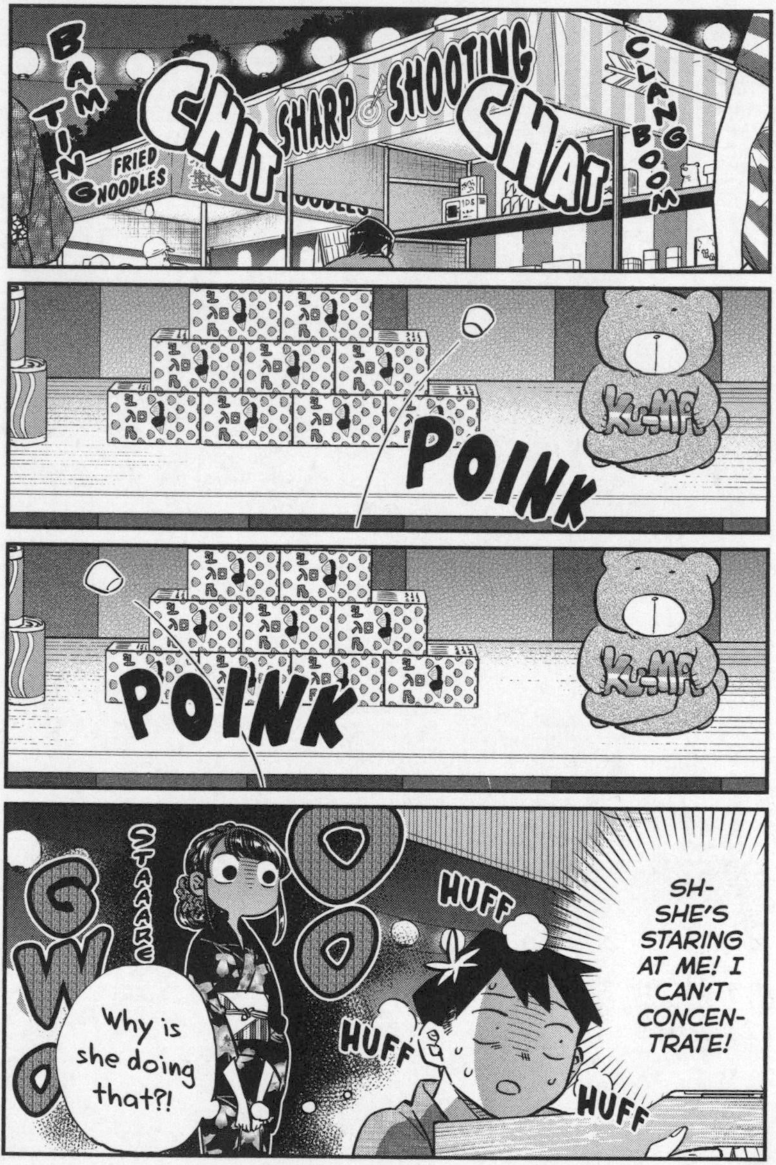
CLANG BOOM
CHAT
SHARP SHOOTING
CHIT
FRIED NOODLES
BAM TING
POINK
KU-MA
POINK
KU-MA
SH- SHE'S STARING AT ME! I CAN'T CONCEN- TRATE!
HUFF
HUFF
HUFF
STAAAARE
Why is she doing that?!

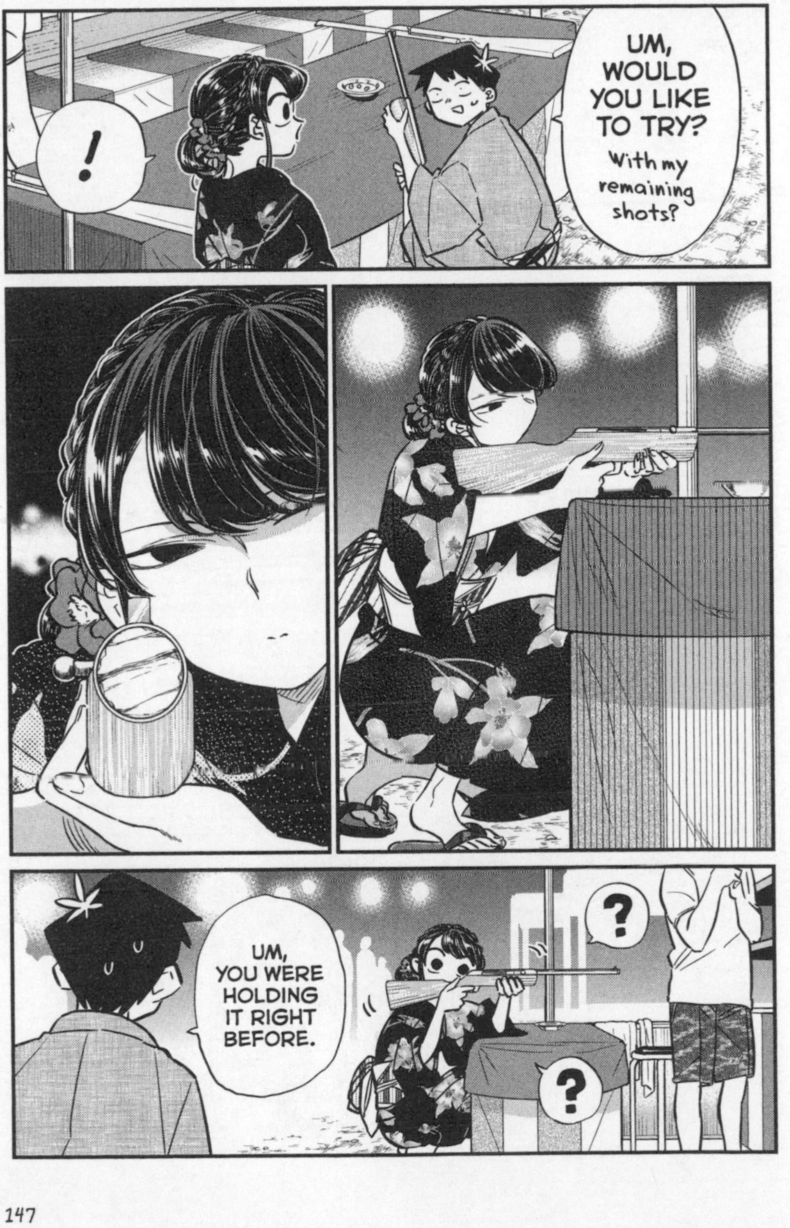
UM, WOULD YOU LIKE TO TRY? With my remaining shots?
!
?
UM, YOU WERE HOLDING IT RIGHT BEFORE.
?

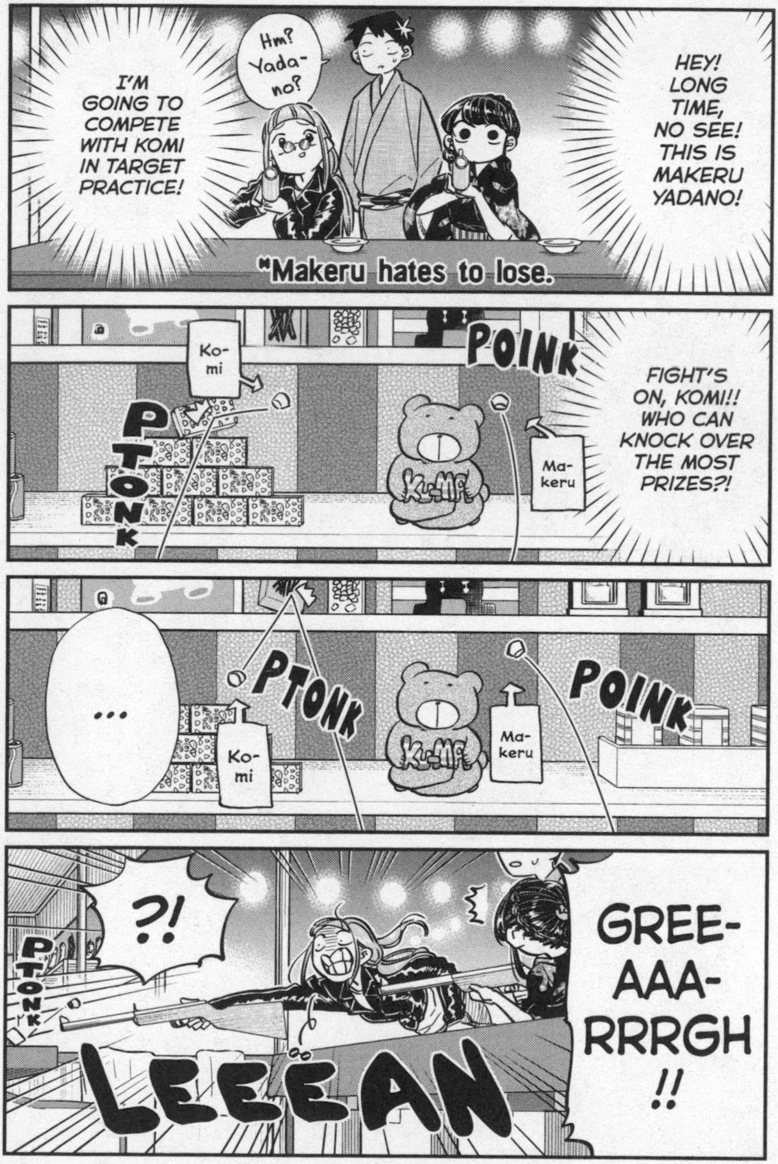
HEY! LONG TIME, NO SEE! THIS IS MAKERU YADANO!
Hm? Yada-no?
I'M GOING TO COMPETE WITH KOMI IN TARGET PRACTICE!
*Makeru hates to lose.
FIGHT'S ON, KOMI!! WHO CAN KNOCK OVER THE MOST PRIZES?!
POINK
Ma-keru
Ko-mi
PTONK
POINK
Ma-keru
PTONK
Ko-mi
...
GREE-AAA-RRRGH!!
?!
PTONK
LEEEAN

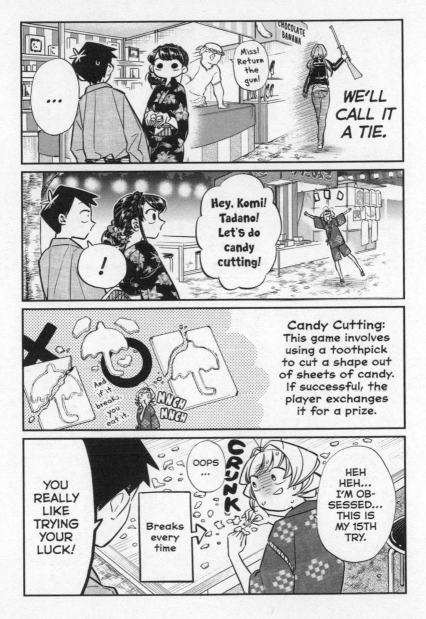

CHOCOLATE BANANA
WE'LL CALL IT A TIE.
Miss! Return the gun!
...
Hey, Komi! Tadano! Let's do candy cutting!
!
Candy Cutting: This game involves using a toothpick to cut a shape out of sheets of candy. If successful, the player exchanges it for a prize.
MNCH MNCH
And if it breaks you eat it.
HEH HEH... I'M OBSESSED... THIS IS MY 15TH TRY.
CRUNK
OOPS ...
Breaks every time
YOU REALLY LIKE TRYING YOUR LUCK!

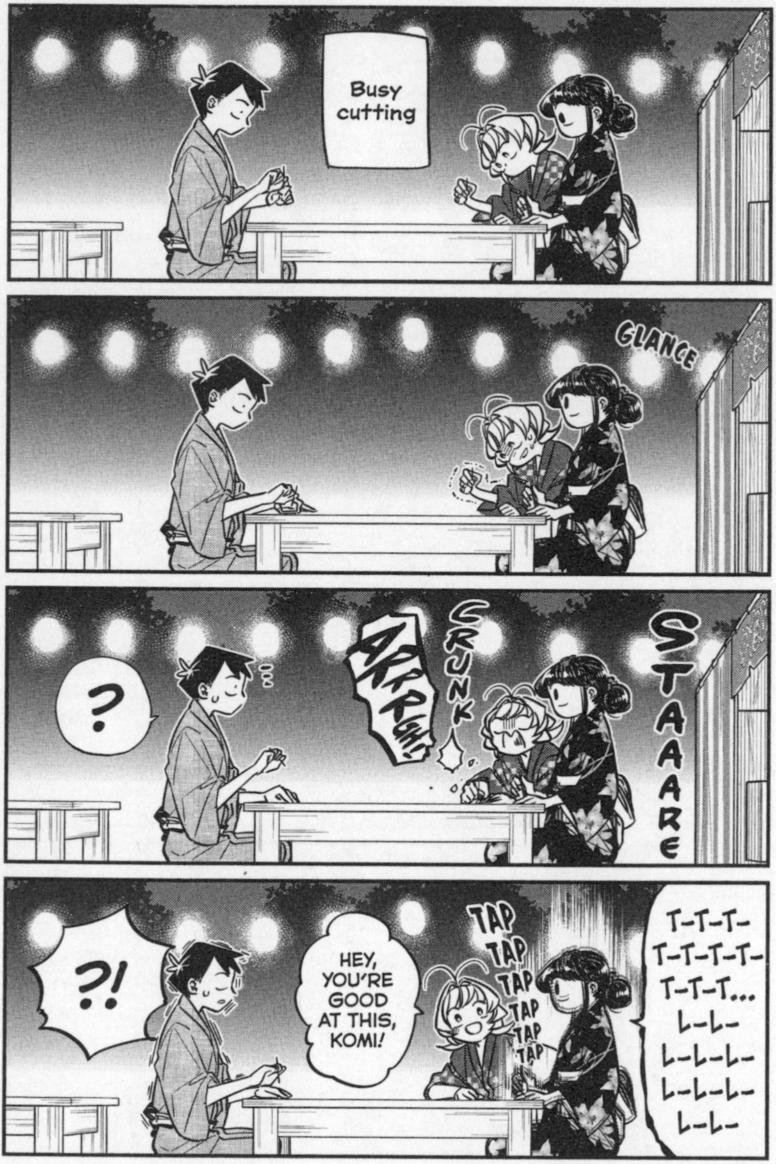
Busy cutting
GLANCE
STAAARE
CRUNK
ARRRGH!!
?
T-T-T- T-T-T-T-T- T-T-T... L-L- L-L-L- L-L-L- L-L-
TAP TAP TAP TAP TAP TAP
HEY, YOU'RE GOOD AT THIS, KOMI!
?!

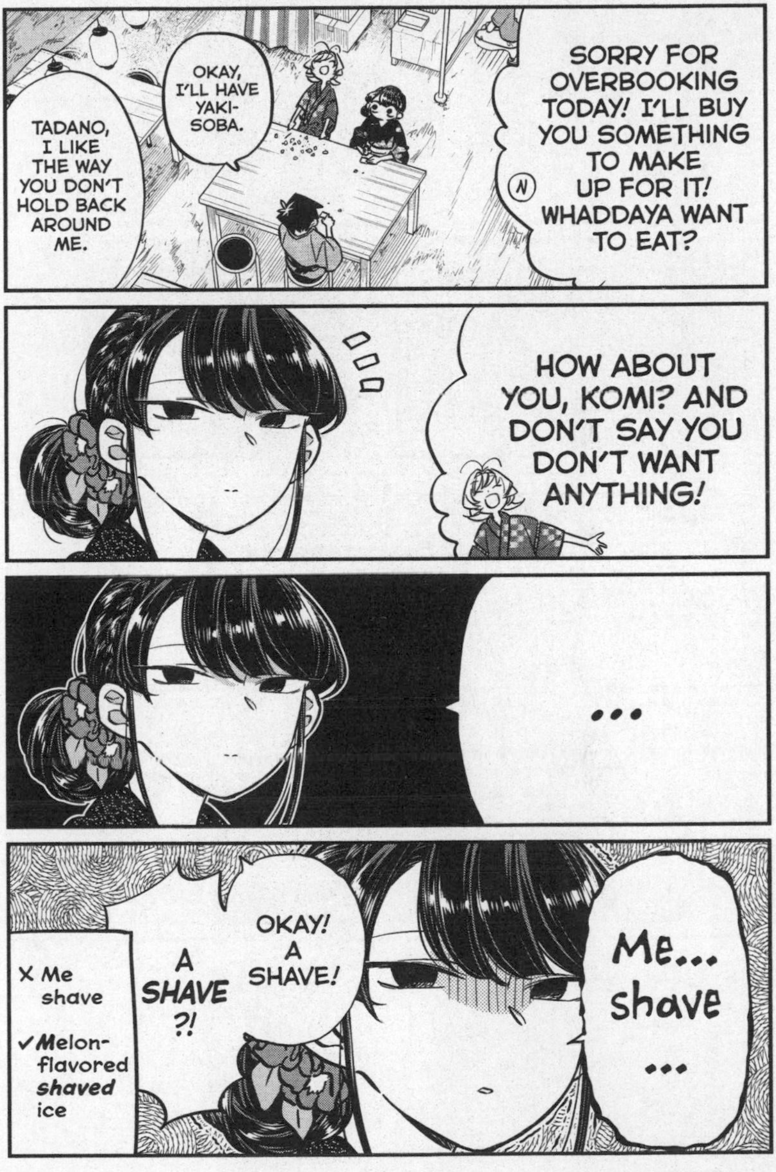
SORRY FOR OVERBOOKING TODAY! I'LL BUY YOU SOMETHING TO MAKE UP FOR IT! WHADDAYA WANT TO EAT?
OKAY, I'LL HAVE YAKI-SOBA.
TADANO, I LIKE THE WAY YOU DON'T HOLD BACK AROUND ME.
HOW ABOUT YOU, KOMI? AND DON'T SAY YOU DON'T WANT ANYTHING!
...
Me... shave ...
OKAY! A SHAVE!
A SHAVE?!
✗ Me shave
✓ Melon-flavored shaved ice

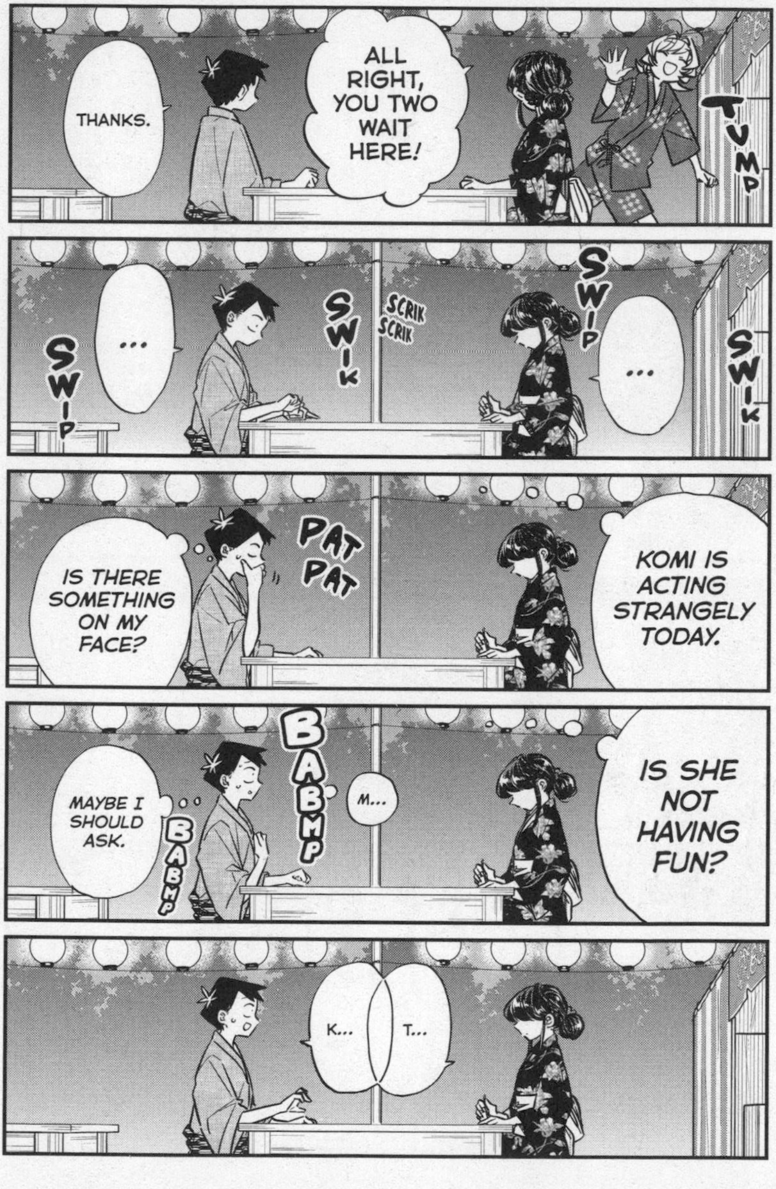
TUMP
ALL RIGHT, YOU TWO WAIT HERE!
THANKS.
SWIP
SWIK
...
SCRIK SCRIK
SWIK
...
SWIP
KOMI IS ACTING STRANGELY TODAY.
PAT PAT
IS THERE SOMETHING ON MY FACE?
IS SHE NOT HAVING FUN?
M...
BABMP
MAYBE I SHOULD ASK.
BABMP
T...
K...

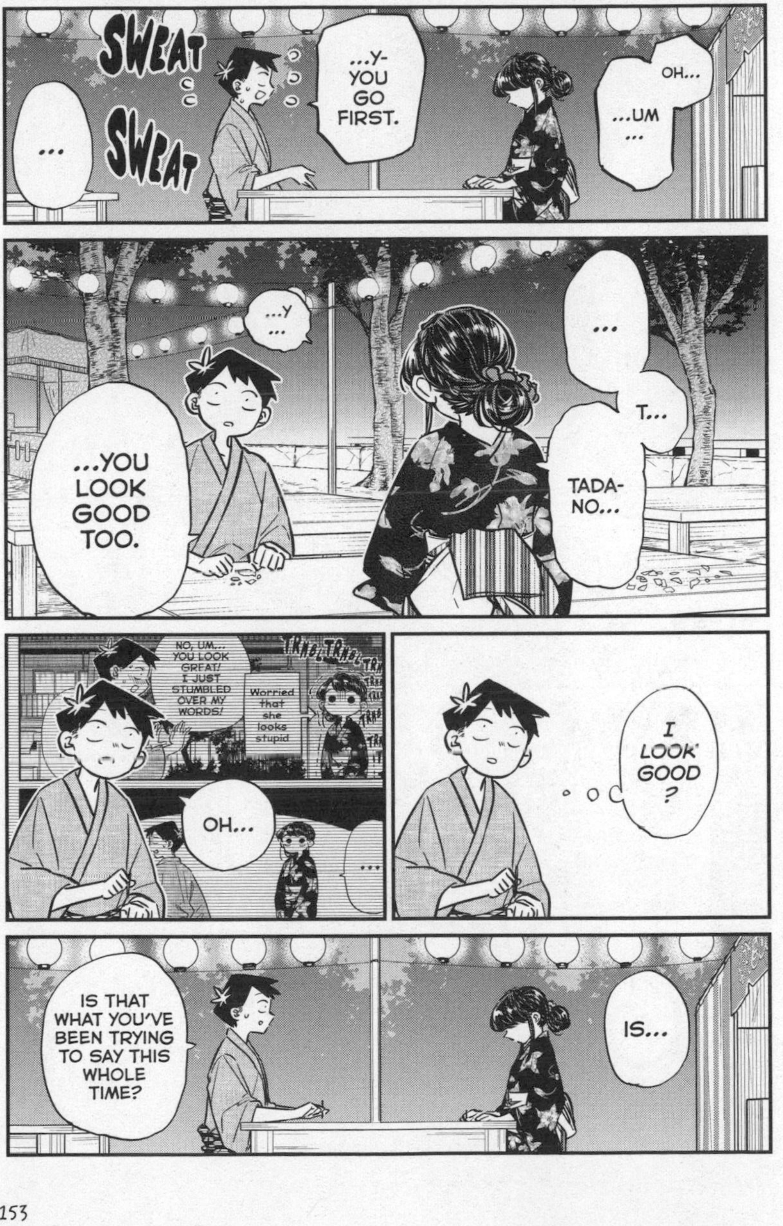
OH...
...UM...
...Y-YOU GO FIRST.
SWEAT
SWEAT
...
...
T...
TADA-NO...
...Y...
...YOU LOOK GOOD TOO.
I LOOK GOOD?
TRMBL TRMBL
NO, UM... YOU LOOK GREAT! I JUST STUMBLED OVER MY WORDS!
Worried that she looks stupid
OH...
...
IS...
IS THAT WHAT YOU'VE BEEN TRYING TO SAY THIS WHOLE TIME?

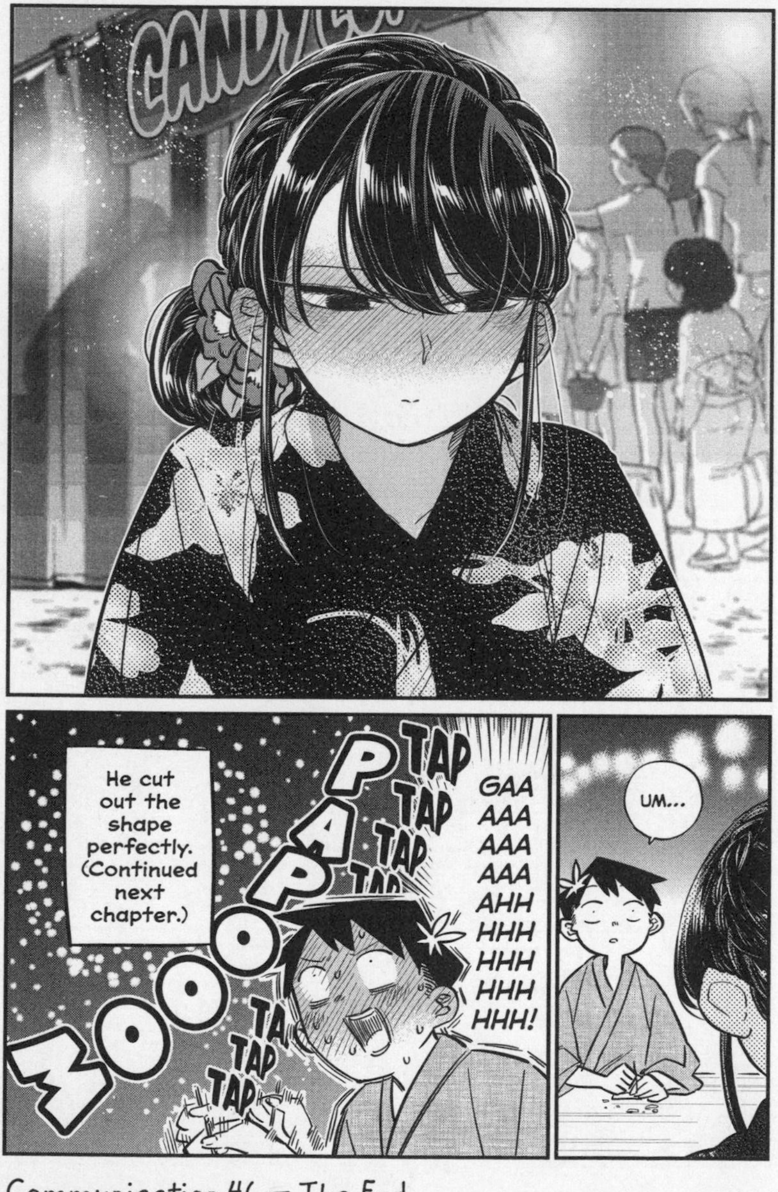
UM...
GAAAAAAAAAAAAAHHHHHHHHHHHHHH!
TAP TAP TAP TAP
PAP
He cut out the shape perfectly. (Continued next chapter.)
ZOOOO
TA TAP TAP

Communication 46 — The End

Komi Can't Communicate

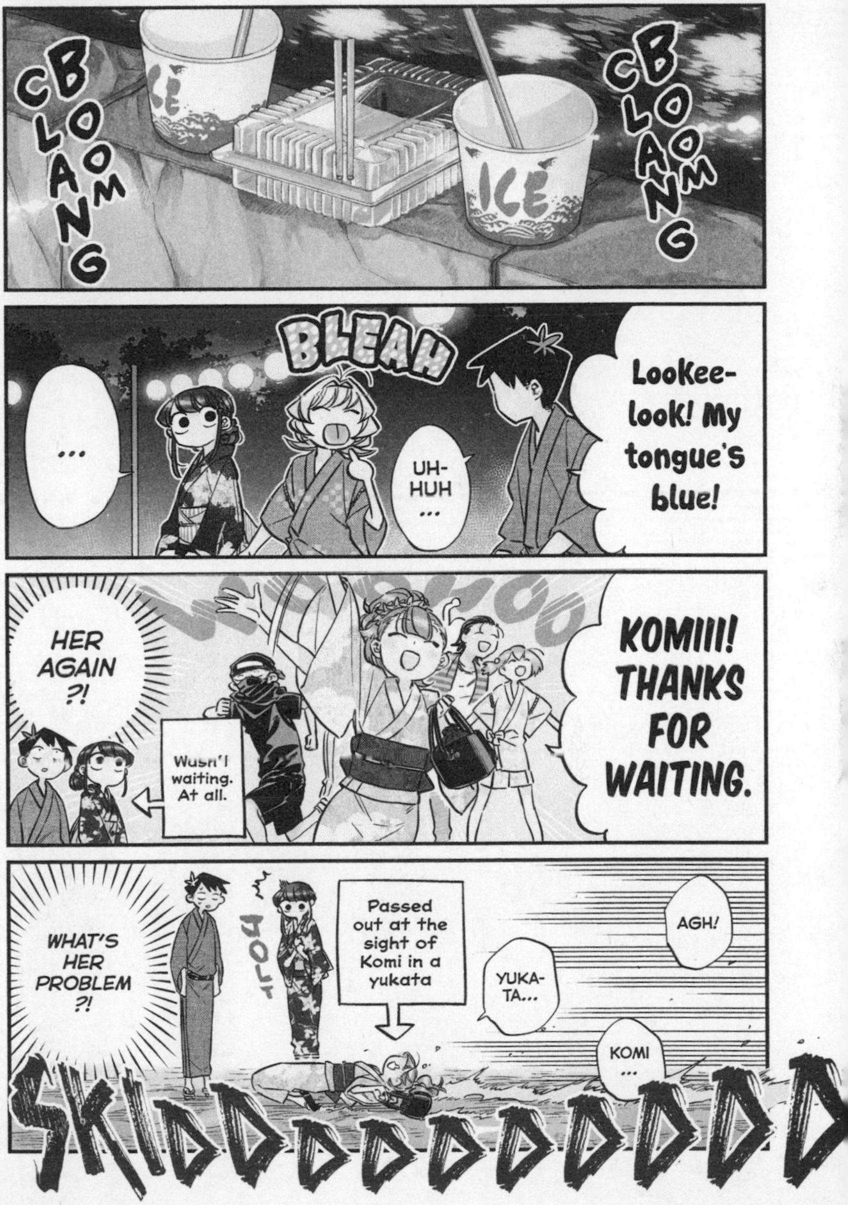

BLOOM
CLANG
ICE
ICE
BLOOM
CLANG
Lookee-look! My tongue's blue!
BLEAH
UH-HUH ...
...
KOMIII! THANKS FOR WAITING.
Wasn't waiting. At all.
HER AGAIN ?!
AGH!
KOMI ...
YUKA-TA...
Passed out at the sight of Komi in a yukata
JOLT
WHAT'S HER PROBLEM ?!
SKIDDDDDDDDDDD

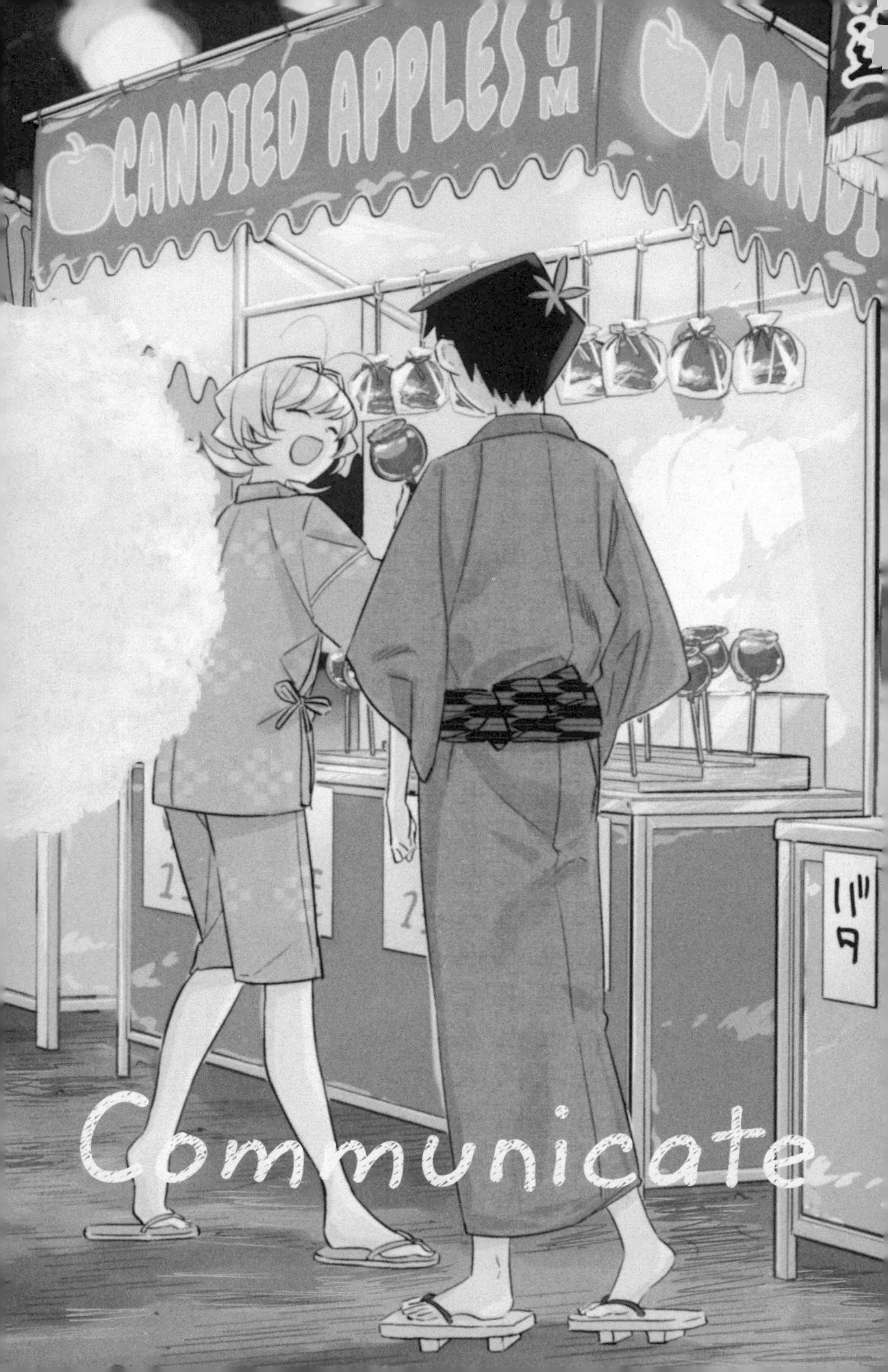
CANDIED APPLES
CAND
Communicate

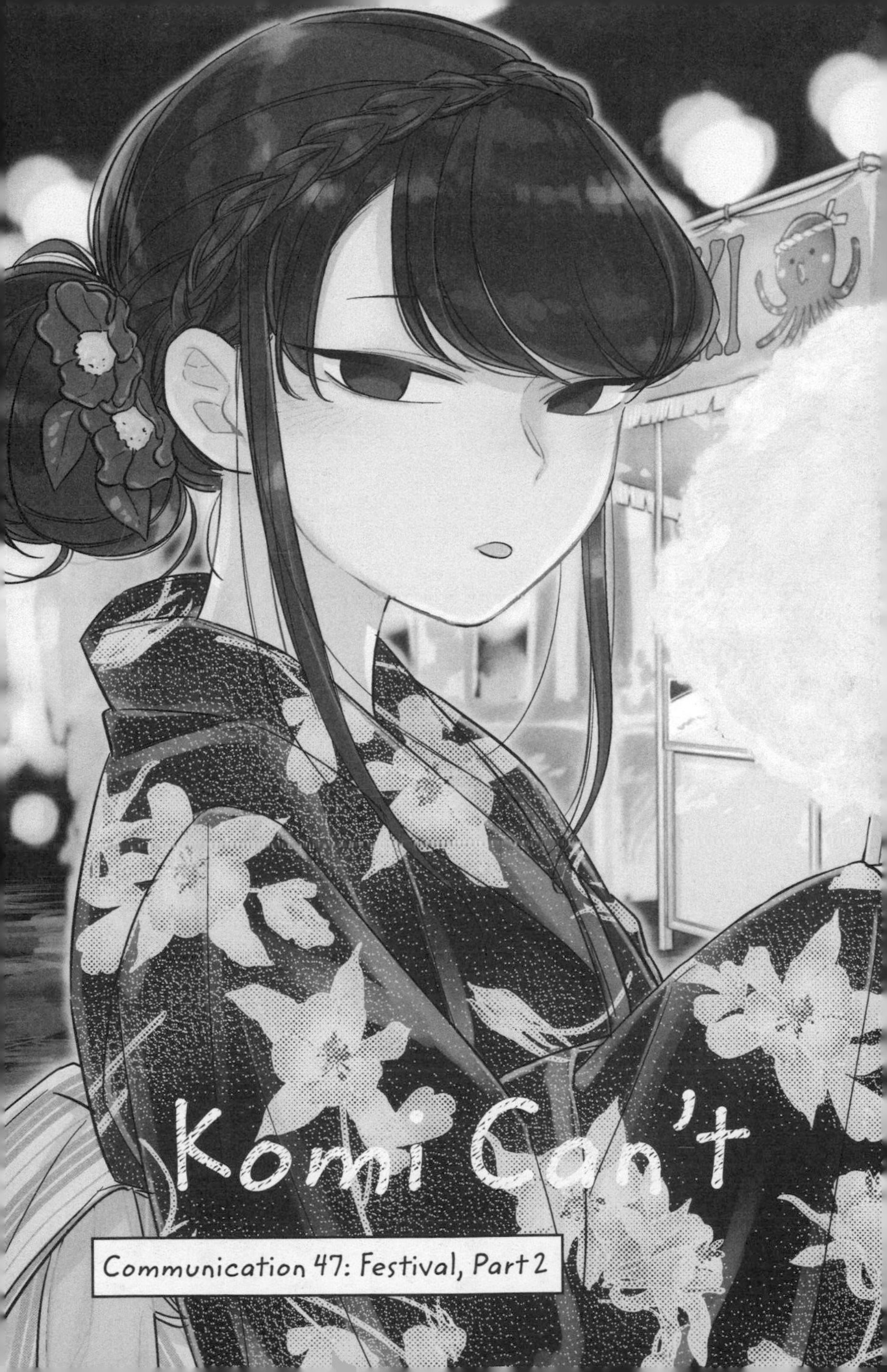
Komi Can't
Communication 47: Festival, Part 2

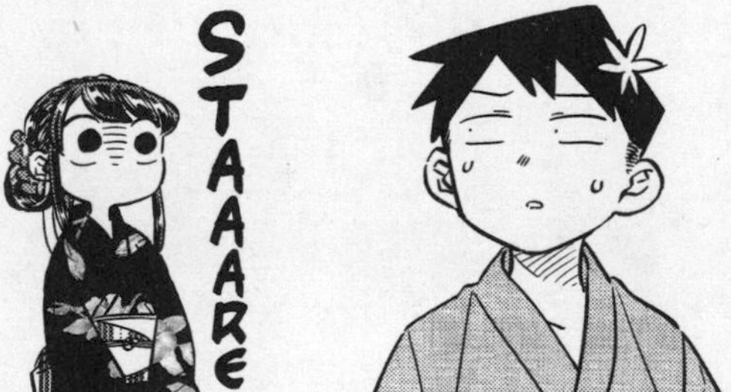
STAAARE

Komi Can't Communicate

Komi Can't Communicate

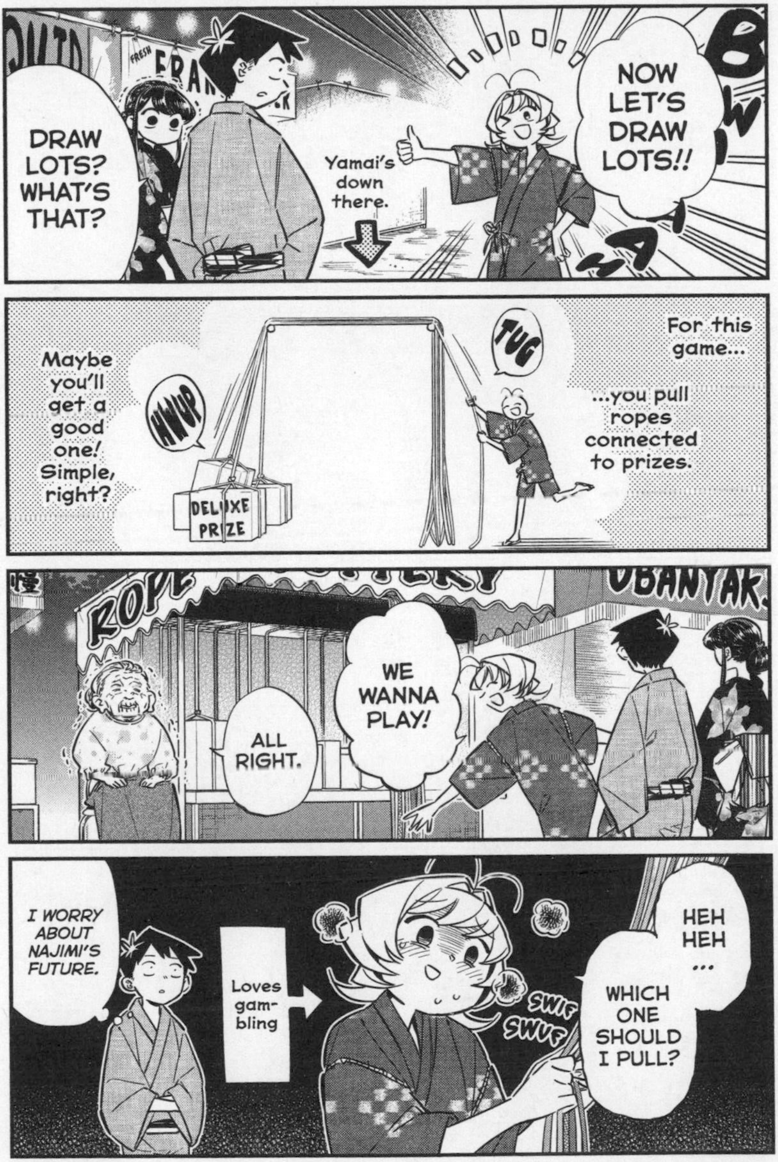
NOW LET'S DRAW LOTS!!
Yamai's down there.
DRAW LOTS? WHAT'S THAT?
For this game...
TUG
...you pull ropes connected to prizes.
HWUP
Maybe you'll get a good one! Simple, right?
DELUXE PRIZE
ROPE
WE WANNA PLAY!
ALL RIGHT.
HEH HEH ...
WHICH ONE SHOULD I PULL?
SWIF
SWUF
Loves gam- bling
I WORRY ABOUT NAJIMI'S FUTURE.

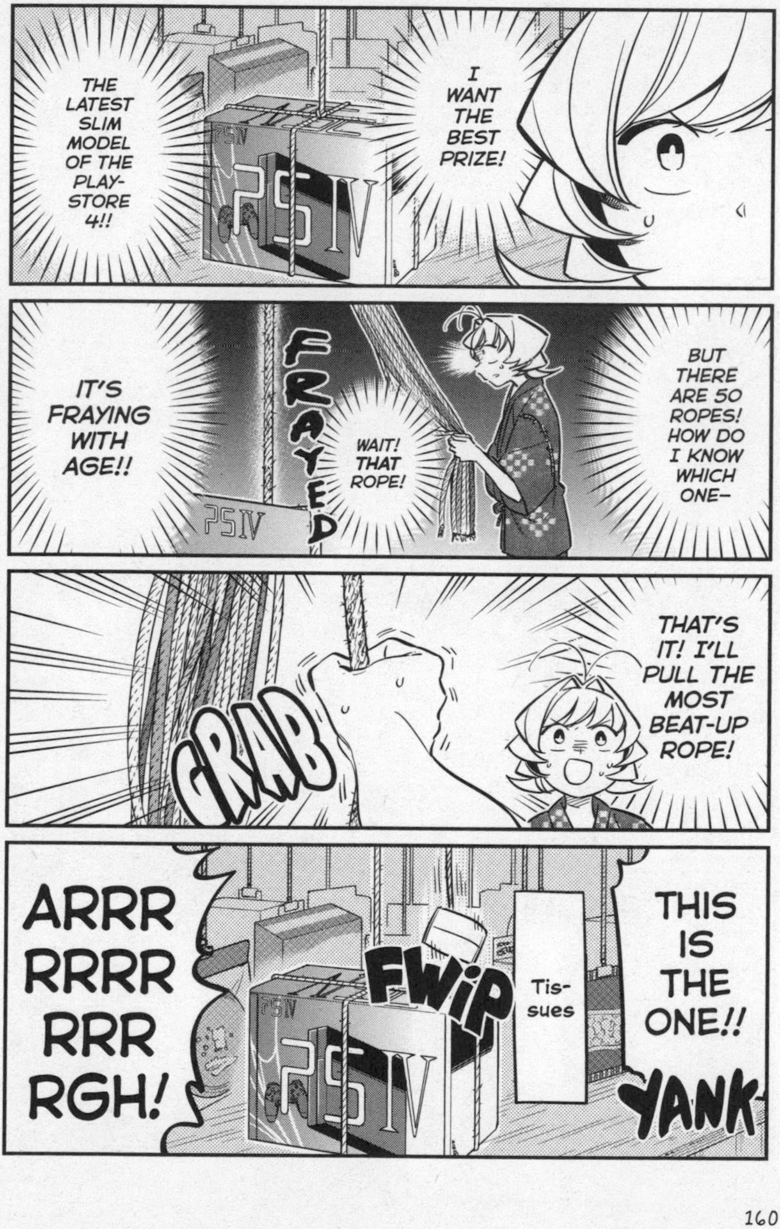
I WANT THE BEST PRIZE!
THE LATEST SLIM MODEL OF THE PLAY-STORE 4!!
PSIV
BUT THERE ARE 50 ROPES! HOW DO I KNOW WHICH ONE–
WAIT! THAT ROPE!
FRAYED
IT'S FRAYING WITH AGE!!
PSIV
THAT'S IT! I'LL PULL THE MOST BEAT-UP ROPE!
GRAB
THIS IS THE ONE!!
YANK
Tis-sues
FWIP
PSIV
ARRRRRRRRRRRGH!

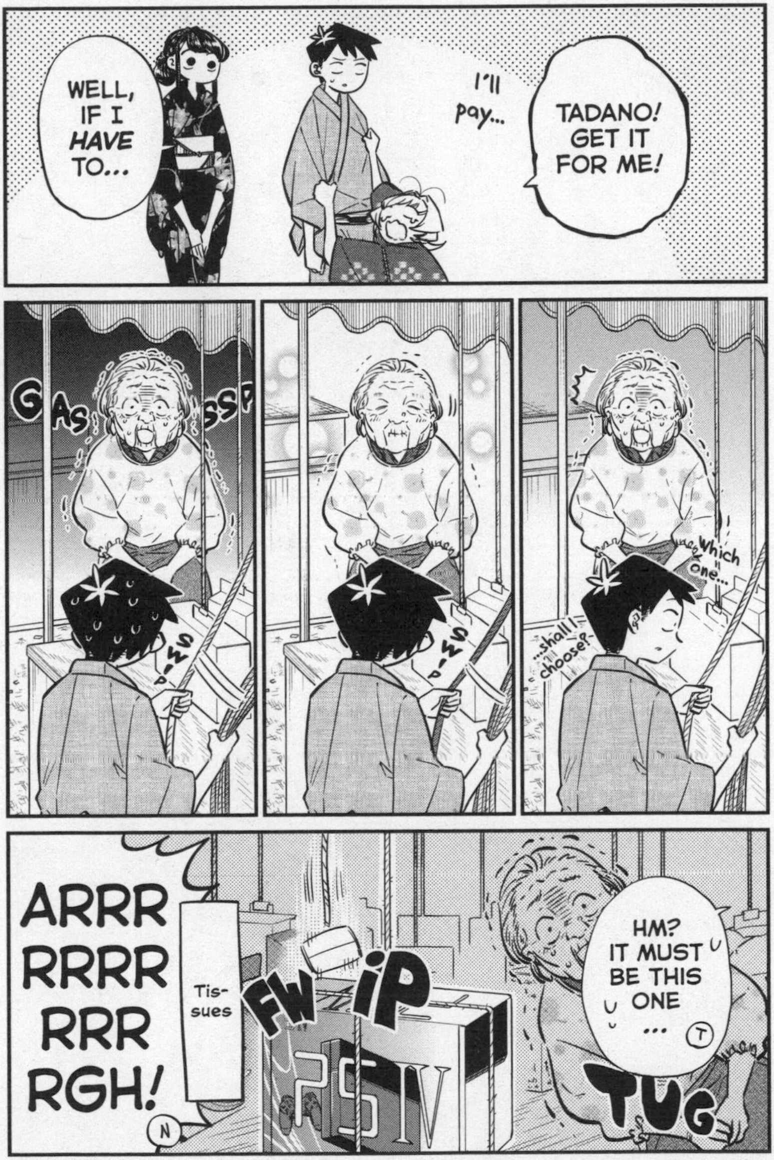
TADANO! GET IT FOR ME!
I'll pay...
WELL, IF I HAVE TO...
Which one...
...shall I choose?
SWIP
SWIP
GAs
SSP
HM? IT MUST BE THIS ONE ...
TUG
FWIP
PS IV
Tis-sues
ARRRRRRRRRRRGH!

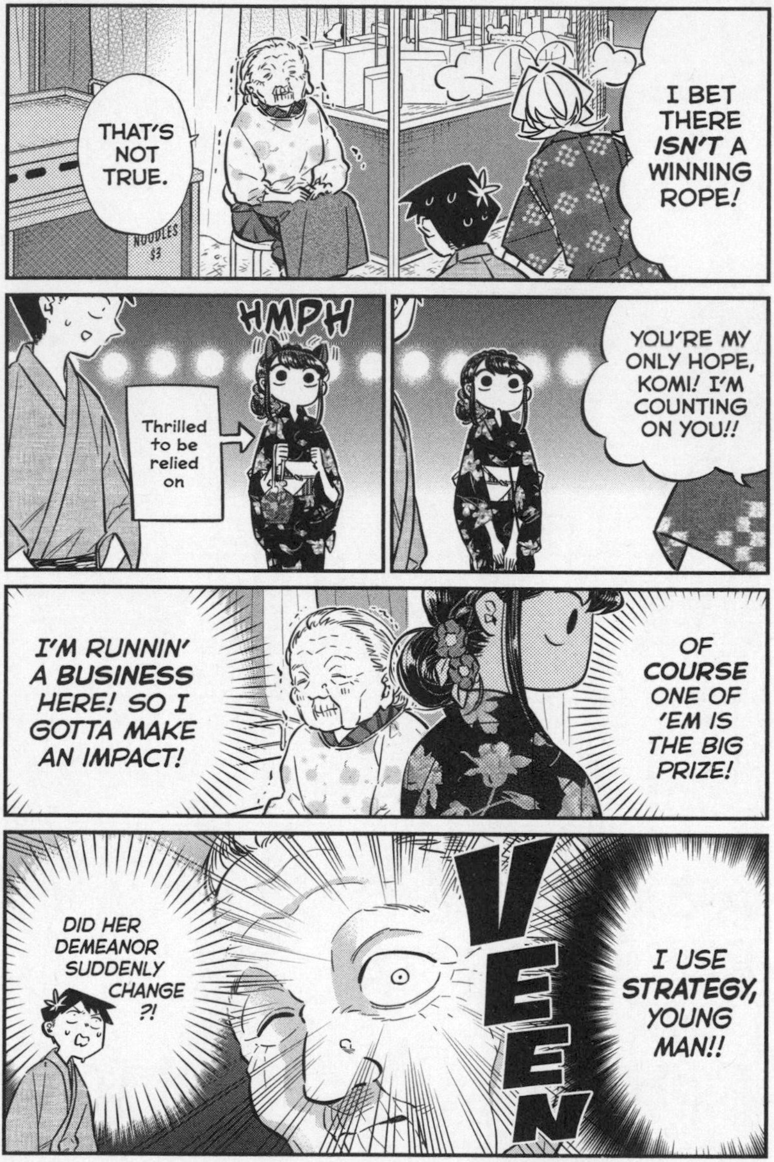
I BET THERE ISN'T A WINNING ROPE!
THAT'S NOT TRUE.
NOODLES $3
YOU'RE MY ONLY HOPE, KOMI! I'M COUNTING ON YOU!!
HMPH
Thrilled to be relied on
OF COURSE ONE OF 'EM IS THE BIG PRIZE!
I'M RUNNIN' A BUSINESS HERE! SO I GOTTA MAKE AN IMPACT!
I USE STRATEGY, YOUNG MAN!!
VEEN
DID HER DEMEANOR SUDDENLY CHANGE?!

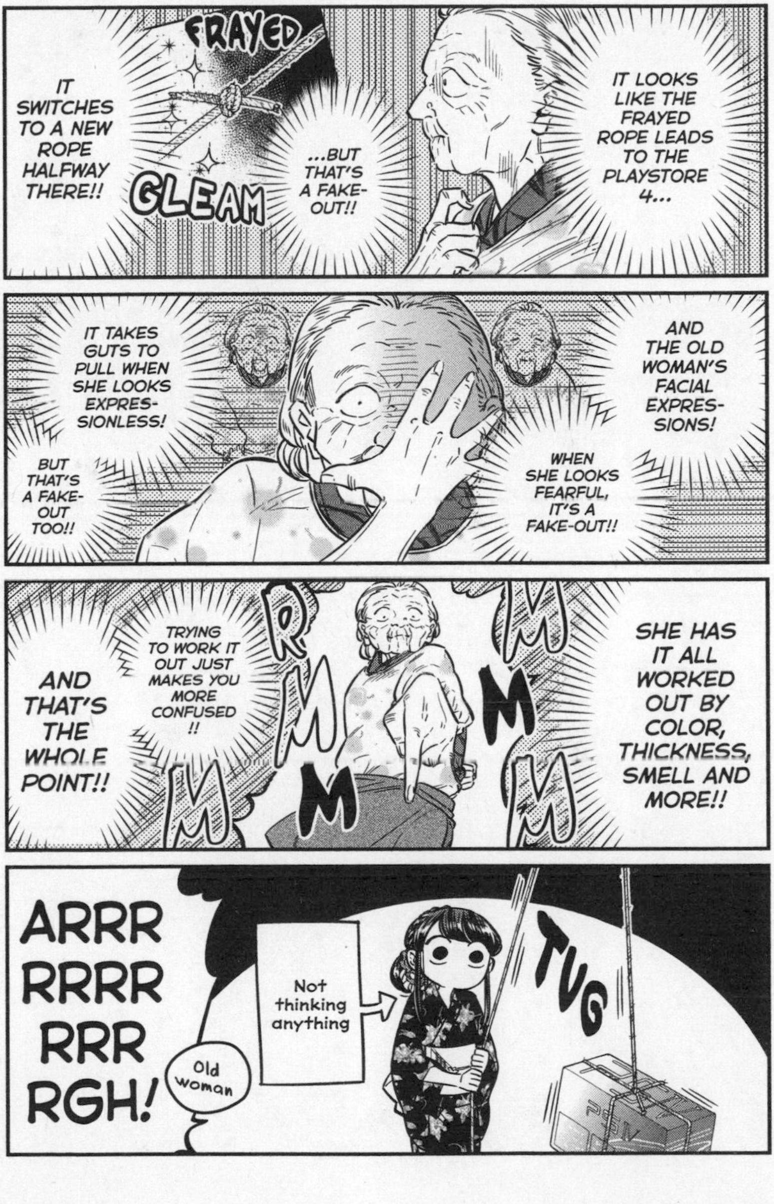
IT LOOKS LIKE THE FRAYED ROPE LEADS TO THE PLAYSTORE 4...
FRAYED
...BUT THAT'S A FAKE-OUT!!
IT SWITCHES TO A NEW ROPE HALFWAY THERE!!
GLEAM
AND THE OLD WOMAN'S FACIAL EXPRESSIONS!
WHEN SHE LOOKS FEARFUL, IT'S A FAKE-OUT!!
IT TAKES GUTS TO PULL WHEN SHE LOOKS EXPRESSIONLESS!
BUT THAT'S A FAKE-OUT TOO!!
SHE HAS IT ALL WORKED OUT BY COLOR, THICKNESS, SMELL AND MORE!!
RMMMMMMM
TRYING TO WORK IT OUT JUST MAKES YOU MORE CONFUSED!!
AND THAT'S THE WHOLE POINT!!
TUG
Not thinking anything
Old woman
ARRRRRRRRRRRRGH!

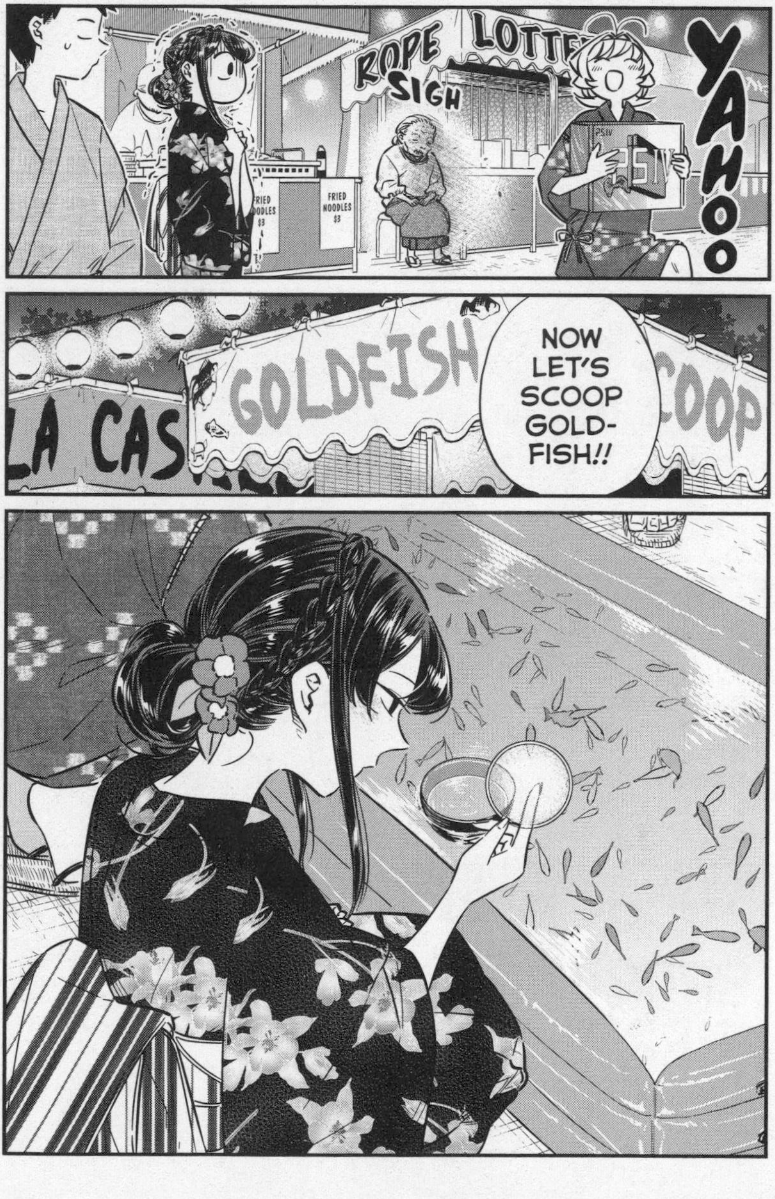
YAHOO
PSIV
ROPE LOTTE
SIGH
FRIED NOODLES $3
FRIED NOODLES $3
COOP
NOW LET'S SCOOP GOLD-FISH!!
GOLDFISH
LA CAS

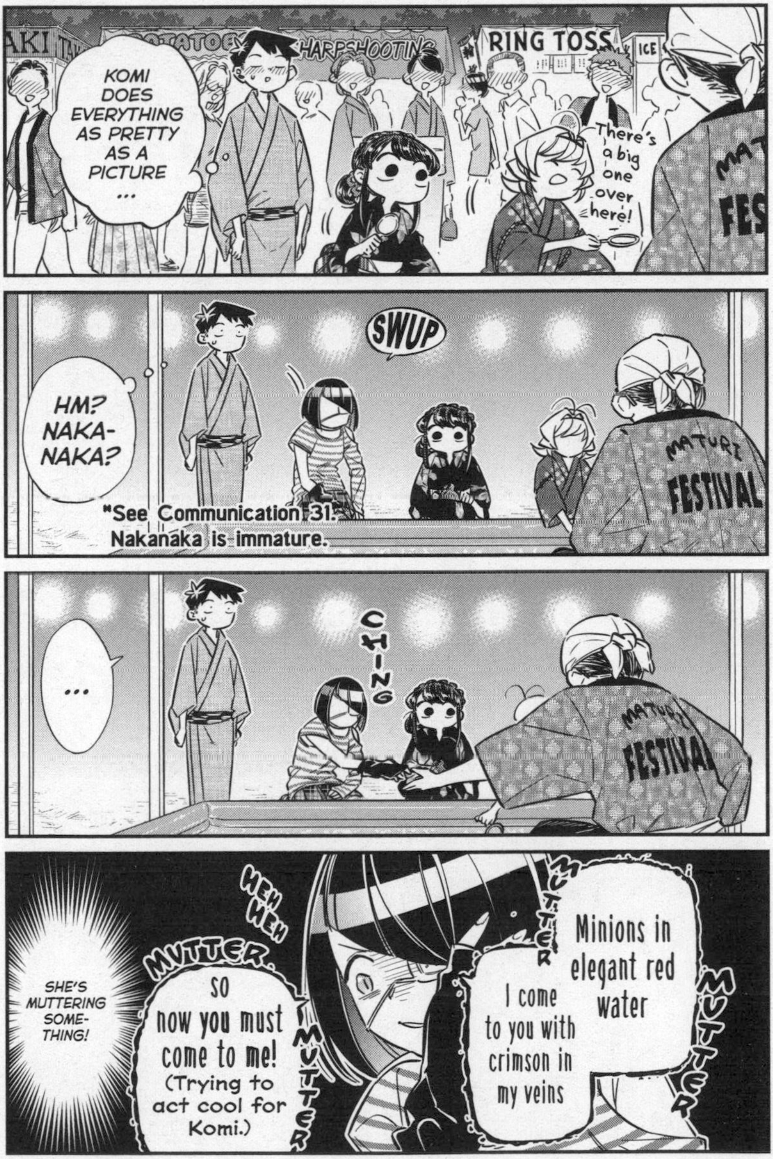
RING TOSS
ICE
There's a big one over here!
KOMI DOES EVERYTHING AS PRETTY AS A PICTURE ...
SWUP
MATURI
FESTIVAL
HM? NAKA-NAKA?
*See Communication 31. Nakanaka is immature.
CHING
MATURI
FESTIVAL
...
MUTTER
Minions in elegant red water
I come to you with crimson in my veins
MUTTER
so now you must come to me!
(Trying to act cool for Komi.)
MUTTER
HEH HEH
MUTTER
SHE'S MUTTERING SOME-THING!

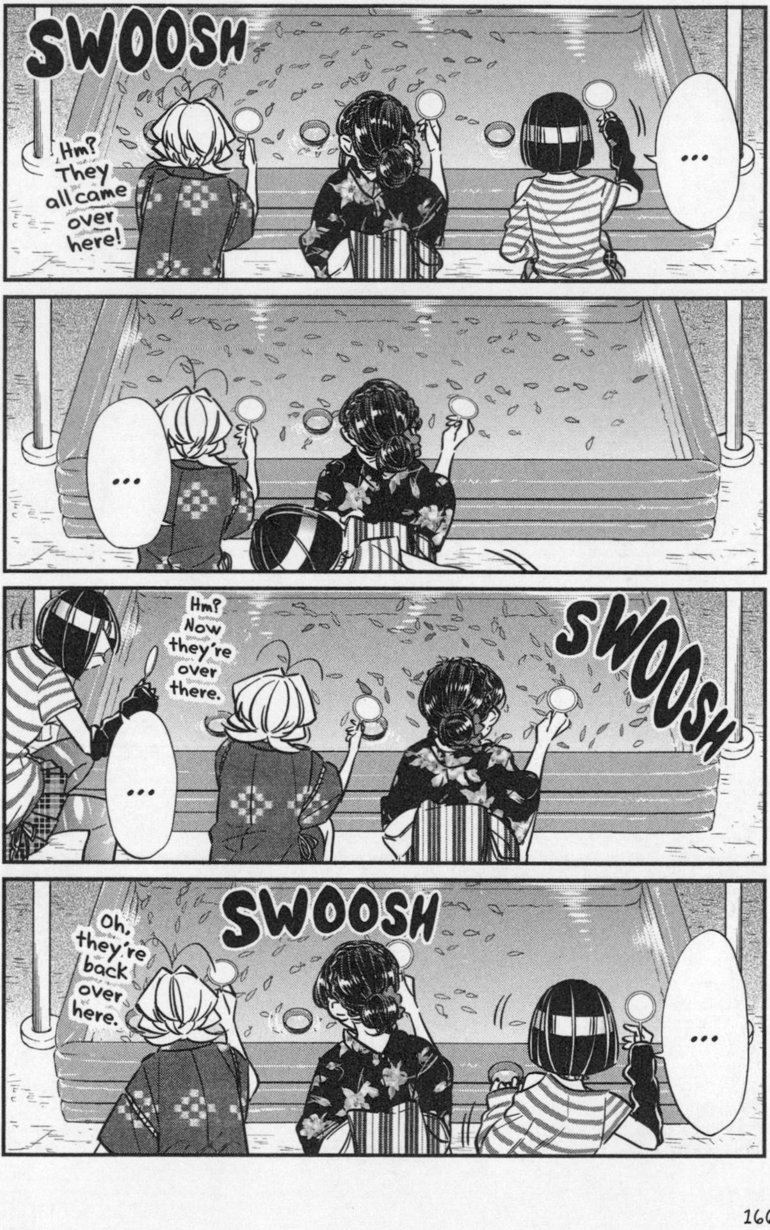
...
SWOOSH
Hm? They all came over here!
...
SWOOSH
Hm? Now they're over there.
...
...
SWOOSH
Oh, they're back over here.

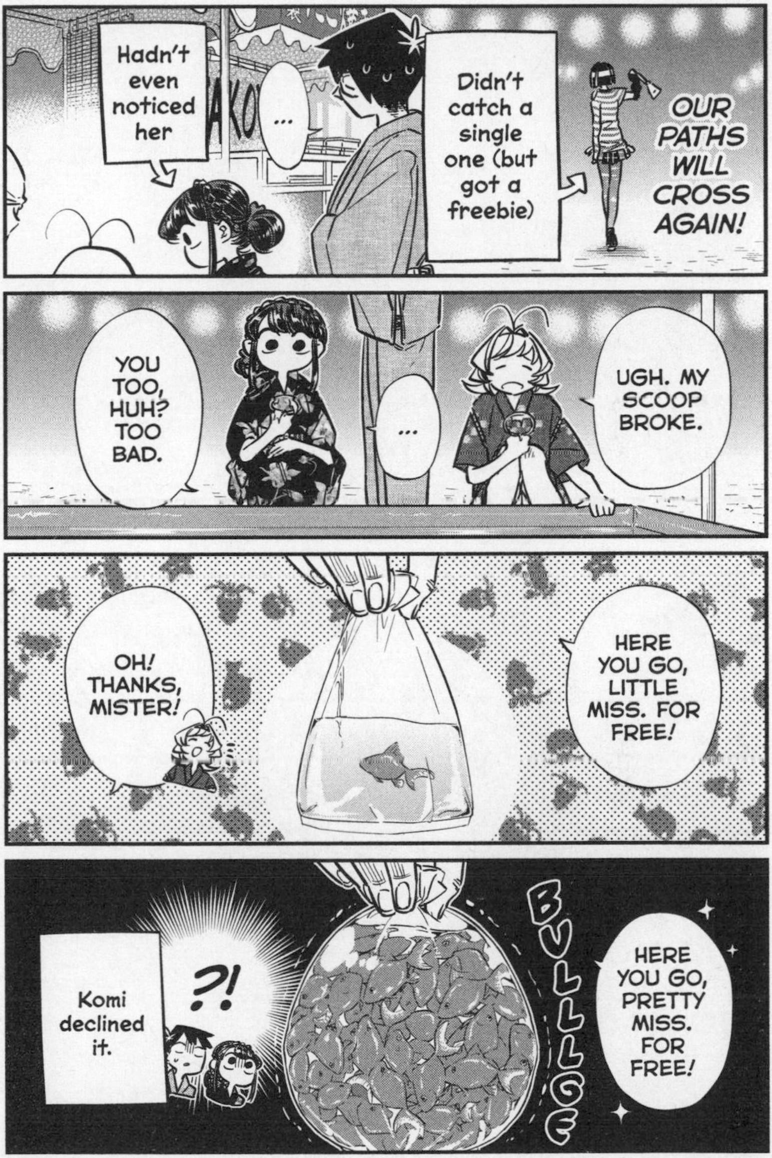
OUR PATHS WILL CROSS AGAIN!
Didn't catch a single one (but got a freebie)
...
Hadn't even noticed her
UGH. MY SCOOP BROKE.
...
YOU TOO, HUH? TOO BAD.
HERE YOU GO, LITTLE MISS. FOR FREE!
OH! THANKS, MISTER!
HERE YOU GO, PRETTY MISS. FOR FREE!
BULLGE
?!
Komi declined it.

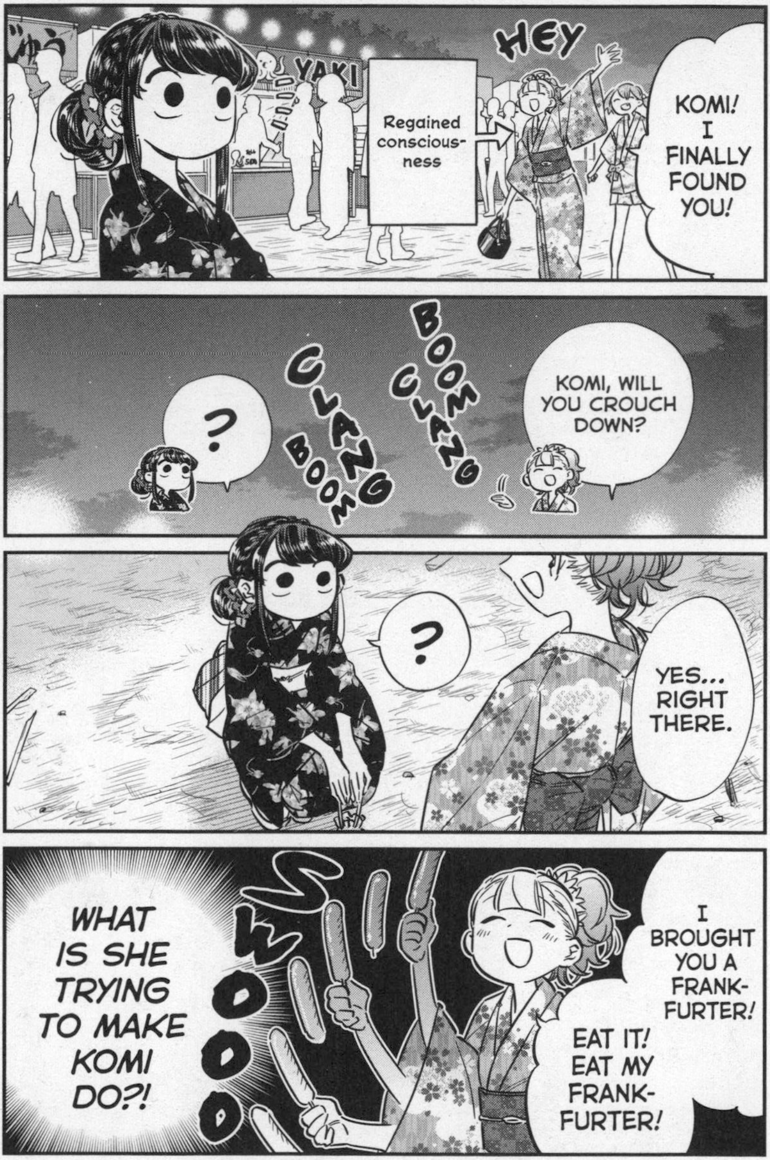
KOMI! I FINALLY FOUND YOU!
HEY
Regained conscious-ness
YAKI
KOMI, WILL YOU CROUCH DOWN?
BOOM CLANG
CLANG BOOM
?
YES... RIGHT THERE.
?
I BROUGHT YOU A FRANK-FURTER!
EAT IT! EAT MY FRANK-FURTER!
SWOOO
WHAT IS SHE TRYING TO MAKE KOMI DO?!

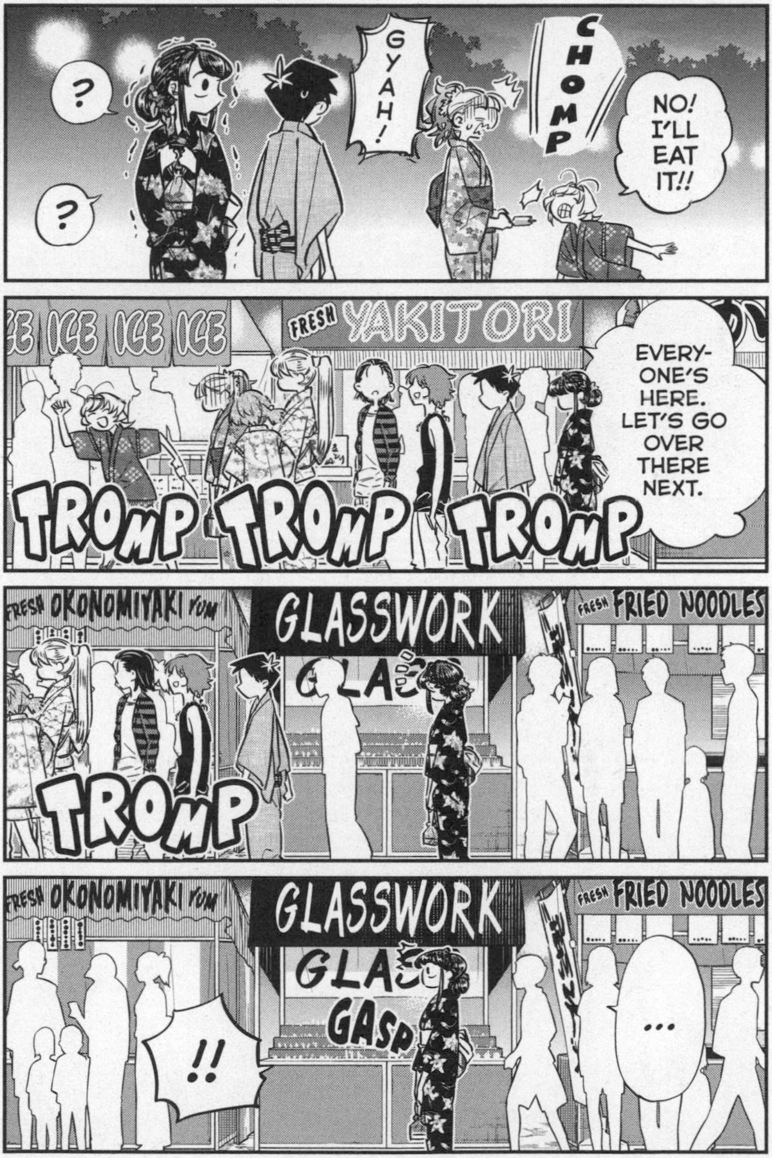
NO! I'LL EAT IT!!
CHOMP
GYAH!
?
?
EVERY-ONE'S HERE. LET'S GO OVER THERE NEXT.
FRESH YAKITORI
ICE ICE ICE
TROMP TROMP TROMP
FRESH FRIED NOODLES
GLASSWORK
FRESH OKONOMIYAKI YUM
TROMP
...
FRESH FRIED NOODLES
GLASSWORK
GASP
FRESH OKONOMIYAKI YUM
!!

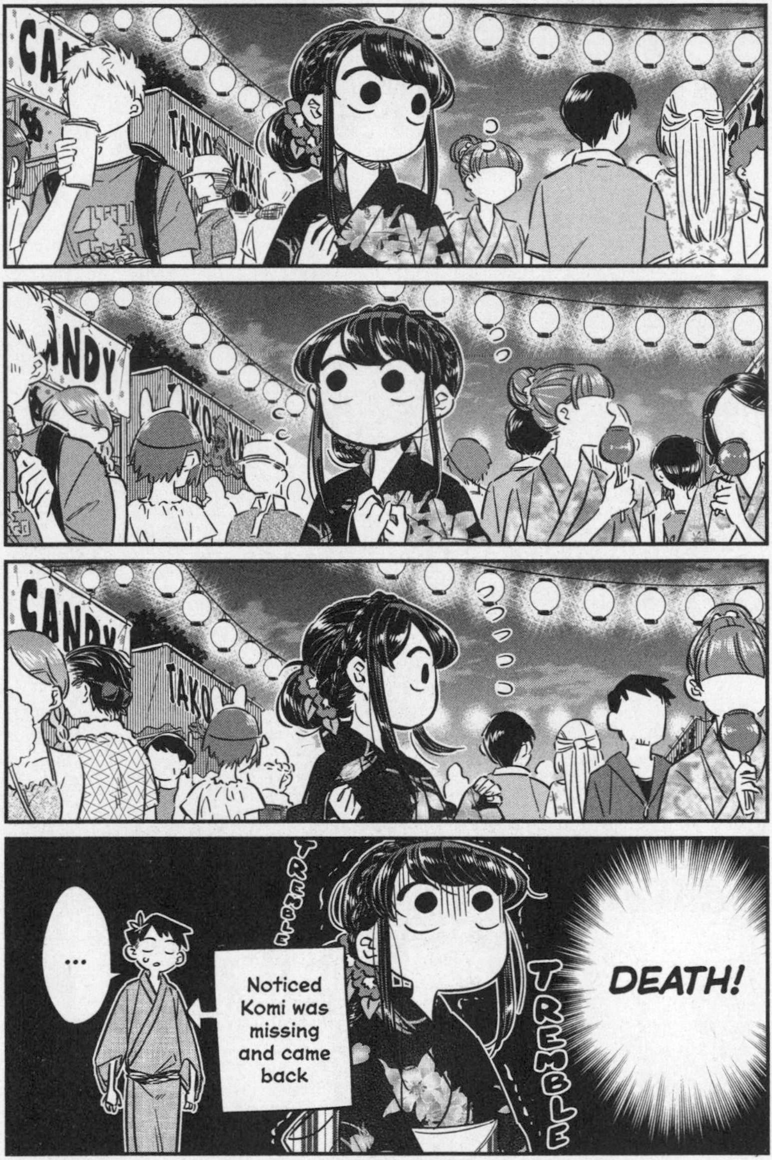
TAKO YAKI
CA
NDY
TAKO YAKI
CANDY
TAKO
DEATH!
TREMBLE
TREMBLE
Noticed Komi was missing and came back
...

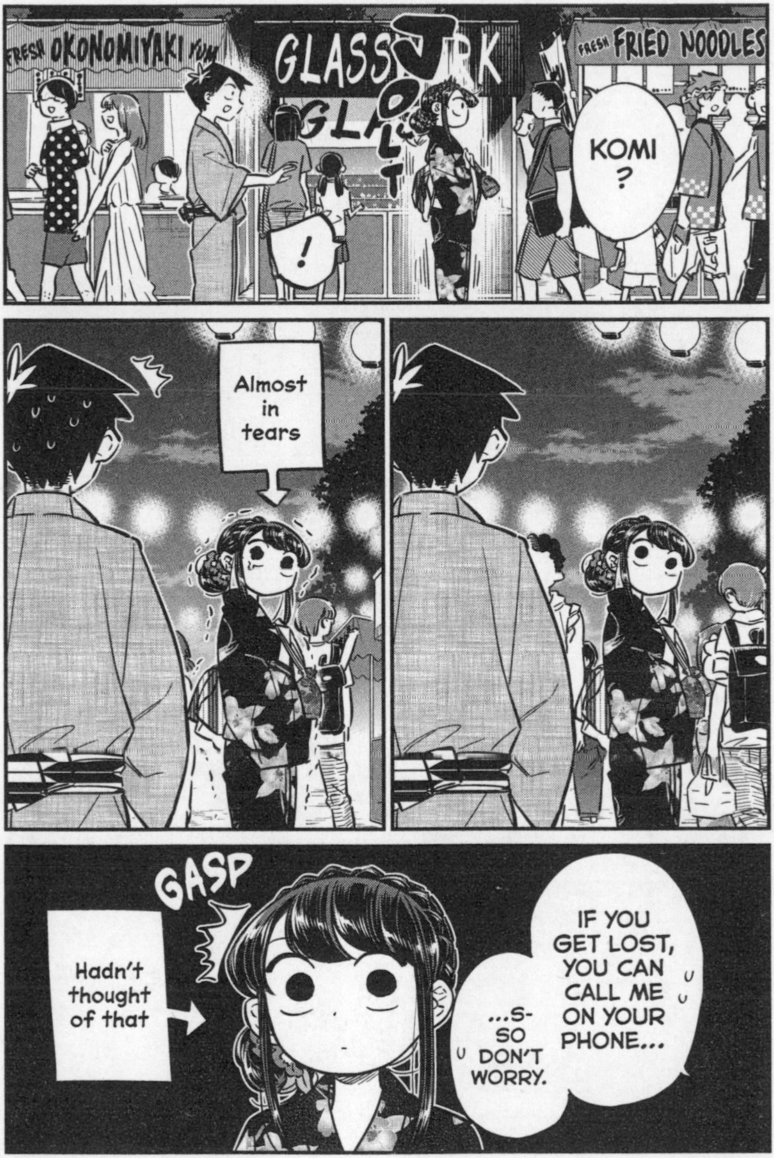
FRESH FRIED NOODLES
KOMI ?
JOLT
GLASS
!
FRESH OKONOMIYAKI YUM
Almost in tears
IF YOU GET LOST, YOU CAN CALL ME ON YOUR PHONE...
...S-SO DON'T WORRY.
GASP
Hadn't thought of that

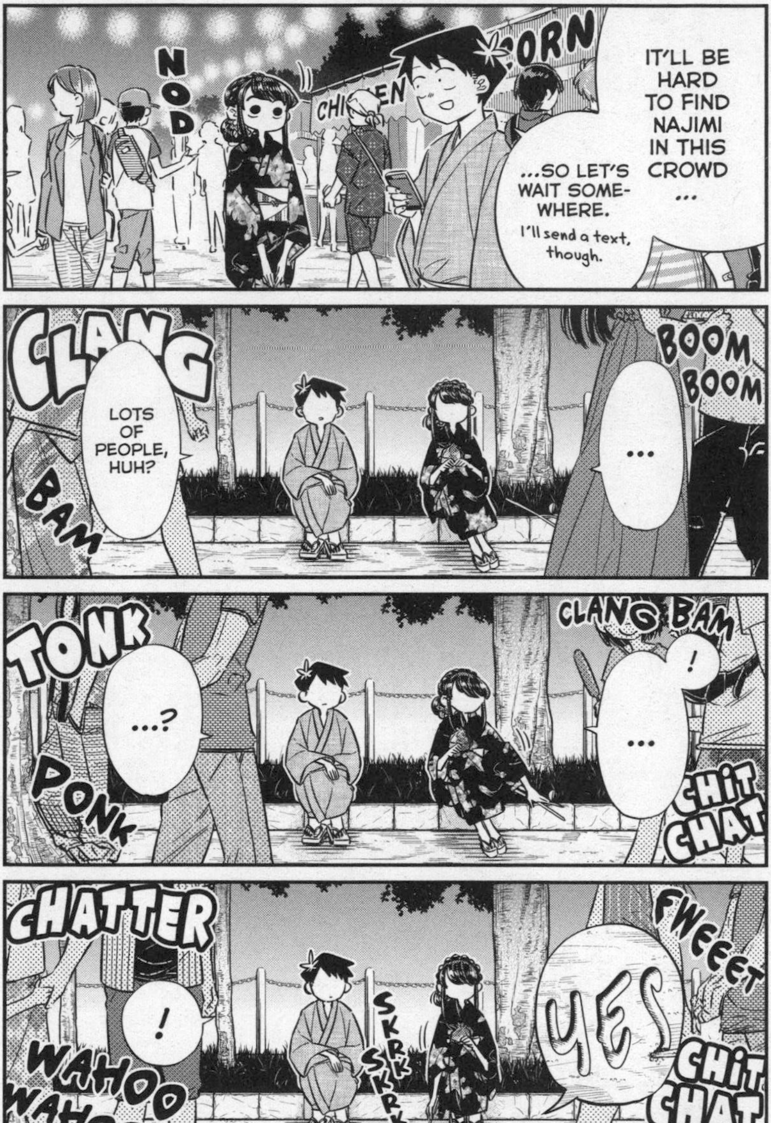
IT'LL BE HARD TO FIND NAJIMI IN THIS CROWD ...
...SO LET'S WAIT SOME-WHERE.
I'll send a text, though.
CORN
NOD
BOOM BOOM
...
LOTS OF PEOPLE, HUH?
CLANG
BAM
CLANG BAM
!
...
CHIT CHAT
...?
TONK
PONK
FWEEET
YES
CHIT CHAT
SKRK SKRK
!
CHATTER
WAHOO WAHOO

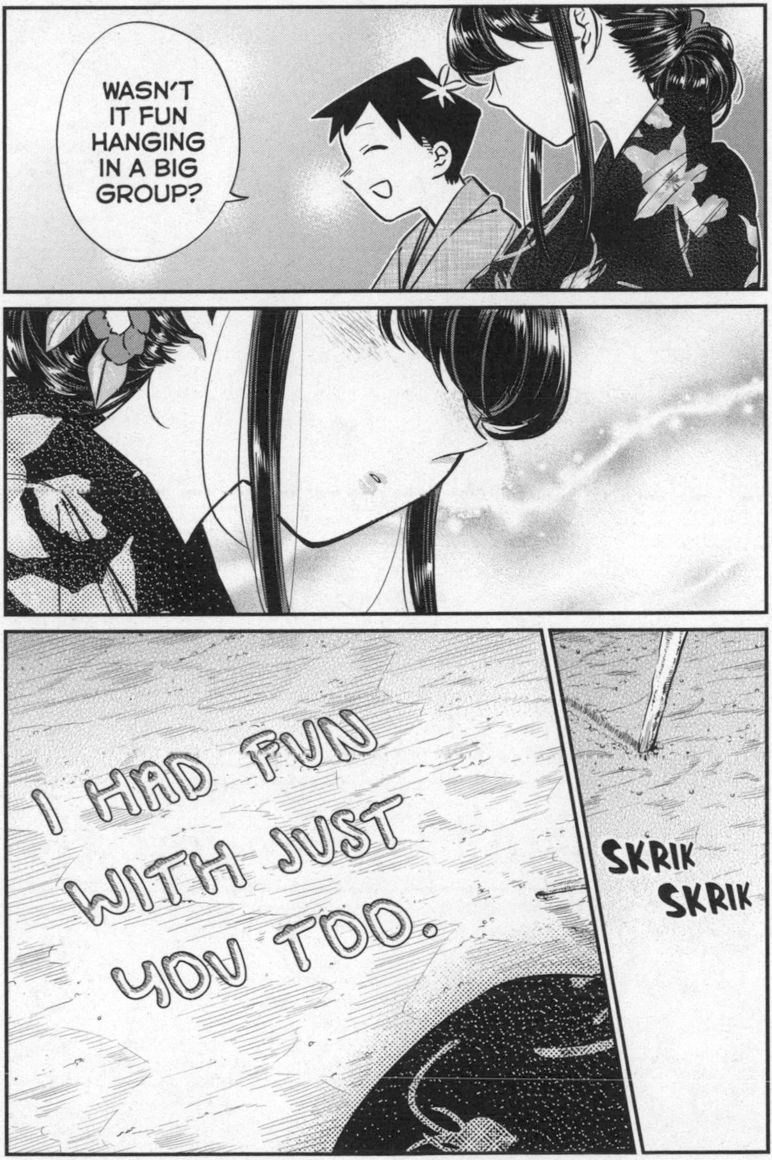
WASN'T IT FUN HANGING IN A BIG GROUP?
SKRIK SKRIK
I HAD FUN WITH JUST YOU TOO.

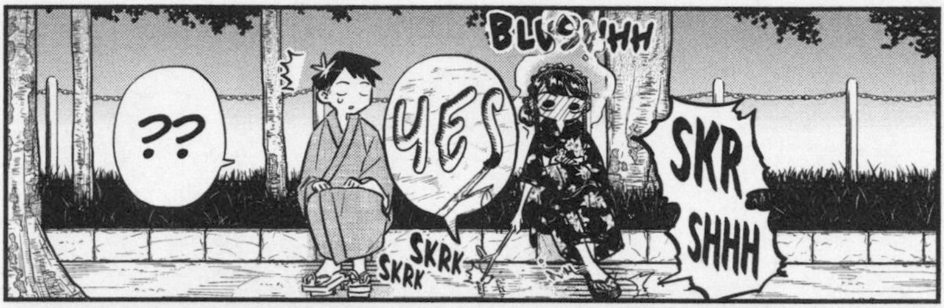
SKR SHHH
YES
SKRK SKRK
??

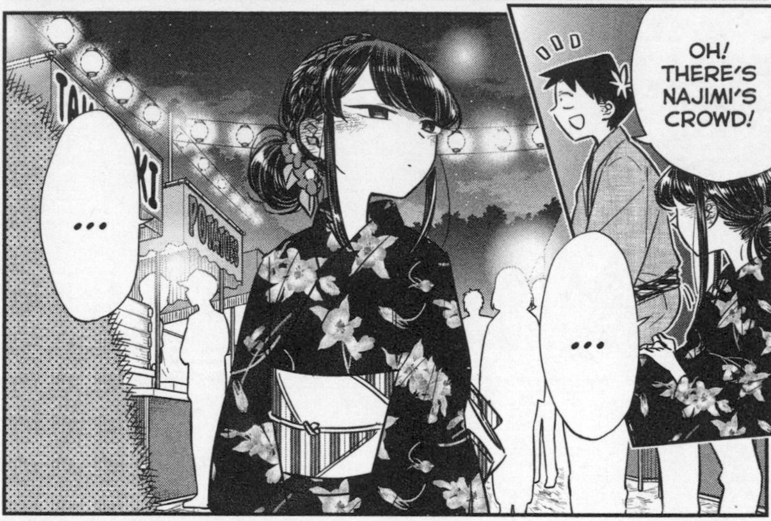
OH! THERE'S NAJIMI'S CROWD!
...
...

Komi Can't Communicate

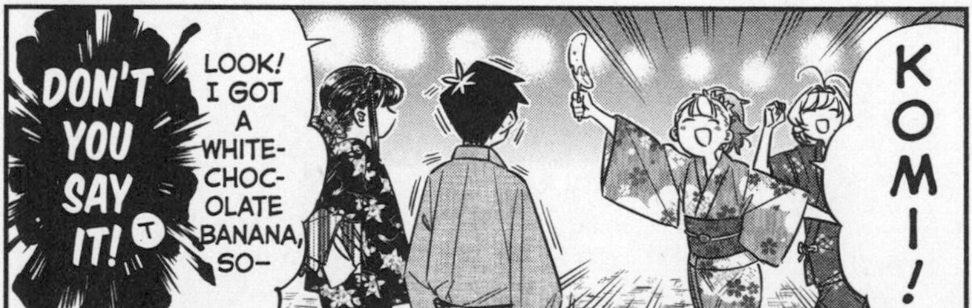
KOMI!
LOOK! I GOT A WHITE-CHOCOLATE BANANA, SO–
DON'T YOU SAY IT!

Communication 47 — The End

Komi Can't Communicate

Komi Can't Communicate Bonus

Looking at Butts Underwater

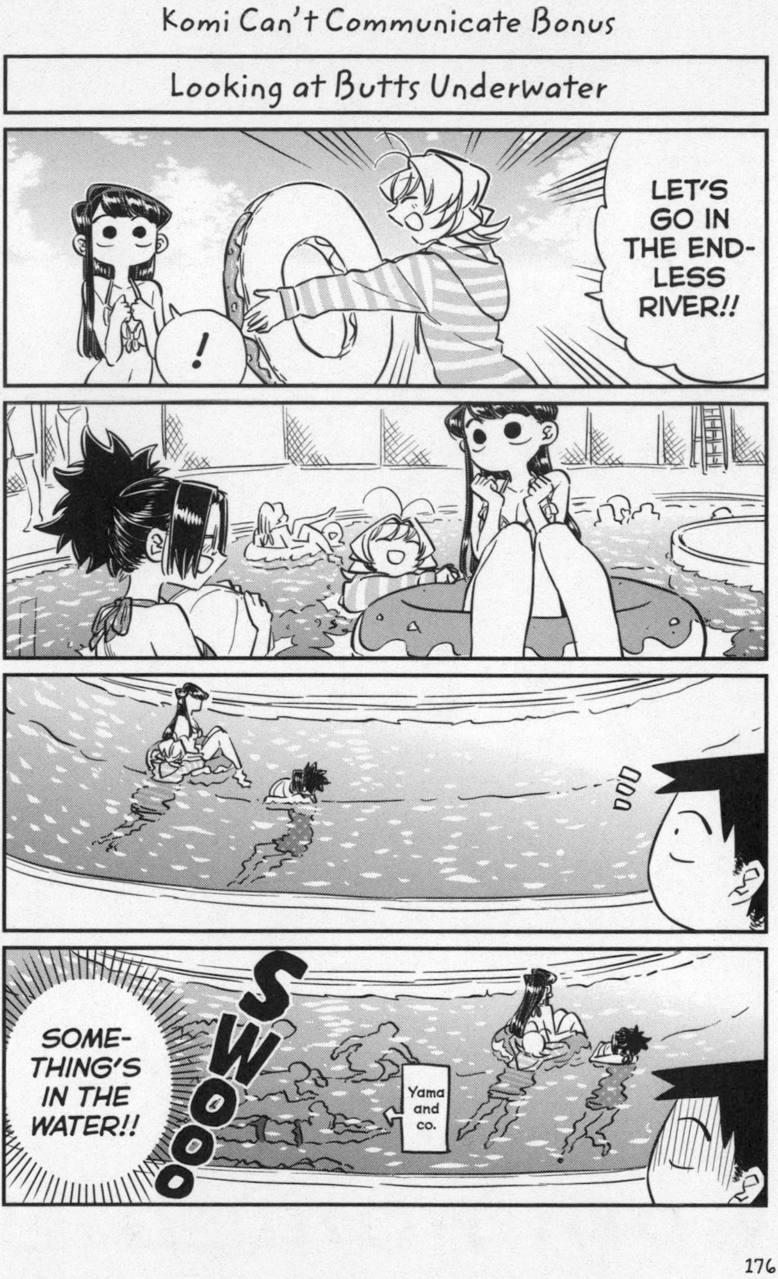

LET'S GO IN THE END-LESS RIVER!!
!
SWOOO
Yama and co.
SOME-THING'S IN THE WATER!!

Komi Can't Communicate Bonus

Can Komi Make 100 Friends? Enjoying Summer Vacation

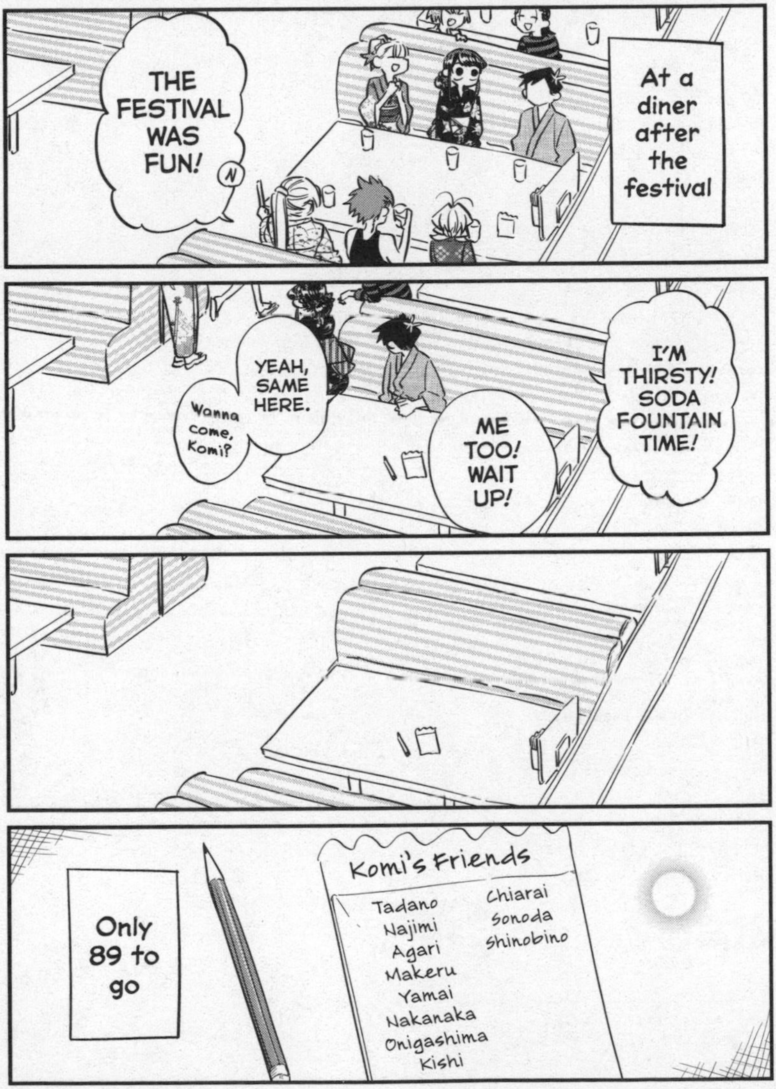

At a diner after the festival
THE FESTIVAL WAS FUN!
N
I'M THIRSTY! SODA FOUNTAIN TIME!
ME TOO! WAIT UP!
YEAH, SAME HERE.
Wanna come, Komi?
Komi's Friends
Tadano
Najimi
Agari
Makeru
Yamai
Nakanaka
Onigashima
Kishi
Chiarai
Sonoda
Shinobino
Only 89 to go

Komi Can't Communicate

VOL. 3
Shonen Sunday Edition

Story and Art by Tomohito Oda

English Translation & Adaptation/John Werry
Touch-Up Art & Lettering/Eve Grandt
Design/Julian [JR] Robinson
Editor/Pancha Diaz

COMI-SAN WA, COMYUSHO DESU. Vol. 3
by Tomohito ODA
© 2016 Tomohito ODA
All rights reserved.
Original Japanese edition published by SHOGAKUKAN.
English translation rights in the United States of America, Canada, the United
Kingdom, Ireland, Australia and New Zealand arranged with SHOGAKUKAN.

Original Cover Design/Masato ISHIZAWA + Bay Bridge Studio

Printed in the U.S.A.

Published by VIZ Media, LLC
P.O. Box 77010
San Francisco, CA 94107

10 9 8 7 6 5 4
First printing, October 2019
Fourth printing, June 2021

viz.com

shonensunday.com

Tomohito Oda won the grand prize for *World Worst One* in the 70th Shogakukan New Comic Artist Awards in 2012. Oda's series *Digicon*, about a tough high school girl who finds herself in control of an alien with plans for world domination, ran from 2014 to 2015. In 2015, *Komi Can't Communicate* debuted as a one-shot in *Weekly Shonen Sunday* and was picked up as a full series by the same magazine in 2016.

Kidnapped by the Demon King and imprisoned in his castle, Princess Syalis is...bored.

SLEEPY PRINCESS IN THE DEMON CASTLE

Story & Art by
KAGIJI KUMANOMATA

Captured princess Syalis decides to while away her hours in the Demon Castle by sleeping, but getting a good night's rest turns out to be a lot of work! She begins by fashioning a DIY pillow out of the fur of her Teddy Demon guards and an "air mattress" from the magical Shield of the Wind. Things go from bad to worse—for her captors—when some of Princess Syalis's schemes end in her untimely—if temporary—demise and she chooses the Forbidden Grimoire for her bedtime reading...

Can Detective Conan solve the toughest cases ....while trapped in a kid's body?

CASE CLOSED™

Story and Art by
Gosho Aoyama

High schooler Jimmy Kudo has had many successes in his young detective career. But what will he do when a pair of shady men feed him a poison that turns him into a little kid?

This is the last page!

Komi Can't Communicate has been printed in the original Japanese format to preserve the orientation of the artwork.

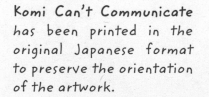

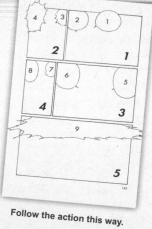

Follow the action this way.